EUROPEAN
SOCCER
WHO'S WHO

Tim Barnett
Ni⸱ ⸱ Hill⸱

GUINNESS PUBLISHING

© **Tim Barnett and Nich Hills 1992**

The right of Tim Barnett and Nich Hills to be identified as the Authors of this work has been asserted in accordance with the Copyright, Design and Patents Act 1988

Published in Great Britain by Guinness Publishing Ltd, 33 London Road, Enfield, Middlesex

Cover design by Ad Vantage Studios
Text Design and layout by Tim Barnett & David Foster

Printed in Great Britain by
BPCC Hazells Ltd
Member of BPCC Ltd

'Guinness' is a registered trademark of Guinness Publishing Ltd

A catalogue record for this book is available from the British Library

ISBN 0-85112-570-0

ABOUT THE AUTHORS

HILLS, Nich
• 19.11.62 • Midfield

Has been the bane of many a sub-editor's life by deliberately spelling his first name with a final 'h' to create problems. Began his career with Reg Hayter's Sports Agency in Fleet Street, where he quickly won a regular by-line in the News of the World, as well as a regular pint of Guinness in The Cartoonist. On leaving Hayter's in 1987, Nich was appointed Sports Editor for the South London Guardian group. Now works as a freelance sports writer, covering anything from Archery to Octopush, but always returning to his beloved Queen's Park Rangers. His main claim to fame is having once bowled out Alec Stewart in a school cricket match. Nich has also written and edited for the 1986 and 1987 News of the World football annuals, and the 1985, 1986 and 1987 International Football Books.

BARNETT, Tim
• 26.09.68 • Midfield

Another graduate of the Hayter's School of Excellence. Tim held a regular by-line in the Sunday Express newspaper in 1987/88, but decided that travelling the world - twice - was a far better idea than working for a living. He returned to England in March 1990, just in time to watch Crystal Palace's 4-3 FA Cup Semi-Final win over Liverpool, and he hasn't stopped talking about it since. Main claim to fame is inviting Kylie Minogue to a party. She refused. Helped write and edit the 1986, 1987 and 1988 News of the World annuals and the 1988 International Football Book. Currently spends much of his time charting the magical career of Roy of the Rovers.

INTRODUCTION

This book features personal and professional details, both statistical and biographical, of players registered in the First Division (or equivalent) sides in the following countries of Europe: Belgium, Eire, France, Germany, Holland, Italy, Northern Ireland, Spain and Portugal.

In addition there are profiles on other top European players that the Authors considered worthy of inclusion.

The Authors would like to thank the following people for their invaluable help in the compilation of this book: Adrian Ford, David Foster, Sean Neville, Laura Meecham, Steve Leven, Karl Mercer, Rob Kemp, Ellie Gingall, Ian Cruise and, of course, the staff and players of all the clubs featured within these pages.

BIBLIOGRAPHY

Soccer Who's Who, by Jack Rollin *(Guinness)*

The European Football Yearbook, by Mike Hammond *(Sports Projects)*

Irish Football Handbook, by Gerry Desmond and Dave Galvin *(Red Card Publications)*

HOW THE BOOK WORKS

A typical entry will consist of the following information:-

SURNAME, First name(s)
(Name of club, Country of club)
• date of birth • position
• international/representative experience and goals scored (where applicable)

Followed by a brief resume of the player's career to date. This will include particular highlights, honours won, unusual information etc.

ABBREVIATIONS

In the interest of expedience, all countries listed after club names have been abbreviated to three letters.

AUS	Austria
BEL	Belgium
BYE	Byelorussia
EIR	Republic of Ireland
FRA	France
GER	Germany
GRE	Greece
HOL	Holland
ITA	Italy
LIT	Lithuania
N.IR	Northern Ireland
NOR	Norway
POR	Portugal
RUS	Russia
SPA	Spain
SWE	Sweden
SWI	Switzerland
LAT	Latvia
UKR	Ukraine
CIS	CIS
YUG	Yugoslavia

ABADIOTAKIS, Yorgo (Panathinaikos, Gre)

• Goalkeeper

Understudy to first choice 'keeper Joszef Wandzik, his first team appearances have been limited. Signed from Korinthos in June 1988.

ABAZI, Edmond (Hajduk Split, Yug)

• Striker
• Albania 3 full caps, 1 goal

One of many players to have defected from Albania over the past three years. Greece is their favourite destination, but Edmond transferred to Hajduk Split in Yugoslavia towards the end of season 1990/91, and scored a goal in his only start. Helped make history in May 1991, when his second half strike against Iceland in a European Championship Qualifier gave Albania their first win in more than six and a half years.

ABBENHUIS, Martin (Den Haag, Hol)

• 18.06.68 • Striker

Signed from local football in July 1985. Although he has played over fifty games for the club, he has yet to score his first goal.

ABDEL-GHANY, Magdy (Beira Mar, Por)

• 27.07.59 • Midfield
• Egypt full caps

Born in Cairo and made his Portuguese First Division debut with Beira Mar during the 1988/89 season. Has spent all his career in Portugal with the club.

ABDELLAH, Nacer (Cercle Brugge, Bel)

• 03.03.66 • Midfield

Moroccan-born wide midfielder who has Belgian citizenship. Began with Mechelen, but failed to make the breakthrough there, and moved on to Second Division Lommel. Cercle gave him his chance in the top flight when they snapped him up at the beginning of season 1990/91.

ABDULLAH, Duran (Ankaragucu, Tur)

• 30.07.68 • Midfield
• Turkey 2 full caps

Made his international debut v Poland in the spring of 1991, when he came on as sub for Yildrin Osman.

ABEELS, Jean-Marie (Waregem, Bel)

• 18.11.62 • Striker

Highly experienced forward who's goal supply seems to have dried up somewhat over the last couple of seasons. Signed for Waregem from Ekeren. He was previously with Stade Warremien, Tongeren and Kortrijk.

ABED, Denis (Metz, Fra)

• 10.02.69 • Striker

Signed from Paris FC in 1990 and made his debut in May the following year, against Lille.

ABEL Jorge Pereira Silva (Maritimo, Por)

• 21.08.69 • Defender

A steady blocker who made just one appearance for Benfica in the 1988/89 season before moving to Penafiel and then on to Maritimo.

ABEL Resino Gomez (Atletico Madrid, Spa)

• 02.02.60 • Goalkeeper

Got his chance in the First Divsion after moving up from the reserves in 1982 and has been regarded as one of the most consistent 'keepers in Spain ever since. He can boast the impressive statistic of having not conceeded a League goal for more than 1,000 minutes during 1991.

ABLANEDO I (Espanol, Spa)

• 22.08.62 • Defender

Central defender who joined Espanol from Sporting Gijon in 1992.

ABLANEDO II (Sporting Gijon, Spa)

• 02.09.63 • Goalkeeper
• Spain 4 full caps

Dependable 'keeper who has spent all hs career with Gijon.

ADAM, Michael (Den Haag, Hol)

• 22.01.68 • Defender
• Holland U21

Local born player who joined Den Haag in July 1985 and finally got his chance in the first team two years later. Has now played more than 140 games for his only League side.

ADAMS, Ian (Distillery, N.Ir)

• Striker

Although small for a striker he finished 1991/92 as comfortably the club's leading scorer. Fast and difficult to knock off the ball - a tremendous prospect.

ADAO Carlos Manuel Pinto
(Penafiel, Por)

• 03.04.60 • Midfield
• Portugal full caps

An experienced midfielder who began his league career with Varzim in 1980/81 season, where he made a total of 82 appearances. He joined Vitoria Guimaraes in 1985 establishing himself as a first choice midfielder for three seasons before moving onto Belenenses. He signed for Penafiel in 1990.

ADEMAR Moreira Marques
(Farense, Por)

• 04.03.59 • Midfield
• Portugal full caps

Now in the twilight of an impressive career spanning thirteen years and four clubs, including Portuguese giants, Sporting Lisbon and Porto. Has been the backbone of the Farense midfield since 1987/88 and has found a goal-scoring touch not seen in his early career.

van AERLE, Berry
(PSV Eindhoven, Hol)

• 08.12.62 • Defender
• Holland full caps

Joined PSV as an amateur in July 1981, and turned professional twelve months later. He was loaned to FC Antwerp of Belgium in 1988. Made over 200 League appearances for PSV since his debut during the 1981/82 season

AFFOH, Atty
(Charleroi, Bel)

• 27.08.71 • Defender

Togo-born central defender who was granted Belgian nationality in the summer of 1991. Signed from FC Semassi de Sokode. Dangerous from dead-ball situations.

AGOSTINI, Massimo
(Parma, Ita)

• 19.01.64 • Striker

Began his career with Cesena and moved on to Roma in 1986 for two seasons. After returning to Cesena he scored 22 goals in 59 Serie A games before being signed by Milan in 1990. Spent just one season at Milan before moving to Parma for £2.5m in part of the deal that took Enzo Gambaro in the opposite direction.

de AGOSTINI, Luigi (Juventus, Ita)

• 07.04.61 • Defender
• Italy 36 full caps, 4 goals

Born in Udine and made his debut for Udinese in 1979. Spent the 1981/82 season on loan at Third Division Trento and the following season with Catanzaro to gain more experience before returning to Udinese and winning a regular place. Joined Verona in 1986 and was signed by Juventus for £3m a year later.

AGUILERA, Carlos (Genoa, Ita)

• 21.09.64 • Striker
• Uruguay full caps

Much travelled South American striker. Has played for Nacional and Penarol in Uruguay. River Plate and Racing in Argentina, Independiente in Colombia and Guadalajara in Mexico. Moved to Italy and Genoa in 1989. Made international debut aged 17.

AGUILERA, Juan Carlos (Atletico Madrid, Spa)

• 22.05.69 • Striker
• Spain youth

Former Atletico reserve who has been with the club for the past six years.

AGUIRRE Beldarrain, Jose Luis (Real Sociedad, Spa)

• 14.09.65 • Midfield

Joined Sociedad from Sestao along with Uria in 1989.

AGUSTIN Rodriguez Santiago (Tenerife, Spa)

• 10.09.59 • Goalkeeper

In and out of the Real Madrid side before finally moving on to Tenerife in 1990.

AIGNER, Rainer (Fortuna Dusseldorf, Ger)

• 04.09.67 • Defender

Signed from Bayern Munich in 1991.

ALBERGA, Giuseppe (Bari, Ita)

• 26.09.66 • Goalkeeper

Made his debut for Bari in Serie B during the 1988/89 season, but did not establish himself as first choice until former Polish international Zbigniew Boniek took over as boss in October 1991. Previously had spells with Altamura and Trani.

ALBERT, Philippe
(Anderlecht, Bel)

• 10.08.67 • Defender
• Belgium 18 full caps, 1 goal

Commanding central defender who likes to get forward at free kicks and corners and create problems with his heading ability. Formerly with Royal Standard Bouillon and Charleroi. He made his international debut in Dublin, against the Republic of Ireland, in April 1987. Was the subject of a big money move to Belgian giants Anderlecht in June 1992.

ALBERTINI, Demetrio
(Milan, Ita)

• 23.08.71 • Midfield

Born in Besana, Demetrio made his League debut for Milan during the 1988/89 season. He was loaned out to Serie B side Padova in November 1990 to help him gain some valuable first team experience before returning to Milan in 1991.

ALBERTO Paulo
Lombardo Grou
(Uniao, Por)

• 24.06.67 • Midfield

Plucked from obscurity at Vitoria Guimaraes, where he played just ten games in two seasons from 1989. Lack of consistency though has meant he has struggled to secure a regular place in the first eleven.

ALBESA Gasulla,
Albert
(Espanol, Spa)

• 06.03.65 • Defender

Tall stopper who returned to his home city when signed by Espanol from Valladolid in 1989.

ALDAIR
(Roma, Ita)

• 30.11.65 • Defender

Brazilian stopper who played his football with Flamengo in South America before signing for Benfica in 1989. Left Portugal after just one season and moved to Serie A club Roma.

ALDANA, Adolfo
(Real Madrid, Spa)

• 05.01.66 • Striker
• Spain U21

Has now been with the first team squad for six seasons after moving up from Castilla, Real's reserve side.

ALEINIKOV, Sergei
(Lecce, Ita)

• 07.11.61 • Midfield
• USSR 77 full caps, 6 goals

Skilful midfielder who moved to Juventus from Dynamo Kiev in 1989. Signed by Lecce after 1990 World Cup. USSR debut v West Germany 1984.

ALEMAO, Ricardo (Napoli, Ita)

• 22.11.61 • Midfield

Brazilian-born player who made his name in South America with Botofago. Bought to Europe by Atletico Madrid in 1987, but spent just one season in Spain before being snapped up by Napoli.

ALESANCO, Jose Ramon (Barcelona, Spa)

• 19.05.56 • Defender
• Spain 34 full caps

Began his career with Atletico Bilbao and received his international call-up before he had even played a dozen league games. Moved on to Barcelona in 1980 for a then Spanish domestic record fee of £650,000. Member of Barcelona's 1982 Cup-Winners' Cup winning side.

ALESSIO, Angelo (Juventus, Ita)

• 29.04.65 • Midfield

Right sided midfielder who began his League career with Avellino, making his debut during the 1984/85 season. Moved to Juventus in 1987, although he did spend the 1988/89 season on loan at Bologna.

ALFANO, Gennaro (Toulon, Fra)

• 06.02.58 • Defender

Italian-born naturalized French citizen. Signed for the club from local football in 1980, and has been there ever since. Lead the club to promotion from Division Two in 1983 and has gone on to play more than 240 First Division games since his top flight debut v Brest in July 1983.

ALFLEN, Rob (Ajax, Hol)

• 07.05.68 • Midfield

Signed from Utrecht prior to the start of the 1991/92 season. Made his League debut for Utrecht during the 1985/86 season and played over 140 senior games before his move to Amsterdam.

ALFREDO da Silva Castro (Boavista, Por)

• 05.10.62 • Goalkeeper

Joined the Rio Ave club as a youngster and made his League debut for the club during the 1981/82 season. Transferred to Boavista in 1984 and has now made more than 150 first team appearances for the club.

ALFREDO, Santaelena Aguado (Atletico Madrid, Spa)

• 13.10.67 • Midfield

Transferred to Madrid from local Third Division side Getofe in 1989. An accomplished ball-winner he has coped successfully with the difference in class between the divisions.

ALI, Gultiken (Besiktas, Tur)

• 27.06.65 • Midfield
• Turkey 7 full caps; U21; Olympic

Played for Turkey's U21s against England in April 1987, and made his full debut six months later in the infamous 8-0 thrashing at Wembley. March 1991 saw his first senior international for three years, when he played against Tunisia. Equally happy in midfield or up front his goals have helped Besiktas in their run to three successive League titles.

ALLEN, Jason (Linfield, N.Ir)

• 8.6.70 • Defender
• N.Ireland Youth

Calm and confident on the ball, Jason joined English League club Oldham straight from school, before moving to Linfield in 1990. His presence has settled the back-four at Windsor Park, and he displays a maturity beyond his years.

ALLIEVI, Sergio (Dynamo Dresden, Ger)

• 17.01.64 • Striker

A forward of Italian descent, Sergio was signed by Dresden from Kaiserslautern in 1990. He had previously been with Wattenscheid.

ALLOFS, Klaus (Werder Bremen, Ger)

• 05.12.56 • Striker
• Germany 56 full caps

Joined Cologne from Fortuna Dusseldorf, before moving to France and appearing for Marseille and Bordeaux. Returned to Germany with Bremen in 1990.

ALLOFS, Thomas (Fortuna Dusseldorf, Ger)

• 17.11.59 • Striker
• Germany 2 full caps

Began his career with Dusseldorf before joining Kaiserslautern and Cologne. Had a spell in France with Racing Strasburg before returning to Dusseldorf in 1990.

ALOISI, Antonio (Ascoli, Ita)

• 28.08.68 • Defender

Central defender who has spent all of his career with Ascoli since signing up as an 18-year-old. Made his League debut for the club in Serie A during the 1987/88 season and has been a regular ever since. Involved in a severe on the field argument with team mate Angelo Pierleoni in April 1992 during a home fixture against Internazionale and was subsequently banned by the club for the remainder of the season.

ALOISIO Pinto Alves (Porto, Por)

• 16.08.63 • Defender
• Brazil full caps

Brazillian born defender who joined Porto prior to the 1990/91 season and ended his first season in Portuguese football with a Cup winners' medal.

ALTAY, Dagdelen (Altay Izmir, Tur)

• 04.03.70 • Goalkeeper
• Turkey U21

Won his first full international call-up for the match v Bulgaria in August 1991.

ALVARO Cervera Diaz (Mallorca, Spa)

• 22.09.64 • Striker

African-born forward who joined Mallorca from Santando in 1987.

ALVARO GREGORIO (Salgueiros, Por)

• 25.08.72 • Defender

Porto born youngster who began his career with the Porto club, but failed to break into the first team. Joined Salgueiros prior to the 1991/92 season.

ALVARO MACIEL (Salgueiros, Por)

• 23.02.67 • Defender

Long serving player with the Salgueiros club. He has experienced the lows of relegation in 1988 and the high of promotion two years later as the team won the Second Division Championship.

ALVARO SOARES (Salgueiros, Por)

• 25.05.60 • Striker

Much travelled forward who began his career with Sporting Bustelo. Gained First Division experience with Rio Ave, Boavista and Penafiel before joining Salgueiros.

AMARAL Rodrigues, Jorge (Sporting Lisbon, Por)

• 01.06.70 • Striker

Born in Mozambique and has spent all his career in Portugal and joined Sporting as a junior. Made his League debut while with Viseu during during the 1988/89 season, but returned to Sporting in 1989.

AMITRANO, Andre (Cannes, Fra)

• 30.11.57 • Goalkeeper

Highly experienced shot-stopper who signed from Nice in 1988 as back up for first choice Michel Dussuyer. Algerian-born, but with French citizenship, he has played less than 100 games in the First Division, despite a professional career stretching back to 1978.

AMOKACHI, Daniel (Club Brugge, Bel)

• 20.12.72 • Striker

Nigerian-born youngster with Belgian citizenship. Signed from Ranchers Bees he has made a handful of first team appearances.

AMOROS, Manuel (Marseille, Fra)

• 01.02.62 • Defender
• France 81 full caps, 1 goal

Captain of the national team, and winner of the record number of caps for a French player. His career has spanned two World Cup campaigns and two European Championships. A tremendous inspiration to all around him, he is without a doubt one of the top five defenders in the world.

ANASTOPOULOS, Nikos (Olympiakos, Gre)

• Striker
• Greece 79 full caps, 23 goals

Along with Panathinaikos star Dimitris Saravakos, he is the greatest forward in Greek history. Holds the national record for both internationals played and goals scored - although both of those totals look set to be surpassed by Saravakos. Very strong in the air, and with deceptive pace, he is still a handful for most defences. Scored 16 goals in 25 games in 1990/91, proving to the world that he is far from washed up.

ANDERBRUGGE, Ingo (Schalke, Ger)

• 02.01.64 • Midfield

Originally got his chance in the German First Division with Borussia Dortmund. Moved to Schalke in 1988 and helped them to promotion in 1991.

ANDERSEN, Henrik (Cologne, Ger)

• 07.05.65 • Defender
• Denmark 26 full caps, 2 goals

After playing for Fremad Amager, Henrik made his name in Belgium with Anderlecht. Brought to Germany by Cologne in 1990. Broke his knee in the semi final of the 1992 European Championships, and had to sit out the historic final. A versatile player who is equally comfortable in defence or central midfield.

ANDERSEN, Jorn (Eintracht Frankfurt, Ger)

• 03.02.63 • Striker
• Norway 27 full caps, 5 goals

Played for Ostsiden IL, Fredrikstad FK and Valerengen Oslo in Norway before joining Nuremburg in Germany. Later moved on to Eintracht Frankfurt before being sold to Fortuna Dusseldorf. Came back to Frankfurt in September 1991.

ANDERSSON, Kennet (Mechelen, Bel)

• 06.10.67 • Striker
• Sweden 16 full caps, 9 goals

Signed on the advice of former IFK Gothenberg team-mate Klas Ingesson at the beginning of season 1991/92. Has won a regular spot in Sweden's national side over the last twelve months, where his scoring record speaks for itself.

ANDRE, Antonio dos Santos (Porto, Por)

• 24.12.57 • Midfield
• Portugal 18 full caps, 1 goal

Began his career with Rio Ave and made his League debut for Varzim during the 1980/81 season. Joined Porto in 1984 and has now made over 200 League appearances for the club.

ANDRINUA, Genaro (Atletico Bilbao, Spa)

• 09.05.64 • Defender
• Spain 28 full caps, 2 goals

Tall stopper who has made himself a regular in the Spanish international side.

ANGLOMA, Jocelyn (Marseille, Fra)

• 07.08.65 • Midfield
• France 10 full caps

Jocelyn has shot into the international frame since the arrival of Michel Platini as national coach. Began with Rennes back in 1986, and then moved, via Lille, to Paris St Germain before joining Olympique Marseille at the beginning of 1991/92. Likes to play wide right midfield, and get among the goals. Scored two League goals in 1991/92.

ANGOY, Jesus Maria (Barcelona, Spa)

• 22.06.66 • Goalkeeper

Spent his early career in the Spanish Third Division with Barcelona Athletico, Barcelona's nursery side. Joined the first team squad last year.

ANTONIOU, Kostas (Panathinaikos, Gre)

• Midfield
• Greece 30 full caps, 6 goals

Goalscoring central midfielder who has been out of favour at international level since 1988, despite playing a major role in two League Championships and three domestic Cup victories.

ANZIANI, Philippe (Toulon, Fra)

• 21.09.61 • Midfield
• France 5 full caps

French-Algerian striker turned wide midfielder who has played more than 400 First Division games. Began with Sochaux, for whom he made his debut in December 1979, v Brest. Has also played for Monaco, Nantes and Matra Racing . Joined Toulon in August 1989. Scored one goal during the 1991/92 League campaign.

ANNONI, Enrico (Torino, Ita)

• 01.07.66 •Defender

Began his career with junior side Seregne before joining Como in 1983. Had two seasons with Sambenedettese before

returning to Como in 1987. Signed by Torino prior to the 1990/91 season.

APOLLONI, Luigi (Parma, Ita)

• 02.05.67 • Defender

Central defender who played in the lower Leagues with Lodigiani, Pistoiese and Reggiana, before getting his chance in Serie B with Parma in 1987. Helped the club gain promtion to the top flight three years later.

APOSTOLAKIS, Stratos (Panathinaikos, Gre)

• Defender
• Greece 41 full caps, 1 goal

An attacking right back who likes to get forward and support the midfield. Signed from rivals Olympiakos Piraeus in March 1990. His tough tackling and intelligent use of the ball played a huge part in the club's tremendous defensive record of 1991/92, when they conceded fewer goals than any other side in Greece.

ARAGON Martinez, Santiago (Valladolid, Spa)

• 03.04.68 • Midfield

Joined Valladolid from Real Madrid in 1992. Previously with Espanol.

ARAGON, Santiago
(Valladolid, Spa)

• 03.04.68 • Midfield

Joined Valladolid from Real Madrid in 1992. Previously with Espanol.

ARAMBASIC, Zlatko
(Mechelen, Bel)

• 20.09.69 • Striker

Like most top Australian players, he is of European descent and came to the Northern hemisphere in a bid to further his professional football career. Signed from Sydney Olympic, he has yet to make a significant impact on the first team at Mechelen.

ARIANO, Sergio
(Kortrijk, Bel)

• 27.10.64 • Striker

One of three attackers to join the club at the beginning of 1991/92 season from lower division clubs. Signed from Roeselare.

ARISVALDO, Pereira
(Genk, Bel)

• 28.11.70 • Striker

Brazilian ball-player who came to Belgium from Moto Club de Sao Luis in 1988/89. Genk signed him from Beerschot after clinching promotion from Division Two in 1989/90.

ARKINS, Vinny
(Shamrock Rovers, Eir)

• 18.09.70 • Striker

Began with Dundee United in Scotland , but failed to make the grade at Tannadice, and transferred to Rovers in October 1989. He didn't have to wait long for his debut in the League of Ireland, playing against Bohemians on October 15 that same year (won 3-1). He was the third highest scorer in the League of Ireland in 1990/91, when he grabbed 14 goals in 25 starts.

ARMANDO Santos
(Gil Vicente, Por)

• 18.10.64 • Striker

Began his career in the Portugese league with Salgueiros making 90 appearances before joining Boavista in 1987, finally moving to Gil Vincente for the start of the 1991/92 campaign. Although not a renowned goalscorer, his height (6ft 2ins) has enabled him to take the role of target man in the front line.

ARMSTRONG, Winston
(Glentoran, N.Ir)

• Striker

Realised a personal ambition when he

signed for Glentoran - the club he supported as a boy - at the back end of the glorious 1991/92 season. Known as 'Winkle'.

ARROYO Ayala, Carlos
(Valencia, Spa)
• 19.02.66 • Midfield

Ball-winner in the middle of the park for the side. Joined Valencia in 1984 from Madrid junior club Alcorcon.

ARSENE, Herve
(Lens, Fra)
• 30.10.63 • Midfield

Born in the poetically titled Madagascan town of Nosy-Be-Hell, he first came to the club in 1987, making his debut at Niort in July of that year. Other than a brief spell on loan at La Roche, Lens has been his only senior club in France.

ASANOVIC, Aliojsa
(Cannes, Fra)
• 14.12.65 • Midfield
• Yugoslavia full caps

Very tall central midfielder, and playmaker of the Cannes side. Formerly with home-town club Hajduk Split, he signed for Metz in 1990, making his French League debut, v Lille, in July of that year. Moved to Cannes in 1991.

ASSADOURIAN, Eric
(Lille, Fra)
• 24.09.66 • Striker
• France U21

Began with INF Vichy, but never made a senior appearance before moving on to Toulouse in 1986. After making his debut, against Monaco, in August that year he was snapped up by Lille. Has now made more than 100 First Division appearances.

ASSELMAN, Patrick
(Standard Liege, Bel)
• 30.10.68 • Midfield

Began with Liedekerke before joining Belgian giants Anderlecht. Standard signed him from Mechelen in 1990. Stocky attacking midfielder who likes to get forward and among the goals.

AUBAMEYANG, Pierre
(Le Havre, Fra)
• 29.05.65 • Midfield

Born in Gabon this tenacious ball-winner is equally happy in defence or central midfield. Signed from Laval in June 1991.

AUMANN, Raimond
(Bayern Munich, Ger)
• 12.10.63 • Goalkeeper
• Germany U21, 4 full caps

Signed from FC Augsburg in 1980. Succeeded Jean-Marie Pfaff as Bayern first choice keeper in 1988. Former U21 international, made full debut v Eire, September 1989. Member of 1990 World Cup winning squad. Missed most of 1991/92 season with serious knee injury.

AVENET, Philippe
(Caen, Fra)
- 16.04.67 • Striker
- France U21

Second string striker who was formerly with Matra, Lens and Racing Paris. Has been at the top for nearly ten years, having made his debut for Racing against Toulouse back in 1984. Was overshadowed by Paille and Pickeu in 1991/92. Did not have the most productive of seasons in 1991/92, when he scored just once in the League.

AYACHE, William
(Nimes, Fra)
- 10.01.61 • Defender
- France 19 full caps

Much travelled full back who made his debut for Nantes, v Lens, in August 1979. Approaching his 300th First Division game, he was previously with Nantes (twice), Paris St Germain, Marseille (twice), Montpellier and Nice. Signed from Marseille in the summer of 1991. Scored once during the 1991/92 League campaign.

AYARZA, Andoni
(Atletico Bilbao, Spa)
- 12.09.65 • Midfield

Rejoined Bilbao in 1991 after spending two seasons with Valladolid.

AZEVEDO Jose Nuno Freire
(Gil Vicente, Por)
- 19.07.69 • Defender

Originally with his home town club Porto but only made his First Division debut on signing for Gil Vicente. In his first season, 1990/91, he made 32 appearences and scored one goal.

AZZOUZI, Rachid
(MSV Duisburg, Ger)
- 10.11.69 • Defender

Began his professional career with Cologne, but failed to make a league appearance with the club. Moved on to Duisburg in 1989. Was a member of the Morocco squad at the 1992 African Nations Cup.

BACCI, Roberto
(Lazio, Ita)

• 15.06.67 • Defender

Versatile defender who failed to make the grade with Turin - who he joined straight from school - and spent his early career in the lower divisions with Derthona, Pavia and Como. Brought back to Serie A by Lazio from Mantova in October 1989.

BACH, Jorg
(Wattenscheid, Ger)

• 20.11.65 • Defender

Joined club from SpVgg Wirges in 1988.

BADE, Alexander
(Cologne, Ger)

• 25.08.70 • Goalkeeper

Joined Cologne from Tennis Borussia Berlin in 1988. Made his first team debut v Wattenscheid in April 1992.

van BAEKEL, Alain
(Anderlecht, Bel)

• 20.06.61 • Midfield

Experienced central midfielder who joined the club, from Waregem, in August 1990. Has made more than 300 First Division appearances and also played for Verb, Meerhout and Lierse.

BAERT, Kris
(Eendracht Aalst, Bel)

• 27.12.69 • Midfield

Exciting young player who was snapped up from Second Division Harelbeke in the summer of 1991.

BAETSLE, David
(Charleroi, Bel)

• 01.01.67 • Goalkeeper

Signed from minor League club Namur at the beginning of 1991/92 as cover for first choice 'keeper Ranko Stojic.

BAFFOE, Anthony
(Fortuna Dusseldorf, Ger)

• 25.05.65 • Midfield
• Ghana 2 full caps

Ex-Cologne, RW Oberhausen and Stuttgarter Kickers. Signed from Fortuna Cologne in 1989.

BAGGIO, Roberto
(Juventus, Ita)

• 18.02.67 • Striker
• Italy 19 full caps, 11 goals

Began his career with little LR Vicenza in the Third Division before moving up in class to the Serie A with Fiorentina in 1985. Signed by Juventus for a then

World record £8m in 1990, prior to representing his country at the World Cup finals that year.

BAHR, Nils
(SV Hamburg, Ger)

• 16.12.69 • Goalkeeper

Reserve team keeper who joined Hamburg from SV Siebeneichen in 1988.

BAIA Amilcar Fonseca
(Uniao, Por)

• 08.08.66 • Defender

One of three players to sign from Familicao before the 1990/91 season, he has failed to find a regular place in the side.

BAIANO, Francesco
(Foggia, Ita)

• 24.02.68 • Striker

Born in Naples and joined his home town club Napoli in 1984. Made just five League appearances for the club before transferring to Foggia in 1990, after brief loan spells with Empoli, Parma and Avelino. Scored a staggering 22 goals in 36 games during the 1991 promotion season.

BAILIE, Noel
(Linfield, N.Ir)

• Midfield
• N.Ireland Youth, U21

Never-say-die midfielder who can also operate in defence or on the wing. He graduated through the ranks at Windsor Park - quite a regular route for Linfield players - and really made the breakthrough to the first team during 1989/90.

BAILS, Pascal
(Marseille, Fra)

• 30.12.64 • Defender
• France 1 full cap

Perpignan-born central defender who began with Montpellier, making his First Division debut against Toulouse on 18th July 1987. Moved to Marseille in 1991.

BAIOCCO, Christophe
(Lens, Fra)

• 29.04.66 • Goalkeeper

Signed for the club on leaving school in 1984. Faces a battle for the first team spot with Bernard Lama. Made his debut in October 1988, v Nantes.

BAKERO, Jose Maria
(Barcelona, Spa)

• 11.02.63 • Midfield
• Spain 16 full caps, 4 goals

Free-scoring midfielder who made his name with Real Sociedad, helping them to win the Spanish Cup in 1987. Was signed by Barcelona, along with Aitor Beguiristain, in 1988 for £3m and has now scored more than 100 League goals in Spain. Made a dramatic impact at international level, scoring a hat-trick v Albania in only his second full appearance for his country, in November 1987.

BALAKOV, Krassimire (Sporting Lisbon, Por)

• 29.03.66 • Midfield
• Bulgaria 6 full caps

Started Sporting's Bulgarian connection when he joined the club from Etar midway through the 1990/91 season. Guentchev and Yordanov followed soon after.

BALINT, Gauril Pele (Burgos, Spa)

• 30.01.63 • Striker
• Hungary full caps

Prolific forward who was Burgos' top scorer in 1991/92.

BALLARD, Derek (Omagh Town, N.Ir)

• Midfield

Veteran of 11 seasons with Omagh, and club captain for several years. A social worker who's seen the club rise from the junior to senior ranks in his time at St Julian's Road.

BALLENGHIEN, Laurent (Germinal Ekeren, Bel)

• 15.12.69 • Striker

Former Kortrijk forward who was one of several players to sign for Ekeren during July 1991.

BALSEIRO Luis Alberto Duarte (Uniao, Por)

• 29.09.63 • Goalkeeper

Signed as a number two to Yugoslavian Goran Zivanovic after spells as understudy at Covilha and Tirsense.

BALTAZAR, Maria Jr (Rennes, Fra)

• 17.07.59 • Striker
• Brazil full caps

Came to Europe with Atletico Madrid, before transferring to Porto in August 1990. Two goals in 19 games (15 as sub) wasn't considered good enough by the Portuguese giants and he was sold to Rennes in July 1991. His experience was expected to be a great asset alongside Kujtin Chala up front for the club, but Rennes still struggled for goals in 1991/92, managing just 25 strikes all season, although Baltazar was joint top scorer with six goals.

BANGO, Ricardo Gonzalez (Oviedo, Spa)

• 18.09.68 • Midfield

Tall player who contributes more than his fair share of goals from the Oviedo midfield.

BANNON, Paul (Cork City, Eir)

• 15.11.56 • Defender

Signed from Greek club Larissa,he's one of several vastly experienced players at Cork. Previously served at Nottingham Forest, Carlisle, Cardiff City, Bristol Rovers, Plymouth, NAC Breda (Hol) and PAOC Salonika. Good reader of the game who always makes time on the ball.

BANY, Ralph (Karlsruher, Ger)

• 01.09.64 • Defender

Formerly with Stuttgart Kickers as a youth, Ralph joined Karlsruher from Pforzheim in 1989.

BARE, Alain (Lyon, Fra)

• 24.08.66 • Striker

Well travelled forward who did not make his First Division debut until signing for Lyon in the summer 1989. He eventually took his bow against Montpellier in August of that year. Previously with Sochaux, Thonon and Montceau.

BARESI, Franco (Milan, Ita)

• 08.05.60 • Defender
• Italy 60 full caps, 1 goal

Highly respected sweeper who has spent his entire career with Milan. Made League debut for the club during 1976/77 season and has now played over 350 games. Franco made his international against Romania in December 1982 and now more than 50 caps. Milan club captain.

BARNES, Steven (Larne, N.Ir)

• Striker

A great favourite at Inver Park. His goals carried Larne to fourth spot in the Irish League in 1991/92 - their best ever finish to a League season. Previously with Distillery.

BARNY, Luis Pedro (Boavista, Por)

• 20.06.66 • Defender

Born in Porto, he first played his football with the Progresso club. Made his League debut with Boavista during the 1985/86 season, but then wjoined Amadora for two years in 1988. returned to Boavista in 1990.

BARONE, Onofrio (Foggia, Ita)
• 04.07.64 • Midfield

Began his career in Serie B with Palmero and had five seasons with his home-town club before joining Messina. Linked up with Foggia in 1987 while they were still a Third Division side and was a mainstay of the side that made their way to Serie A.

BARRABE, Claude (Montpellier ,Fra)
• 19.11.66 • Goalkeeper
• France U21

Joined the club from Brest in July 1990, and quickly established himself as first-choice 'keeper'. Very confident on crosses, using his height (6ft 2in) to good effect. Previously with INF Vichy and Paris St Germain.

BARRETT, Claude (Nancy, Fra)
• 10.11.60 • Defender

A veteran of more than 300 First Division appearances. Formerly captain at Auxerre, this two-footed defender has given Nancy's defence some much needed balance since signing from Bordeaux in 1990.

BARRIGA Joaquim Angelo Pereira (Pacos De Ferreira, Por)
• 27.09.64 • Defender

After four seasons in the League has returned to his home club as a utility defender. Brief spells with Porto, Sporting Espinho and Maritimo before claiming a place in the Pacos De Ferreira side.

BARROS, Rui Gil (Monaco, Fra)
• 24.11.65 • Midfield
• Portugal 17 full caps, 1 goal

Left the glamour of Juventus in Italy for the comparative tranquility of Monaco in 1990. Tiny midfield general (5ft 3in) who is as adept at scoring goals as he is at creating them. Man of the match in Monaco's 1991 French Cup Final win over Marseille. Seven goals in 34 games in his first season (1990/91) showed he was a wise investment. Scored six League goals in 1991/92.

BARROSO, Oliveira (Anderlecht, Bel)
• 24.03.69 • Striker

Also known as Luis Oliveira. Began with SE Tupan, but has made his mark over the past three seasons with Anderlecht. Described as the "new Scifo" by coach Aad De Mos he was runner up in the voting for the 1990 Belgian Footballer of the Year, while still only 21. His partnership up front with teenager Nii Lamptey rocketed Anderlecht to the 1991 League title.

BARRY, Dave (Cork City, Eir)

• 16.09.61 • Midfield
• League of Ireland Representative

Played in Cork's first ever League game (v Dundalk, 16.09.84), and also became first Cork player to be selected for a League of Ireland Representative team, in 1987. Also a talented Gaelic Footballer, he scored Cork's goal in the historic draw with Bayern Munich in the of 1991/92 UEFA Cup.

BARTHOLOMEEUSSEN, Joel (Mechelen, Bel)

• 02.03.66 • Midfield

Signed from Germinal Ekeren prior to the start of season 1991/92. Previously with Zoersel (twice), Lierse and Poederlee. He is the fetcher and carrier for Klas Ingesson.

BASAULA Lemba (Vitoria Guimaraes, Por)

• 03.03.65 • Midfield
• Zaire full caps

Born in Kinshasa, Basaula was signed by Vitoria in the 1986/87 season. After just seven games he moved to Elvas for a season and then on to Est Amadora . Scored three times for them between 1988 and 1990 and was then re-signed by Vitoria in 1990/91.

BASILIO Fernandes Marques (Vitoria Guimaraes, Por)

• 09.05.66 • Defender

Born and brought up in Guimaraes, he signed for Vitoria in 1986. Played just six games in his first season but has since become a regular member of the side.

van BASTEN, Marco (Milan, Ita)

• 31.10.64 • Striker
• Holland 53 full caps, 24 goals

Joined Milan for £1.5m from Ajax in his native Holland. Was voted European Footballer of the Year in 1989 and was the Italian League's top scorer in 1989/90. Over 50 caps and more than 20 goals for Holland, including the spectacular winner in the 1988 European Championship Final, when he hooked the ball in from what seemed an impossible angle. Played, but was disappointing, in 1990 World Cup finals but followed that with two impressive seasons at club level in Italy as Milan swept all before them. Couldn't repeat his European Championship success at Sweden 1992 and cruelly had his vital spot-kick saved by Peter Schmeichel as

Holland bowed out to Denmark in the Semi Final after a thrilling 2-2 draw.

BASTERE, Nicolas (Toulouse, Fra)

• 19.09.69 • Striker
• France U21

Another product of Toulouse's fruitful youth policy, he signed straight from school in 1986. Five goals from 30 games may not be a staggering return, but he did enough to persuade the club to sign him on a four-year contract at the end of 1990/91.

BATAILLE, Kurt (Beveren, Bel)

• 05.03.70 • Striker

Signed from KV Oostende in the summer of 1991.

BATS, Joel (Paris St Germain, Fra)

• 04.01.57 • Goalkeeper
• France 51 full caps

Veteran of the 1986 World Cup who played a huge part in Paris-SG's title win in 1986. Previously with Sochaux and Auxerre he joined the club in 1985. Has been playing top level football for almost 20 years, having first donned his gloves for Sochaux v St Etienne in September 1976. Announced his retirement from top level football at the end of 1991/92.

BAUMANN, Karsten (Cologne, Ger)

• 14.10.69 • Defender

Signed from VfB Oldenburg in 1988. Previously with TuS Eversten.

BAXTER, Stephen (Linfield, N.Ir)

• Striker

At 6ft 2in Baxter is every defender's nightmare in the air. Excellent header of the ball, he's averaged around 20 goals a season since joining Linfield in 1987. Previously with Glentoran and Ards.

BAYLY, Martin (Athlone Town, Eir)

• 14.09.66 • Midfield

Prolific wide midfielder who scored three goals in his first five games after joining the club in February 1991. Previously with St James Gate, where he played alongside older brother Ritchie.

BAZDAREVIC, Mehmed (Sochaux, Fra)

• 28.09.60 • Midfield
• Yugoslavia 50 full caps, 4 goals

Born in Sarajevo, this right-sided midfielder signed from Zeljeznicar in

1987. Made his French League debut on 16th July the following year against Strasbourg. Not a regular goalscorer, but he supplies a good stream of crosses for Caveglia and Carrasco up front.

BAZULEV, Sergei (Spartak Moscow, CIS)

• 10.10.57 •Defender

Experienced sweeper who played for Krasnaya Presniya, Kirov Dynamo, Nefchi Baku and Moscow Lokomotiv before joining Spartak in 1984.

BEATTY, Stephen (Linfield, N.Ir)

• 01.09.69 • Midfield

A defensive midfielder who began his career with Chelsea, but failed to break into the first team. He transferred to Danish club Aarhus before joining Linfield in 1990/91. Dangerous at free-kicks, he possesses a tremendous shot.

BECK, Robert (Glenavon, N.Ir)

• Goalkeeper

Signed from Distillery in October 1983, has now made more than 350 first team appearances. A fibreglass laminator by profession. One of the top 'keepers in N.Ireland and a candidate for the international side.

de BEER, Wolfgang (Borussia Dortmund, Ger)

• 02.01.64 • Goalkeeper

Tall keeper who moved to Dortmund from MSV Duisburg in 1986.

BEGGS, Brian (Shamrock Rovers, Eir)

• 08.01.71 • Midfield

Has struggled to establish himself at Rovers since making his first team debut in a League game at Limerick City on 9th September, 1990 (won 2-1).

BEGUIRISTAIN, Aito (Barcelona, Spa)

• 12.08.64 • Striker
• Spain 10 full caps, 1 goal

Began his career in the nursery side at Real Sociedad before moving to Barcelona as part of a £3m deal in 1988. Has a younger brother who still plays for Sociedad.

BEIERSDORFER, Dietmar (SV Hamburg, Ger)

• 16.11.63 • Defender
• Germany 1 full cap

Came to SV Hamburg from SpVgg Furth in 1986 and has now made over 150 First

Division appearances for the club. His international debut came against Belgium in May 1991 (won 1-0).

BEIN, Uwe (Eintracht Frankfurt, Ger)

• 26.09.60 • Midfield
• Germany 14 full caps, 3 goals

Highly rated defender who joined Frankfurt from SV Hamburg in 1989. Prior to that he had played for Cologne and Kickers Offenbach.

BEJENAR, Sergei (Dnepr, CIS)

• Defender
• USSR full caps

Overlapping full back who was formerly an international at Olympic level before progressing to full honours.

BELL, Joseph-Antoine (St Etienne, Fra)

• 08.10.54 • Goalkeeper
• Cameroon 7 full caps

Outspoken and hugely experienced 'keeper who missed much of Cameroon's glorious World Cup 90, when Thomas N'Kono was preferred in goal. Has spent the majority of his pro career at the very pinnacle of French football. He was spotted by giants Marseille playing for Arab Contractors and signed for 'OM' in 1985, making his debut at Le Havre. Moved to Toulon and then spent several seasons with Bordeaux where his great shot-stopping and bravery endeared him to the fans. Joined St Etienne in 1991 and is now a veteran of more than 230 First Division games. Played in the 1988 African Nations Cup Final.

BELLONE, Bruno (Cannes, Fra)

• 14.03.62 • Striker
• France 34 full caps

Experienced goalscorer who's enjoyed the highlife with Monaco and Montpellier. Now in his second spell at Cannes. His League debut came back in 1980, for Monaco v Lyon.

BELLUCI, Francesco (Bari, Ita)

• 23.02.73 • Defender

A left-sided defender and the youngest member of Bari's first team squad last season. Francesco made his League debut away to Napoli in November 1991.

BELODEDIC, Miodrag (Valencia, Ita)

• 20.05.64 • Defender
• Romania 20 full caps

Born in Serbia, but raised in Romania. Joined army club Steaua Bucharest and won the European Cup in 1986. He made his international debut v China in August 1984. Made 20 appearances for his country before going to Yugoslavia on a tourist visa and seeking political asylum in December 1988. Eventually recieved permission to join Red Star. Became first man to win European Cup winners' medal with two different clubs when Red Star beat Marseille in 1991 Final. Made a return to international competition against Latvia in April 1992. Spanish club Valencia signed him for £4 millionin May 1992.

BELSUE Arias, Alberto
(Zaragoza, Spa)
• 02.03.68 • Defender

Full back who joined Zaragoza from local junior club Endera-Andorra in 1988.

BENATELLI, Frank
(Bochum, Ger)
• 19.08.62 • Midfield

Frank originally joined Bochum from Westfalia as a 19 year old and has now been with the club for over a decade.

BENDER, Manfred
(Bayern Munich, Ger)
• 24.05.66 • Midfield

Joined Bayern in 1989 after playing for SpVgg Unterhaching and TSV 1860 München. Has made more than 70 first team appearances without ever claiming a regular first team place.

BENEDET, Alain
(Le Havre, Fra)
• 20.10.60 • Striker

Journeyman goalscorer who is approaching his tenth season in top flight football, having made his debut for Toulon in July 1983 (v Brest). Has also played for St Etienne, Nimes and Metz.

BEN MABROUK, Alim
(Lyon, Fra)
• 25.06.60 • Midfield
• Algeria full caps

Experienced ball player and fierce tackler. Born in Lyon of Algerian parents, he began his career with AS Minguettes in 1980. His First Division bow came four years later with Racing Paris, after a brief spell with Paris FC. Moved to Bordeaux, and then on to his home town club in the summer of 1991.

BENARRIVO, Antonio
(Parma, Ita)
• 21.08.68 • Defender

Exciting full back who joined local club Brindisi in 1986 and spent three years with the Third Division side before moving up a level to join Serie B side Padova. Made it into Serie A when signed by Parma in 1991.

BENEDETTI, Silvano (Torino, Ita)

• 05.10.65 • Defender

Central defender who started his career with Torino in 1983, but made just one League appearance before moving onto Parma the following year. Also spent one season at both Palermo and Ascoli before returning to Turin in 1987.

BERGKAMP, Dennis (Ajax, Hol)

• 10.05.69 • Striker
• Holland 16 full caps, 9 goals

Has spent all his career at Ajax and made his first team debut v Roda JC in December 1986. Has now made over 150 appearances for the club, scoring more than 50 times. He was outstanding for Holland at the 1992 European Championship in Sweden.

BERGODI, Cristiano (Lazio, Ita)

• 04.10.64 • Defender

Right-back who began his career with Abano before joining Pescara in 1984. Helped Pescara to win promotion to Serie A in 1987 and joined Lazio two years later.

BERGOMI, Giuseppe (Internazionale, Ita)

• 22.12.63 • Defender
• Italy 77 full caps, 6 goals

One club player who first played for Inter during the 1980/81 season. Has now played over 250 Serie A games for the club.

BERNADET, Gerard (Nimes, Fra)

• 07.03.57 • Midfield

If there was an award for the most travelled player in France, Algerian-born Bernadet would win it hands down. Nimes is his ninth club in 12 years as a professional. It took him three transfers before he made his debut, for Valenciennes against Lyon, in July 1980. Before that match he had also plied his trade with Brest, Montpellier and Olympique Marseille. Later moved to Cannes, Brest (again), Mulhouse and Toulon, before joining Nimes and guiding them to promotion in 1990/91. Was the club's second highest goalscorer in 1991/92, with five strikes in the League.

BERTHOLD, Thomas (Bayern Munich, Ger)

• 12.11.64 • Defender
• Germany 49 full caps, 1 goal

Sweeper who made his name with Eintracht Frankfurt. Moved to Italy with

Verona in 1986. Signed by Bayern from Roma in 1991 as a replacement for Klaus Augenthaler. Member of 1990 World Cup winning side, but missed 1992 European Championships through suspension.

BERTI, Gianluca
(Genoa, Ita)

• 20.05.67 • Goalkeeper

Spent five seasons with Third Division side Prato before dropping down yet another division to join Olbia. Bought to Serie A by Genoa in 1991.

BERTI, Nicola
(Internazionale, Ita)

• 14.04.67 • Midfield
• Italy 23 full caps, 3 goals

Began his career with Parma while they were still a Third Division side.Moved into serie A in 1985 when signed by Fiorentina. Joined Inter three years later.

BERTO
(Oviedo, Spa)

• 27.10.62 • Midfield

Alberto Martinez Diez was signed from junior club Cuadal Deportivo in 1984.

BERTRAND, Eric
(Nancy, Fra)

• 30.03.64 • Defender

Never-say-die full back who was previously with Metz. Signed for Nancy in September 1986, making his debut, v Lens, the following month. Strong in the air and highly determined.

BES, Alexandre
(Lyon, Fra)

• 10.04.67 • Defender

Cameroon-born defender who loves to get forward and among the goals. Was an integral part of the side that won the Division Two title in 1989.

BEST
(Salgueiros, Por)

• 24.12.68 • Goalkeeper

Previously with Vitoria Guimaraes. Artur Paulo Silva, to give him his full name, is currently Salgueiros' second choice keeper behind Jorge Madureira.

BEST, Robbie
(Athlone Town, Eir)

• 12.09.67 • Defender

Solid and uncompromising defender who joined the club on loan from St Patrick's Athletic during 1990/91. Ironically, his League of Ireland debut came against Athlone in September 1989.

BESTER, Marinus
(Werder Bremen, Ger)

• 16.01.69 • Striker

Joined Bremen from Suderelbe Hamburg
in 1990 and made his first team debut v
Borussia Dortmund in December 1991
while still an amateur at the club.

BEUCKELAERS, Olivier
(RWD Molenbeek, Bel)

• 02.12.63 • Defender

Signed from VC Groot-Bijgaarden. Has
now played more than 100 senior games.

BEUGNIES, Didier
(Charleroi, Bel)

• 14.03.61 • Midfield

Wide midfielder who is equally happy as
an out and out striker. Has formed one
half of a not particularly productive
partnership with Marc Wuyts over the past
couple of seasons. Signed from Mons.

BEUKENKAMP, Roy
(Den Haag, Hol)

• 12.01.68 • Goalkeeper

Resrve team keeper who has made just 8
appearances for Den Haag since signing in
July 1990. Previously had spells with
DWV (twice) and Ajax.

BEULS, Norbert
(Genk, Bel)

• 13.01.57 • Defender

His career got off to a slow start in the
lower divisions, where he began with Rapid
Spouwen and Tongeren before moving into
the big time with first Antwerp and then
Charleroi. Has now played more than 300
First Division games.

BEYEL, Jorg
(MSV Duisburg, Ger)

• 02.10.69 • Striker

Played his junior football with Baesweiler and
Brachelen, before moving on to Alemannia
Aachen. Joined Duisburg in 1990.

BEYENS, Luc
(Club Brugge, Bel)

• 27.03.59 • Midfield
• Belgium 2 full caps

Belgian Cup winner in 1991, and League
Champion in 1990 and 1992, he's
experiencing the high-life with Brugge(?)
having spent much of his early career in
the lower divisions with Turnhout,
Louvieroise and Tongeren.

BIATO, Enzo Maurizio
(Bari, Ita)

• 30.07.63 • Goalkeeper

Very tall keeper who joined Bari from Triestina in 1990. Started his career with Genoa, but failed to make an impression. Spent time with Acqui, Casale, Entella and Centese before getting his chance in Serie B with Triestina in 1989.

BICKEL, Thomas (Grasshoppers, Swi)
• 10.10.63 • Midfield
• Switzerland 25 full caps, 2 goals

Began career with FC Biel. Joined Grasshoppers in 1988 from local rivals FC Zurich.

BIGLIARDI, Tebaldo (Atalanta, Ita)
• 05.02.63 • Defender

Joined Palermo in 1981 and spent five seasons with the club before getting his chance in Serie A with Napoli. Four years and 31 League games later he moved on to Atalanta.

BINDEWALD, Uwe (Eintracht Frankfurt, Ger)
• 13.08.68 • Defender

Joined Frankfurt as a teenager from Kickers Offenbach but originally struggled to establish himself in the side.

BINZ, Manfred (Eintracht Frankfurt, Ger)
• 22.09.65 • Defender
• Germany 12 full caps

Talented defender who has become an integral part of the Frankfurt side since joining the club from VfR Bockenheim 1979.

BIRA (Beira-Mar, Por)
• 23.02.65 • Striker

Brazilian Ubiraci Souza de Souza made his Portuguese First Division debut with Beira-Mar during the 1988/89 season. Returned to the club from Agueda in 1991.

BIRNEY, Nigel (Larne, N.Ir)
• Defender
• Irish League Representative

Made a sensational start to senior football, after signing from local minor League club Dungannon Swifts at the start of season 1990/91. His tremendous form was rewardede with his first Irish League Representative cap - in a match v Kilmarnock - just a couple of months after taking his League bow. Remarkably calm and confident on the ball he has adapted well to life in the top flight.

BIURRUN, Jose Vicente Fernandez (Espanol, Spa)

• 01.09.59 • Goalkeeper

Although born in Brazil he qualified to play for Spain through his parents. Joined Espanol from Atletico Bilbao in 1990 as a replacement for Tommy N'Kono.

BLACKLEDGE, Gary (Crusaders, N.Ir)

• Striker

One of a string of ex-Glenavon players at the club. He was a great favourite at Glentoran, where he earned a reputation as one of the Irish League's most potent strikers. Has also had spells with Manchester City, Portadown and French club Chaumont.

BLACKSON, Dwight (Feyenoord, Hol)

• 16.10.71 • Striker

Made his League debut during 1989/90 season, but has struggled to gain a regular place in the side. He is of Dutch West Indian descent.

BLANC, Andre (Toulon, Fra)

• 19.11.66 • Defender

Centre back who has been with the club since 1989. Previously with Avignon and, on loan, Grenoble.

BLIND, Danny (Ajax, Hol)

• 01.08.61 • Defender

• Holland 19 full caps, 2 goals

Spent seven seasons in the Sparta Rotterdam first team squad before moving to Ajax in 1986. Has now played more than 200 matches for the club. Captained the side to their 1991/92 UEFA Cup triumph which equalled Juventus' record of winning all three Euro club competitions. Barcelona became the third club to achieve that feat when they won the Champions' Cup at Wembley in May.

BLINKER, Regi (Feyenoord, Hol)

• 04.06.69 • Striker

Rastafarian left winger who made debut in Feyenoord first team when still a teenager. Spent much of 1988/89 season on loan to Den Bosch. Over 100 League appearances for the Rotterdam club.

BLONDEAU, Patricke (Monaco, Fra)

• 27.01.68 • Defender

• France U21

Signed from Division Two club Martigues

in 1989. Took his top flight bow in July of that year, against Racing Paris. Despite his comparative lack of height he is very commanding in the air and likes to bring the ball out from the back.

BLONDEAU, Stephane (Montpellier, Fra)

• 04.03.68 • Defender
• France U21

Tall central defender who was signed from Racing Paris in 1990. He was a member of Montpellier's victorious 1990 French Cup winning squad.

BOBAN, Zvonimir (Milan, Ita)

• 08.10.68 • Midfield
• Yugoslavia 8 full caps, 1 goal

A talented playmaker who likes to attack, Zvonimir was signed by Milan from Dinamo Zagreb in 1991. Loaned out by Milan to Bari for the 1991/92 season. Was due to transfer to Marseille in 1992/93 as part of a deal taking Jean-Pierre Papin, but contracted viral hepatitis in April 1992 and the deal was put on hold. He was banned from taking part in the 1990 World Cup after he assaulted a policeman during ethnic violence which erupted after Zagreb's game against Red Star Belgrade in May 1990. He was an important member of Yugoslavia's 1987 World Youth Cup winning side, many of whom, graduated to the full national side.

BOBO Djalo, Mamadu (Boavista, Por)

• 09.02.63 • Midfield

Began hsi career with Porto but failed to gain a regular first team place and moved to Varzim in 1984. Had spells with Guimaraes, Maritimo and Amadora but joining Boavista in 1990.

BOCANDE, Jules (Lens, Fra)

• 25.11.58 • Striker
• Senegal full caps

Highly experienced player who had scored 64 goals in 197 senior games when he signed for Lens in July 1991. Formerly with Tournay, Seraing, Metz, Paris St Germain and Nice. Was signed as an elder-statesman to help the club consolidate in its first season back in top flight.

BOCKENFELD, Manfred (Werder Bremen, Ger)

• 23.07.60 • Defender
• Germany 1 full cap

Very experienced member of the Bremen side with over 300 First Division games to his credit. Signed by Werder from Waldhof Mannheim in 1989. Previously with Fortuna Dusseldorf.

BODART, Gilbert (Standard Liege, Bel)

• 02.09.62 • Goalkeeper
• Belgium 7 full caps; Olympic; U21; Youth

Signed from CS Verlaine. Experienced 'keeper who would undoubtedly have been Belgium's number one for the best part of a decade but for the not insubstantial presence of the extraordinary Jean-Marie Pfaff. He has made more than 230 First Divison appearances. Made his international debut against Bulgaria on 23rd April 1986.

BODDEN, Olaf (Hansa Rostock, Ger)

• 04.05.68 • Striker

Began his career with Viktoria Goch and then made a handful of first team appearances in Bundesliga A with Borussia Moenchengladbach before signing for Rostock in 1991.

BODE, Jorg (SV Hamburg, Ger)

• 22.08.69 • Midfield

Young playmaker who was signed from Arminia Bielefeld in 1989. Began his career with another minor League club, Osnabruck, before hitting the big time with Hamburg.

BODE, Marco (Werder Bremen, Ger)

• 23.07.69 • Striker

Joined Bremen from VfR Osterode in 1988.

de BOER, Frank (Ajax, Hol)

• 15.05.70 • Defender
• Holland full caps

Has spent all his career with Ajax and made his first team debut at PEC Zwolle in September 1988. Has now made more than 100 appearances for the club.

BOES, Rudy (Waregem, Bel)

• 26.02.67 • Defender

Full back who likes nothing more than haring down the flanks and taking on opponents. Signed from Second Division club Patro Eisden at the beginning of the 1990/91 season, he scored five goals in 23 starts that campaign - which was a better record than striker David Nakhid.

BOFFIN, Danny (Anderlecht, Bel)

• 10.07.65 • Midfield
• Belgium 7 full caps

Creative playmaker and new central figure

of the Anderlecht midfield. Began with STVV and was signed from Liege in Jun 1991. Helped Liege to the 1990 Belgian Cup.

BOGAERTS, Marnik (Beveren, Bel)

• 16.04.67 • Midfield

Signed in the summer of 1991 from SK Lommel.

BOGDAN, Srecko (Karlsruher, Ger)

• 05.01.57 • Defender
• Yugoslavia 15 full caps

Experienced defender who move to the Bundesliga seven years ago and has made over 130 League appearances since then. Signed from Dinamo Zagreb.

BOGER, Stefan (Hansa Rostock, Ger)

• 01.06.66 • Midfield
• East Germany 4 full caps

Joined Rostock in 1991 from Carl Zeiss Jena. Previously with Rot-Weiss Erfurt.

BOGERS, Adri (Mechelen, Bel)

• 04.05.65 • Defender

Uncompromising Dutchman who joined

from RKC at the beginning of the 1990/91 season. Previously with Boeimeer and NAC.

BOGNAR, Gyorgy (Standard Liege, Bel)

• 05.11.61 • Defender
• Hungary 43 full caps, 8 goals

Formerly with MTK Budapest and Toulon in his native Hungary.

BOLI, Basile (Marseille, Fra)

• 02.01.67 • Defender
• France 37 full caps, 1 goal

A defender with a real taste for goals at club level. Ever-present during his first season with Marseille (90/91) his presence at the heart of defence carried them to the 1991 Champions' Cup Final. Born on the Ivory Coast, he was signed from Auxerre. Was at the centre of controversy during the 1992 European Championship, when he blatantly head-butted England's Stuart Pearce on "live" television.

BOLI, Roger (Lens, Fra)

• 26.09.65 • Striker

Elder brother of Marseille and France star Basile Boli. Like Basile, began with Auxerre, where he made his debut against Racing Club Paris in December 1984. Moved on to Lille, before joining Lens in

1989. His goals helped the club to promotion from Division Two B in 1990/91.

BONALAIR, Thierry (Nantes, Fra)
• 14.06.66 • Defender
• France 1 full cap

Came up through the ranks at Nantes to make his bow for the first team, against Metz, in February 1987. Had a very brief spell at Amiens in 1989 before returning to his first club. Strong tackling full back.

BONAN, Heiko (Bochum, Ger)
• 10.02.66 • Midfield
• East Germany 2 full caps

Former international who played his early football in the eastern Germany with Magdeburg. Later signed by FC Berlin and moved to the West with Bochum in 1991.

BONETTI, Ivano (Sampdoria, Ita)
• 01.08.64 • Defender

Left-back who began his League career with his home town club, Brescia, in 1981. Later had spells with Genoa, Juventus and Atalanta, before joining Sampdoria from Bologna in 1991.

BONNER, Denis (Sligo Rovers, Eir)
• 24.05.60 • Defender

Solid central defender who was signed from Finn Harps

BONNER, Seamus (Omagh Town, N.Ir)
• Forward

Omagh's longest serving player. Signed straight from school in 1978, and has stayed there ever since. Sales rep by profession he signed a new three-year contract in September. 1991.

BONOMI, Mauro (Cremonese, Ita)
• 23.08.72 • Defender

Locally born teenager who has been with Cremonese for all of his short career. Made his League debut during the 1990/91 season.

BORDIN, Roberto (Atalanta, Ita)
• 10.01.65 • Midfield

Made his League debut during the 1982/83 season while at Third Division Sanremese. Moved up a division to join Taranto in 1984 and then went on to Parma a year later. Transferred to Cesena in

1986 and helped the club gain promotion to Serie A in his first season. Picked up by Atalanta in 1989.

BORKELMANS, Vital
(Club Brugge, Bel)

• 01.06.63 • Midfield
• Belgium 1 full cap

Ball-winning midfield general, who is more than happy to drop back and defend when necessary. His only international experience so far has been 10 minutes as sub against Denmark in August 1989. Consistent and hard-working he was signed from Waregem.

BORO, Salvador Gonzalez
(Valencia, Spa)

• 09.10.63 • Defender

Locally born defender who began his career with Valencia, but left for a spell with Tenerife. Returned to the club in 1985.

BORODJUK, Alexander
(Schalke, Ger)

• 30.11.62 • Midfield
• USSR 7 full caps, 1 goal

Bought to Western Europe from Dynamo Moscow by Schalke in 1989. Helped the club to the Second Division Championship in 1990/91.

BOROWKA, Uli
(Werder Bremen, Ger)

• 19.05.62 • Defender
• Germany 6 full caps

Signed from Borussia Moenchengladbach in 1987 and was a member of the Bremen side that won the German League title in 1988.

BORRELLI, Luc
(Toulon, Fra)

• 02.07.65 • Goalkeeper

Home grown number one who has played more than 80 senior games since his debut against Metz in November 1986. Has had strong competition for his position from Cameroon's Jacques Songo'o over the past three seasons.

BORTOLAZZI, Mario
(Genoa, Ita)

• 10.01.65 • Midfield

Began career with Mantova in 1980 and played for Fiorentina, Parma, Atalanta, Milan and Verona. Joined Genoa in 1990. Won League title with Milan 1988.

BOSMAN, Johnny
(Anderlecht, Bel)

• 01.02.65 • Striker
• Holland 22 full caps

Was billed as Holland's brightest new star prior to the 1988 European Championships, but missed the opening games due to injury and has since lived in the shadow of Marco van Basten. Eleven goals in 27 starts for PSV Eindhoven during the 1990/91 Championship season obviously wasn't enough to convince coach Bobby Robson and he was sold to Anderlecht at the beginning of season 1991/92. Also formerly with Ajax and Mechelen.

BOSMANS, Frank
(Lokeren, Bel)
• 14.10.67 • Midfield

After struggling to make the grade in Belgium he finally got a break with Israeli club Eke Nazereth. Realising he had slipped through their net, he was quickly signed up by Anderlecht before moving on to Lierse in 1989. Equally happy as a combative midfielder or in defence.

BOSZ, Peter
(Feyenoord, Hol)
• 21.11.63 • Midfield
• Holland 6 full caps

Defensive midfield player who made League debut with Vitesse Arnhem. Moved on to RKC Waalwijk before joining Toulon of France. Bought back to Holland for £150,000 by Feyenoord, summer 1991. Made international debut as a substitute v Greece, December 1991.

BOUAFIA, Ali
(Lyon, Fra)
• 05.08.64 • Striker
• Algeria full caps

Giant front-runner who was signed from Marseille, where he had struggled to make an impression thanks to the presence of Jean-Pierre Papin. Formerly with Mulhouse. Made his French League debut, with Marseille, against Monaco in July 1987 and has now played more than 100 senior games.

BOUDERBALA, Abdel Aziz
(Lyon, Fra)
• 26.12.60 • Striker
• Morocco full caps

Began his career with home town club WAC Casablanca before moving, via Sion and Racing Paris, to Lyon in 1990. Speedy front-man with exceptional close control.

BOUMNIJEL, Ali
(Nancy, Fra)
• 13.04.66 • Goalkeeper

Tunision-born giant 'keeper (6ft 4in) who was signed as back up for first choice number one Sylvain Matrisciano. Previously with Gueugnon.

BOVRI, Pascal
(Lierse, Bel)

• 04.10.64 • Defender

Formerly with SK Halle and Anderlecht.

BOWERS, Barney
(Glentoran, N.Ir)

• Defender

Penalty kick expert. He is equally happy playing in central midfield or the sweeper position, where he is very comfortable coming out with the ball. Consistent and reliable player.

BOYD, Alan
(Larne, N.Ir)

• Midfield

Previously with Linfield, where he had trouble breaking into the first team set-up. Joined Larne at the beginning of the 1991/92 season and helped guide the club to fourth place in the Irish League - their best ever finish.

BOZOVIC, Boban
(Lens, Fra)

• 24.11.63 • Midfield

• Yugoslavia full caps

In what has become the norm for Yugoslav players abroad, he is the creative axis around which the Lens team operates. A superb ball-player he signed for the club from home- town club Sarajevo in 1990.

BRADY, Austin
(Drogheda United, Eir)

• 17.04.55 • Defender

Former Athlone Town player who signed for Drogheda in the summer of 1990, and the following season helped the club to promotion from the First Division.

BRADY, Keith
(Bohemians, Eir)

• 10.10.71 • Defender

Joined the club from minor League side Belvedere in July 1990. His First Division debut came at Derry City in September 1990.

BRADY, Kevin
(Derry City, Eir)

• 02.12.62 • Defender

Signed for the club in the summer of 1988 from Shamrock Rovers and helped Derry to their historic League and Cup double the following year. Solid and reliable central defender.

BRAGLIA, Simone
(Genoa, Ita)

• 22.07.62 • Goalkeeper

Played for Como, Legnano, Pavia,

Sambene-dettese, Lecce and Monza, before signing for Genoa in 1989.

BRANCO, Claudio
(Genoa, Ita)

• 04.04.64 • Defender
• Brazil full caps

Highly rated attacking left back who left Fluminense in his native Brazil after the 1986 Mexico World Cup to join Brescia in Italy. Later moved on to Porto in Portugal before returning to Italy with Genoa in November 1990. Powerful shot at free-kicks.

BRATSETH, Rune
(Werder Bremen, Ger)

• 19.03.61 • Defender
• Norway 41 full caps, 4 goals

Signed from Rosenborg Trondheim in 1986 and twice voted Best Overseas Player in the Bundesliga. Intends to return to Norway at end of 1992/93 season. Has a 19-year-old brother who had a trial with Bremen in 1992.

BRAVO, Daniel
(Paris St Germain, Fra)

• 09.02.63 • Striker
• France 13 full caps

Troublesome forward who likes to run at the defence with the ball at his feet. Started his senior career as a 17-year-old with Nice, making his debut v Metz in July

1980. Had a brief spell at Monaco, before retuning to Nice, from where Paris-SG snapped him up in 1989. Has now made more than 300 First Division appearances. Scored five goals during 1991/92.

BRAY, Jose
(Cannes, Fra)

• 23.12.64 • Midfield

Formerly with Antibes, he has now played more than 120 first-class games for Cannes. Comfortable as a wide midfield player, or pushing up from defence.

BREHME, Andreas
(Internazionale, Ita)

• 09.11.60 • Defender
• Germany 73 full caps, 8 goals

Played for Saarbrucken, Kaiserslautern and Bayern Munich in Germany, before joining Internazionale after the 1988 European Championships. He won the Italian League in 1989 and UEFA Cup in 1991 with the Milan based club. Made his international debut against Belgium in 1984. An attacking left back, he scored the winning goal, from the penalty spot, against Argentina in 1990 World Cup Final in Rome.

BREITZKE, Gunter
(Borussia Dortmund, Ger)

• 29.06.67 • Midfield

Formerly on the books of Bayer Leverkusen and Fortuna Cologne, Gunter joined Dortmund from SC Bruck in 1988.

BREMSER, Dirk (MSV Duisburg, Ger)
• 01.10.65 • Midfield

Formerly with Bochum, Dirk arrived at Duisburg in 1990 via Preussen Munster.

BRERETON, Graham (Drogheda United, Eir)
• 07.10.71 • Defender

Fine young prospect who helped the club to promotion to the Premier Division in the 1990/91 season. Formerly with Belvedere, his League of Ireland debut came at Home Farm in October 1990.

BRESCIANI, Giorgio (Torino, Ita)
• 23.04.69 • Striker

Began his career with Torino in 1985 but had to wait until the 1987/88 season before breaking into the League side. Spent the 1989/90 campaign with Atalanta, but returned to Turin in 1990.

BRESLIN, Tom (Cliftonville, N.Ir)
• Midfield

Home-grown hero who used to watch

from the terraces at Solitude Park. Signed for the club in 1982 and has remained there ever since.

BRETON, Christophe (Lyon, Fra)
• 21.05.66 • Goalkeeper

Third in line, behind Gilles Rousset and Jean-Phillipe Foret, for the keeper's jersey at Stade Gerland. Home grown player who has progressed through the ranks at the club. Had a spell on loan at Le Puy in 1990/91.

van BREUKELEN, Hans (PSV Eindhoven, Hol)
• 04.10.56 • Goalkeeper
• Holland 71 full caps

Formerly with Utrecht, signed from Nottingham Forest in July 1984. Won the European Cup with PSV in 1988 and has now played more than 400 First Division games in England and Holland. Intensely competitive, he has been known to resort to obvious gamesmanship in an attempt to win matches.

BRICON, Pierre-Yves (Sochaux, Fra)
• 11.10.63 • Defender

Left back who was previously with Louhans-Cuiseaux, Guingcamp and Brest. Made his debut v Nantes in September

1988 and is now approaching 100 League games with Sochaux. Scored one goal during the 1991/92 campaign.

BRISSON, Francois (Lille, Fra)

• 09.04.58 • Striker
• France 2 full caps

The elder statesman of the Lille side, and a perfect foil to Patrice Sauvaget up front. Hugely experienced, he has scored more than 100 goals in over 400 appearances with Paris St Germain, Laval (twice), Lens, Strasbourg, Marseille and Lyon. His first senior game came way back in December 1975, for Paris-SG against Reims.Spent the 1990/91 season on loan at Lille before making the move permanent in July 1991. Celebrated his first full season at the club by scoring five League goals in 1991/92.

van BRITSOM, Mark (Beveren, Bel)

• 19.01.66 • Midfield

Former WS Sombeke player who has experienced the highs and lows with Beveren. A member of the side that was relegated to Division Two in 1989/90, he battled on and was rewarded as the club romped to the 1990/91 Division Two Championship.

BRNOVIC, Dragoslav (Metz, Fra)

• 02.11.63 • Midfield

Born in Titograd, Yugoslavia, he joined his home town club straight from school. Transferred to Partizan Belgrade before moving to France with Metz in 1989. His French League debut came in July of that year against Bordeaux.

BROCHARD, Rene (Feyenoord, Hol)

• 15.12.68 • Defender

Product of Feyenoord youth team, he came up through the ranks at the club to make his League debut during the 1989/90 season. Further appearances have been limited due to the stability of the Dutch club's back four.

BROCKEN, David (Lierse, Bel)

• 18.02.71 • Defender

Former youth team player who joined the club straight from school in 1987. Broke into the first team during the 1990/91 season and has remained almost ever present in the last two campaigns. Played a big part in the club's impressive run of the 1991/92 campaign, when they finished 7th in the League.

BROECKAERT, Nico (Antwerp, Bel)

• 23.11.60 • Defender
• Belgium 2 full caps

Played with minor League club Zottegem before joining Antwerp, where he has now made more than 250 First Division appearances. Made his international debut comparatively late in his career, when he played v East Germany on 12th September 1990. It was an historic occasion on which to take a bow, as it was the country's last ever national match.

BROGNO, Dante (Charleroi, Bel)

• 02.05.66 • Striker

Not especially prolific front-man who has dual Italian-Belgian citizenship. Reliable back-up for the first choice forwards Malbasa, Wuyts and Beugnies.

BROLIN Tomas (Parma, Ita)

• 29.11.69 • Striker
• Sweden 20 full caps, 12 goals

Began his career with Sundsvall in Sweden and moved on to Norrkoping in 1990. Made his name with the national side during the World Cup finals that summer and, although Sweden where disappointing, he did enough to earn a big money move to Parma prior to the 1990/91 season. His late goal, after a superb one-two with Martin Dahlin, knocked England out of the 1991/92 European Championship in Sweden.

BROUARD, Regis (Montpellier, Fra)

• 17.01.67 • Midfield
• France Olympic, U21

Began with Rodez before moving to Montpellier in July 1990. HIs first appearance in the top flight came on 8th February 1991, at Toulon.

BROWN, Stephen (Bangor, N.Ir)

• 25.12.62 • Defender
• Irish League Representative

Very dangerous in the air, he joined the club from Cliftonville in the summer of 1987. Was voted "Player of the Year" for 1990/91, when he scored eight goals from central defence. Ever-present that season, and also a member of the 1991/92 Lombard Ulster Cup winning side.

BRUJOS, Nick (Sligo Rovers, Eir)

• 22.06.63 • Goalkeeper

Born in Philadelphia, he moved to Sligo Rovers in August 1989. Previously with Shelbourne, for whom he made his League of Ireland debut on 22nd December, 1985, against St Patrick's Athletic (drew 0-0).

BRUNNER, Martin
(Grasshoppers, Swi)

• 23.04.63 • Goalkeeper
• Switzerland 31 full caps

The older brother of Ulrich Brunner who is also a goalkeeper and is also on the club's books. Made his international debut against Algeria in May 1986.

BRUNNER, Thomas
(Nuremburg, Ger)

• 10.08.62 • Defender

Long serving defender who has made more than 250 League appearances for Nuremburg - a club record.

BRUNO, Pasquale
(Torino, Ita)

• 19.06.62 • Defender

Central defender who spent four season in the Second Division with Lecce before joining Como in 1983. Helped his new side gain promotion to Serie A in his first term and was snapped up by Juventus after just one year in the top flight. Arrived at Torino in 1990.

BRYLLE, Kenneth
(Lierse, Bel)

• 22.05.59 • Striker
• Denmark 15 full caps

Hugely experienced front-runner who was brought in at the beginning of the

1991/92 season to lend some experience to the club's lightweight attack. Lierse is his ninth senior club, having already played with Hvdrove IF, Vejle BK, Anderlecht, PSV Eindhoven, Marseille, Sabadelle, Club Brugge and Beerschot. His goals helped fire the club to 7th in the League in 1991/92 - their best finish for many years.

BUCHWALD, Guido
(VfB Stuttgart, Ger)

• 24.01.61 • Defender
• Germany 54 full caps, 1 goal

His headed goal six minutes from time clinched the 1992 Bundesliga title for Stuttgart on the final day of the season. Joined VfB in 1983 - the year before their last championship success - from Stuttgart Kickers and has now made more than 250 First Division appearances.

BUCK, Andreas
(VfB Stuttgart, Ger)

• 29.12.67 • Midfield

Joined Stuttgart from Freiburg in 1990. Previously had spells with Kirchheim and Geslingen as a youth.

BUCKMAIER, Eduard
(Wattenscheid, Ger)

• 09.06.66 • Midfield

Signed from Eintracht Braunschweig in 1988.

BUISINE, Jean-Luc (Lille, Fra)

- 05.10.61 • Defender
- France U21

Giant centre back (6ft 5in) who is currently Lille's longest serving player, having been at the club since 1986. Formerly with Rouen and Strasbourg. Has played more than 200 First Division games.

BULENT, Korkmaz (Galatasaray, Tur)

- 24.11.68 • Defender
- Turkey 7 full caps

Powerful centre back who made his international debut against Eire in May 1990 and has gone onto establish himself in the national side alongside Keskin Gokhan.

BUNCOL, Andrzej (Bayer Leverkusen, Ger)

- 21.09.59 • Midfield
- Poland Full

Veteran midfielder who joined Leverkusen from Homburg in 1987. Previously with Legia Warsaw and Ruch Chorzow in his native Poland. Was a member of Bayer's 1988 UEFA Cup winning side.

BURGER, Henning (Schalke, Ger)

- 16.12.69 • Midfield

Former Motor Zeulenroda and Carl Zeiss Jena midfielder who joined Schalke in West Germany prior to the 1991/92 season.

BURROWS, Jackie (Crusaders, N.Ir)

- Defender

Elder brother of Crues skipper Sid Burrows. A loyal, one-club man who made his senior debut back in October 1982. Uncomplicated defender who is equally happy at full back or in central defence. Was the club's Player of the Year in 1988/89.

BURROWS, Sidney (Crusaders, N.Ir)

- Midfield
- Irish League Representative

Now in his second spell at Seaview. Began with the club in 1982, and attracted interest from Liverpool and Millwall before opting to join Linfield in September 1986. Re-joined his first club in April 1991.

BURRUCHAGA, Jorge (Nantes, Fra)

- 09.10.63 • Midfield
- Argentina full caps

Hugely experienced Argentine central midfield general. Tough tackling ball-winner and creative with it, he has experienced two World Cup Finals with Argentina, as well as a whole host of honours at club level with Argentinian side Independiente. Joined Nantes in 1985, making his debut v Toulon in July of that year. Injuries have severely restricted his appearances over the last two seasons.

BURSAC, Milos
(Lyon, Fra)
• 23.06.64 • Striker

Experienced goalscorer who began in his native Yugoslavia with Hajduk Split and Partizan Belgrade, before moving to France with Toulon in the summer of 1989. His French First Division debut came against St Etienne in July of that year.

BUSO, Renato
(Sampdoria, Ita)
• 19.12.69 • Striker

Discovered by Juventus playing for Montebeiluna. Came to prominence with Fiorentina and joined Sampdoria in summer 1991.

BUSQUETS, Carlos
(Barcelona, Spa)
• 19.07.67 • Goalkeeper
• Spain youth

A product of Barcelona's youth policy, Carlos was given a baptism of fire when he made his first team debut in the 1991 European Cup-Winners' Cup Final defeat against Manchester United. Despite being thrown in at the deep end, he coped well and has impressed any observers with his calmness under pressure.

BUSTARD, Ian
(Ards, N.Ir)
• Midfield

Hard-man central midfield player who was snapped up from Glenavon for £4,500 at the beginning of the 1991/92 season. He was well known to Ards boss Paul Malone, having previously played under him for five years with Larne.

BUSUTILL, Carmel
(Genk, Bel)
• 29.02.64 • Midfield

Equally happy playing wide midfield or up front. Formerly with Rabat Ajax and AC Verbania.

BUTRAGUENO, Emilio
(Real Madrid, Spa)
• 22.07.63 • Striker
• Spain Olympic, U21, 67 full caps, 26 goals

Rejected by Real and Atletico Madrid as boy. Joined Real's Second Division nursery team, Castilla. 22 goals in first half of

1982-83 season earned him call-up to Real squad. Scored twice when making his debut as half-time substitute v Cadiz. Member of Spanish squad for 1984 European Championship, but did not play. Made debut in World Cup qualifier v Wales and scored. Voted 3rd in 1986 and 1987 European Footballer of Year polls. Scored 4 goals v Denmark in 1986 World Cup finals. Nicknamed 'El Buitre' (the Vulture).

BUTTNER, Steffan
(Dynamo Dresden, Ger)

• 02.11.63 • Defender
• East Germany 3 full caps

Joined Dresden as a schoolboy in 1977 and went on to progress from the first team to the East German international set up. Didn't take the opportunity to move West after the collapse of the Berlin Wall, preferring to stay with his first club.

BUYENS, Robby
(Beveren, Bel)

• 21.12.64 • Midfield

Came up through the ranks at the club, which he joined straight from school in 1980. One of several players to stay at the club despite relegation in 1989/90, his midfield prompting was a great help in the successful fight for promotion during the following campaign.

BUYO, Francisco
(Real Madrid, Spa)

• 10.09.59 • Goalkeeper
• Spain Youth, Olympic, U21, U23, 7 full caps

Vastly experienced player with a fiery temper who has now made more than 400 appearances in the Spanish First Division. Joined Real in May 1986 from Seville.

van den BUYS, Stan
(RWD Molenbeek, Bel)

• 08.06.57 • Midfield

Experienced central midfielder who signed from Lierse midway through the 1990/91 season. Formerly with Wuustwezel and Berchem Sport.

de BUYSER, Marc
(Cercle Brugge, Bel)

• 13.11.63 • Midfield

Signed for the club in the summer of 1990 after spells with FC Boom (twice), Anderlecht and Molenbeek.

BWALYA, Kalusha
(PSV Eindhoven, Hol)

• 16.08.63 • Striker
• Zambia full caps

Began career with Mufulira Wanderers in Zambia. Moved to Cercle Brugge in 1986 and joined PSV in July 1989. Member of Zambia's 1992 African Nations Cup squad.

BYRNE, Alan
(Bohemians, Eir)

• 12.05.69 • Midfield

Combative and tough tackling midfielder who joined the club from local side Lakelands in Jul 1987, making his League of Ireland debut away at Cobh Ramblers in September the following year.

BYRNE, Jodi
(Shelbourne, Eir)

• 30.04.63 • Goalkeeper

Signed from Shamrock Rovers in July 1990.

BYRNE, John
(Sligo Rovers, Eir)

• 29.08.62 • Midfield

Former Bohemians and Home Farm player who moved to Sligo prior to the 1990/91 season. Made his League of Ireland debut against St Patrick's Athletic on 22nd November 1981 (lost 2-0).

BYRNE, Pat
(Shelbourne, Eir)

• 15.05.56 • Midfield

Elder brother of goalkeeper Jodi Byrne, he was also snapped up from Shamrock Rovers during the summer of 1990.

BYRNE, Paul
(Bangor, N.Ir)

• 30.06.72 • Midfield

Began with Dublin junior club Bluebell United, before signing for Oxford United straight from school. Played just five League games for the Manor Ground club before moving to Arsenal. Failed to make the grade at Highbury and returned to Northern Ireland. Skilful playmaker who grabbed five League goals in 1991/92.

BYRNE, Paul
(Bohemians, Eir)

• 25.11.65 • Midfield

Hard working midfielder who likes to chip in with his share of the goals. Signed from Athlone Town.

BYRNE, Paul
(Glenavon, N.Ir)

• Defender

Veteran of more than 400 senior games for Glenavon since signing from Drogheda United in 1983. Has established himself in the sweeper's role and is widely regarded as one of the Irish League's top defenders.

BYRNE, Sean
(Shamrock Rovers, Eir)

• Defender

Solid and reliable centre back who made his League of Ireland debut, for Shamrock Rovers, at Galway United in December 1989 (lost 1-2).

CABANAS, Roberto
(Lyon, Fra)

• 11.04.61 • Midfield
• Paraguay full caps

Signed from Brest in June 1990 to help the club consolidate on their return to Division One after winning the Division Two title the previous season. Originally signed as a striker, he was switched to wide midfield by coach Raymond Domenech. Has averaged a goal every 2.5 games while in France with Lyon and, previously, Brest. Began with America Cali, in Colombia.

CACIOLI Junior, Milton
(Sporting Braga, Por)

• 11.05.65 • Midfield

Brazilian midfielder who joined Portuguese side Famalicao in 1990. Made 38 appearances during his debut First Division season and then moved on to Sporting Braga in 1991.

CADETE, Jorge Paulo
(Sporting Lisbon, Por)

• 27.08.68 • Striker
• Portugal 7 full caps, 1 goal

Originally from the AA Santarem club, he made his First Division debut for Sporting during the 1987/88 season. Spent the following year with Vitoria Setubal, but returned to Sporting as a first team regular in 1989.

CAETANO Antonio de Oliveira (Vitoria Guimaraes, Por)

• 05.07.66 • Defender

Made his League debut when he was just seventeen for Boavista. Spent five seasons there before switching to Est Amadora in 1988/89. Was re-signed by Amadora for the 1990/91 campaign before being released to Vitoria.

CAIRNS, Adrian (Bray Wanderers, Eir)

• 15.11.63 • Defender

Coventry-born player who is equally happy playing in midfield or central defence.

CALCATERRA, Fabio (Bari, Ita)

• 13.05.65 • Defender

A tough man marker who spent his early career with Internazionale and Lazio. Signed by Bari prior to the 1991/92 season from Cesena, who had just been relegated to Serie B. Despite his hard work and tough tackling he failed to keep Bari in Serie A.

CALDERARO, Francois (Metz, Fra)

• 15.06.64 • Striker

Formerly with Stade de Reims he has averaged a goal every three games since his First Divison debut, for Metz v Lille, in July 1990. Was the club's leading scorer, with 17 goals, in the League in 1991/92.

CAMARASA Castellar, Francisco Jose (Valencia, Spa)

• 27.09.69 • Defender
• Spain Youth

Young central defender who was called up from the reserves into Valencia's first team squad in the 1988/89 season.

CAMILO Casal Fernandez (Albacete, Spa)

• 25.05.63 • Midfield

Previously with Celta de Vigo and Osasuna, he joined Albacete in 1991.

CAMPBELL, Brian (Ards, N.Ir)

• Defender

Fullback who joined the club as a 15-year-old in 1983. Has progressed through the youth and colts ranks to the first team.

CAMPBELL, David
(Cliftonville, N.Ir)

• 02.06.65 • Midfield
• N.Ireland 10 full caps

Began with Oxford Boys' Club before
travelling to England with Nott'm
Forest in 1983. Spent six years at the
City Ground, and a loan spell at Notts
County, before moving to Chalrton.
Also played with Plymouth and
Bradford City before returning home
with Cliftonville at the end of the
1991/92 season

CAMPBELL, David
(Shamrock Rovers, Eir)

• 02.06.65 • Midfield
• N.Ireland 10 full caps

Began with the Oxford Boys' Club - a
breeding ground for many top League of
Ireland players. Nottingham Forest
snapped him up in 1983, and he went on
to spend five seasons at the City Ground,
with a brief spell on loan at Notts
County, before joining Charlton Athletic
in 1987. Also had a spell at Plymouth,
and two seasons at Bradford City, before
retuning to Ireland with Derry City in
December 1990. Made his League of
Ireland debut with Derry on December
16, 1990, v Waterford (won 6-2).
Shamrock Rovers snapped him up in
January 1991.

CAMPBELL, Raymond
(Glentoran, N.Ir)

• Midfield

Came off the production line of quality
young players at Nottingham Forest,
where he won a Central League
Championship medal in 1989. Failed to
make the first team at the City Ground,
though, and moved to Glentoran in 1990.
Tricky, wide player who can operate down
either flank. His flair played a big part in
the club's astonishing 12-point
Championship win. Reportedly a target of
Howard Kendall at Everton.

CAMPBELL, Rob
(Linfield, N.Ir)

• Midfield

Like older brother Brian he has been with
the club since his schooldays. Won the
Irish Youth Cup with Ards and shortly
afterwards became a target of Chelsea, but
seems settled at Castlereagh Park. Moved
to Linfield in June 1992 in a part exchange
deal which took David Jeffrey to Ards.

CANDLISH, Neil
(Ballymena United,
N.Ir)

• Striker

Signed from Motherwell in 1990, he was
United's leading scorer in 1991/92 with
17 goals. A tremendously skilful performer

who works in the Ballymena Leisure Centre for a living.

di CANIO, Paolo (Juventus, Ita)

• 09.07.68 • Striker

Born in Rome and joined Lazio as a teenager. Went to Ternana for the 1986/87 season to gain some League experience and got his chance in the Lazio first team two years later. Signed by Juventus for £3.5m in 1990.

CANNIGGIA, Claudio (Roma, Ita)

• 09.01.67 • Striker
• Argentina full caps

South American star who spent three years with River Plate in Argentina before moving to Italy and Verona in 1988. After only one season he moved to Atalanta and then transferred to Roma for season 1992/93. Was the outstanding member of Argentina's 1990 World Cup side, which reached the Final before losing 1-0 to West Germany. Transferred to Roma in June 1992 for a fee of £4.5 million.

CAPRON, Eddy (Nantes, Fra)

• 15.01.71 • Defender

Home-grown full back who joined the club from local football in 1988. Had to wait until July 1990 for his first senior game.

CARBONE, Angelo (Bari, Ita)

• 23.03.68 • Midfield
• Italy 2 full caps

Born in Bari and began his career with the local club, making his debut during the 1988/89 season as Bari won promotion to Serie A. Left the club for Milan in 1990, but returned to Bari last season.

CARBONI, Amedeo (Roma, Ita)

• 06.04.65 • Defender

Joined his home town club Arezzo in 1982 and then had spells at Bari, Empoli and Parma before joining Sampdoria in 1988. Moved to Roma in 1990.

CARECA (Napoli, Ita)

• 05.10.60 • Striker
• Brazil full caps

Antonio de Oliveira Filho began his career with Benfica, a minor side in Brazil. Helped Guarani to win the Brazilian title aged only 17 and made his full international debut against Czechoslovakia in March 1982. Signed by Sao Paulo later that year and won another Championship medal in 1987. Signed by Napoli that same year for £3m and helped his Italian side to win the UEFA Cup in 1989 and the League in 1990. Scored five goals in the 1986 World Cup finals and was voted Brazil's 'Sportsman of the Year' that season.

CARICOLA, Nicola (Genoa, Ita)

• 13.02.63 • Defender

Began career with Bari. Later spent four seasons at Juventus before signing for Genoa in 1987.

CARL, Eberhard (Karlsruher, Ger)

• 13.05.65 • Striker

Previously with Boblingen and Gundringen, Eberhard joined Karlsruher from Pforzheim in 1989 and is enjoying life in the Bundesliga 1.

CARLOS JORGE Camacho Dantas (Maritimo, Por)

• 08.11.66 • Defender

Locally born, he made his First Division debut with Maritimo in 1986 and has been with the club ever since. He likes to attack and in 1990/91 scored five goals in his 38 games.

CARLOS MANUEL (Boavista, Por)

• 15.01.58 • Midfield
• Portugal full caps

Spent eight seasons with Benfica before signing for Sporting Lisbon in 1988. After just two seasons at Sporting he was on the move again, signing for Boavista prior to the 1990/91 season.

CARLOS XAVIER (Real Sociedad, Spa)

• 26.01.62 • Midfield

Born in Mozambique of Portuguese descent, he joined Sociedad from Sporting Lisbon in the summer of 1991.

CARLYLE, Paul (Derry City, Eir)

• Midfield

Attacking midfielder who loves to get forward and score goals. Signed from Shamrock Rovers.

CARLY, Peter (Cercle Brugge, Bel)

• 14.05.62 • Defender

Came up through the ranks at Cercle to sign pro in 1979. Had a spell with Eeklo before returning to his first club, has now made nearly 200 senior appearances.

CARLYLE, Mark (Ballymena United, N.Ir)

• Defender

One of several players to have joined the club in summer of 1992. Signed from B Division club Chimney Corner he was previously on the books at Port Vale in England.

CARNEVALE, Andrea (Roma, Ita)

- 12.01.61 • Striker
- Italy full caps

Began his career with Third Division Latina before being signed by Avellino of Serie A in 1979. Joined Reggiana in 1981 and had spells with Cagliari, Catania and Udinese before moving to Napoli in 1986. Signed by Roma in 1990. Was banned for 12 months after failing a dope test in 1990. He had previously scored four goals in five games that season.

CARRACEDO, Marcello (Fortuna Dusseldorf, Ger)

- 16.04.70 • Midfield

Bought to Europe by Dusseldorf in 1989. Previously played his football with Atlanta in Argentina.

CARRASCO, Francisco (Sochaux, Fra)

- 06.03.59 • Striker
- Spain full caps

Experienced front man who was signed from Barcelona in 1989. Has yet to really find his shooting boots in France, but is a master at holding up the ball for the midfield to come through.

CARRERA, Massimo (Juventus, Ita)

- 22.04.64 • Defender

After spells with Pro Sesto, Russi, Alessandria and Pescara, he finally settled when joining Bari in 1986. Helped the club to win promotion to Serie A in 1989 and joined Juventus for £900,000 in 1991.

CARROLL, Derek (Galway United, Eir)

- Defender

Signed in August 1991 from Bohemians he has settled well into the role of sweeper for the Tribesmen. He was previously with Athlone Town.

CARSON, Bobby (Ballymena United, N.Ir)

- Defender

Re-joined the club in August 1991 after a spell at Linfield.

CARTIER, Albert
(Metz, Fra)
- 22.10.60 • Defender
- France full caps; Olympic

Came to the club from Nancy in July 1987, and was so impressed he immediately signed a seven year contract. Has now made more than 300 senior appearances. Member of Metz's 1988 French Cup winning squad.

CARTON, John
(Drogheda United, Eir)
- 08.08.72 • Midfield

Home grown youngster who is tipped for big things at Drogheda. Made his League of Ireland debut at Galway United in October 1989 (lost 2-0), and played a big part in the club's rise from the First Division to the Premier in 1990/91.

CARVALHAL
(Sporting Braga, Por)
- 04.12.65 • Defender

Carlos Augusto Faria began his career with Sporting Braga and made his First Division debut for the club during the 1983/84 season. Spent the 1985/86 campaign with Chaves, but returned to Braga the following season. Was on the move again in 1988 joining first Porto and then Beira-Mar, before returning to Braga in 1990.

CARVALHO Antonio
Jose Pereira
(Pacos De Ferreira, Por)
- 10.12.60 • Midfield

Golden boy of the Pacos De Ferreira side who runs the show from midfield, using his decade of experience in the League. After spells at Salgueiros, Portimonense and Vitoria Guimaraes, joined his current club when they moved into the First Division in 1991/92.

CARVALHO, Philippe
(Toulon, Fra)
- 28.09.67 • Defender

Joined the club straight from school, and made his first senior appearance against Auxerre in August 1987.

CASACA, Rui Manuel
Magalhaes
(Boavista, Por)
- 18.10.59 • Midfield

Originally with Sporting Braga he made his League debut while at Rio Ave during the 1982/83 season. Moved to Boavista two years later and has now established himself as a first team regular.

CASAGRANDE, Walter (Torino, Ita)

• 15.04.63 •Striker
• Brazil full caps

Played for Corinthians, Caidense and Sao Paolo in his home land before being brought to Europe by Porto in 1986. Left Portugal for Italy and Ascoli in 1987. Joined Torino prior to the 1991/92 season and won a UEFA Cup runners-up medal.

CASANOVA, Alain (Marseille, Fra)

• 15.10.61 • Goalkeeper
• France Olympic

Formerly with INF Vichy and Le Havre, he joined Marseille in 1990. Ironically, his First Division debut came against his present club back in July 1985. A broken leg in the latter stages of 1991/92 put paid to his season.

CASH, Michael (Crusaders, N.Ir)

• Midfield

Reformed bad-boy, who now has a reputation for being hard, but fair. Completed his 200th appearance for the club during 1991/92, having made his debut back in May 1986. One of the most competitive players in the Irish League his tackling is legendary.

CASINI, Didier (Metz, Fra)

• 19.08.62 • Defender
• France U21

Began with Nancy, making his First Divison bow against Lens in August 1982. Has now made more than 300 First Division appearances. Moved to Toulouse before signing for Metz in 1989. Failed to score dring the 1991/92 season.

CASIRAGHI, Pier Luigi (Juventus, Ita)

• 04.03.69 • Striker
• Italy 4 full caps, 1 goal

Talented front runner who began his career with Monza. Helped the club gain promotion to Serie B in 1988 and finally got his chance in the top flight when signed by Juventus in 1989. His international debut came against Belgium in February 1991 (drew 0-0).

CASKEY, Billy (Glentoran, N.Ir)

• Midfield
• N.Ireland 7 full caps, 1 goal

Described as the "most influential player around" by manager Tommy Jackson, he is a leader by example at Glentoran. First played for the Glens back in 1974, and has had successful spells with Derby County

and Tulsa Roughnecks in the USA. A
tremendous inspiration

CASONI, Bernard
(Marseille, Fra)

• 04.09.61 • Defender
• France 26 full caps

Formerly with Cannes, Toulon and,
briefly, Racing Paris, he has now played
more than 250 senior games. Forms a
formidable defensive rock with Basile Boli.

CASSIDY, Kevin
(Galway United, Eir)

• 11.07.56 • Defender

Longest serving player at Terryland,
having joined from Galway Rovers in
1979. Previously with local side Our
Lady's Boys.

CASTILLO Monte,
Ezequiel Marcelo
(Espanol, Spa)

• 13.06.67 • Midfield

Flamboyant Argentinian who left
Argentinos Juniors in his home land to
join Espanol in 1988.

CASTRO, Laurent
(Montpellier, Fra)

• 11.12.69 • Striker

Home grown player who made his debut
against Nantes in February 1990. Joined
the club in 1986, straight from school.

CATALANO, Michel
(Nimes, Fra)

• 04.11.59 • Defender

Experienced full back who began with
Lens, making his debut away to St Etienne
in January 1982. Moved to Auxerre before
signing for Nimes on their return to
Division One in the summer of 1991.
Approaching his 300th senior appearance
in the top flight.

CATANESE, Tarcisio
(Parma, Ita)

• 06.09.67 • Midfield

Failed to make the grade at Napoli and
had to move on to Third Division Reggina
before getting a chance of first team
football. Joined Parma in 1989 and helped
the club win promoiton to Serie A in his
first year.

CAUET, Benoit
(Caen, Fra)

• 02.05.69 • Midfield

Speedy wide right midfielder who was
previously with Nantes and Marseille. First
senior game came for Marseille, v Matra, in
February 1988. Joined Caen in July 1990.

CAUGHEY, Mark
(Bangor, N.Ir)
• 27.08.60 • Striker
• N.Ireland 2 full caps

Became the club's most expensive signing when he joined from Ards in August 1989. Something of a soccer nomad he has played for seven clubs - RUC, Linfield, Hibernian, Burnley, Hamilton Academicals, Motherwell and Ards - as well as Bangor. Was a member of Northern Ireland's 1986 Mexico World Cup squad, although he failed to make an appearance in the competition. Missed much of 1991/92 through injury, but still scored four goals in 11 starts.

CAULFIELD, John
(Cork City, Eir)
• 11.10.64 • Striker

Comfortably Cork's leading scorer of all time. Signed from Wembley in July 1986 he was also formerly with Athlone Town. Has played in every position, including 'keeper, for City.

CAVALIERE, Giancarlo
(Ascoli, Ita)
• 18.01.69 • Midfield

After playing for Alessandria, Moncalieri and Campobasso in the Italian junior leagues, Giancarlo moved to Ascoli in 1989.

CAVEGLIA, Alain
(Sochaux, Fra)
• 28.03.68 • Striker

Former midfielder who scored two goals in six games in his first season and was promptly pushed up front. Signed from Gueugnon his debut came against Brest in July 1990.

CAYASSO, Juan
(Stuttgart Kickers, Ger)
• 24.06.61 • Midfield
• Costa Rica 31 full caps

Bought to Germany by Kickers in 1990. Previously played for Deportivo Saprissa.

CECCARELLI, Gilbert
(St Etienne, Fra)
• 04.10.62 • Goalkeeper

Understudy to Cameroon international 'keeper Joseph-Antoine Bell. Began with St Etienne, but failed to break into the first team and moved to Bastia. Returned to St Etienne in 1989 and has now played more than 50 senior games.

CEDRUN Ibarra, Andoni
(Zaragoza, Spa)
• 05.06.60 • Goalkeeper

Very tall keeper who was originally from the Basque country. He was signed by

Zaragoza from Cadiz in 1984. Had to wait more than seven years before establishing himself as the first choice goalkeeper for his new club.

CEREZO, Toninho (Sampdoria, Ita)

- 21.04.55 • Midfield
- Brazil 58 full caps

Made his name in his native Brazil with Atletico Mineiro before moving to Italy, along with fellow Brazilian Falcao, in 1983 with Roma. He played in the 1984 Champions' Cup Final v Liverpool (lost on penalties) and joined Sampdoria two years later. He was a member of the Brazilian World Cup squads in 1978 and 1982, but unfortunately missed the 1986 tournament in Mexico with a hamstring injury. He is the adopted son of a circus clown.

CERVETTI, Antoine (Lille, Fra)

- 19.09.61 • Defender

Former Bastia and Niort player who joined Lille in 1990. He made his French First Division debut for Bastia against Lyon in October 1982 and is approaching 100 senior games. Attacking left back.

CERVONE, Giovanni (Roma, Ita)

- 16.11.62 • Goalkeeper

Joined Avellion from Juve Stabia in 1980 but had to wait three seasons for his chance in the Serie A. Moved to Genoa in 1984 and then on to Parma in 1987 and Verona a year later. Arrived at Roma prior to the 1989/90 season.

CEULEMANS, Jan (Club Brugge, Bel)

- 28.02.57 • Midfield
- Belgium 96 full caps, 23 goals

Along with Eric Gerets, Jan has been at the heart of Belgium's international success over the last 15 years. The most capped Belgian player ever he is still prompting and creating from his advanced midfield position, as well as banging in the goals at club level. Signed from Lierse in the wake of Brugge's 1978 UEFA Cup Final defeat by Liverpool he's now made more than 530 First Divsion appearances. A veteran of three World Cups, four League Championships and three domestic Cup wins.

CHALA, Kujtin (Rennes, Fra)

- 13.07.64 • Striker

Former Partizan Belgrade and Dinamo Zagreb forward who joined the club to partner Maria Baltazar up front with limited success. Rennes scored only 25 goals all season as they struggled in their second season back in Division One. Scored five goals in 1991/92.

CHAPUISAT, Stephane (Borussia Dortmund, Ger)

- 28.06.69 • Striker
- Switzerland 19 full caps, 2 goals

The son of former Swiss international Pierre-Albert Chapuisat. Nottingham Forest were interested in signing him, but he eventually moved to Germany in January 1991, joining Bayer Uerdingen from Lausanne for £1.1 million. Could not save Uerdingen from relegation, but made a good impression and was signed by Dortmund in the summer of 1991 for £860,000. Was the top scorer in the Bundesliga in 1991/92 with 20 goals as Dortmund finished runners-up in the title chase. Made his international debut against Brazil in June 1989 (won 1-0).

CHENDO (Real Madrid, Spa)

- 12.10.61 • Defender
- Spain U19, U21, 26 full caps

Club captain whose real name in Miguel Porlan Noguera. Right sided defender who, like so many of the Madrid squad, learned his trade at Castilla, Real's reserve side.

CHERCHESOV, Stanislav (Spartak Moscow, RUS)

- 02.09.63 • Goalkeeper
- USSR 11 full caps

Joined Spartak from Lokomotiv Moscow in 1984 where he took over from the legendary Rinat Dasayev. Soviet Player Of The Year runner-up in 1989. Made his international debut against Trinidad and Tobago in November 1990.

di CHIARA, Alberto (Parma, Ita)

- 29.03.64 • Defender

Full back who began his career with Roma, making his League debut during the 1980/81 season. He had just one season with Reggiana and then moved on to Lecce in 1983. Signed by Fiorentina in 1986 and eventually arrived at Parma in 1991.

CHICO OLIVEIRA Francisco (Pacos De Ferreira, Por)

- 27.04.64 • Defender

Born in Mozambique joined Amadora in the Portuguese league in 1989/90 before moving to Maritimo a season later. A regular in their first team he was snapped up by Ferreira just a season later.

CHINA
(Beira-Mar, Por)
• 13.09.59 • Midfield

Henrique Valmir Conceicao was born in
Brazil and moved to Portugal in 1988
when he joined Penafiel. Spent two years
with the club before moving to Beira-Mar
prior to the start of the 1990/91 season.

CHOVANEC, Jozef
(PSV Eindhoven, Hol)
• 07.03.60 • Midfield
• Czechoslovakia 48 full caps, 2 goals

Joined the Eindhoven club in January
1989 having previously spent more than
10 seasons with Sparta Prague in his native
Czechoslovakia.

CHRISTENSEN, Bent
(Schalke, Ger)
• 04.01.67 • Striker
• Denmark 16 full caps, 7 goals

Signed from Brondby for £1.4m in June
1991. Previously with Vejle. He helped
make history in 1990/91 when his five
goals for Brondby took a Danish club to
the Semi Finals of a European competition
for the first time. His four goals in the
European Championship qualifiers helped
Denmark qualify for Sweden 1992. He
was the Danish League's top scorer in both
1990 and 1991.

CHRISTIAENS, Hans
(Brondby, Den)
• 12.01.64 • Striker
• Belgium 2 full caps

International debut came as sub v Brazil,
in October 1988, when he came on for the
great Enzo Scifo. Signed from Waregem he
was previously with Eendrecht Zele and
Beveren. Scored twice in three full games
in 1990/91, but injury has restricted him
over the past two seasons. Signed for
Brondby mid-way through 1991/92, after
a short spell at Club Brugge in Belgium.

CHRISTOFTE, Kim
(Cologne, Ger)
• 24.08.60 • Midfield
• Denmark 16 full caps, 1 goal

Versatile performer who is equally happy in
defence or midfield. Filled in admirably for
the injured Henrik Andersson, at left back,
in the 1992 European Championship final
against Germany and was a key player in
Denmark historic 2-0 win. Transferred to
Cologne for £500,000 in July 1992.

CHUNGA, Moses
(Eendracht Aalst, Bel)
• 17.10.65 • Midfield

Zimbabwe-born wide player who has come
up through the ranks at the club. Member
of the side which won the Second Division
play-offs in 1990/91.

CIGANDA Lacuiza, Jose Angel
(Atletico Bilbao, Spa)

• 01.10.66 • Striker

Exciting front runner who joined Atletico Bilbao from Osasuna prior to the 1991/92 season.

CLAESEN, Nico
(Antwerp, Bel)

• 01.10.62 • Striker
• Belgium 36 full caps, 12 goals

Diminutive front-man who is well known to English fans, having spent two seasons with Tottenham (1986- 1988). Played in the 1987 FA Cup Final with Spurs. Played with Patro Eisden, Seresien, VfB Stuttgart and Standard Liege before Spurs paid £600,000 for his services in October 1986. Moved to Antwerp in April 1988.

CLAESSENS, Peter
(Waregem, Bel)

• 31.07.65 • Midfield

Signed from Beerschot prior to the start of the 1991/92 season. Formerly with Berchem Sport, he has now played more than 200 senior games.

CLARKE, Denis
(Athlone Town, Eir)

• 10.04.59 • Defender

Experienced centre back who signed from Limerick City.

CLAUDIO Barragan Escobar
(Coruna, Spa)

• 10.04.64 • Striker

Joined Coruna in 1991 from Mallorca. Previously with Elche.

CLEARY, John
(Galway United, Eir)

• 07.08.58 • Defender

Scored the winning goal in the 1988 FAI Cup Final (v Derry) to clinch the double for Dundalk. Began with Ballyfermot United before moving to St Pat's Athletic and then Dundalk. Moved to Galway in November 1990. Dead-ball specialist and excellent in the air.

CLIJSTERS, Leo
(Mechelen, Bel)

• 06.11.56 • Defender
• Belgium 40 full caps, 3 goals

Highly experienced and successful full back who, along with 'keeper Michel Preud'homme, was a major reason behind Mechelen conceding just 23 goals in 1991/92 - the best record in Belgium. Formerly with Opitter, Club Brugge, Patro Eisden, Tongeren, Thor Wattershei and Malinois. He has played

more than 350 senior games.
International debut came v East Germany in March 1983.

COADY, John
(Derry City, Eir)
• 25.08.60 • Midfield

Like several players at The Brandywell, he began his career with Shamrock Rovers. Signed for Chelsea at the beginning of 1986/87, and played 16 games, scoring twice, for the West London club before returning to Ireland with Derry in the summer of 1989. Equally comfortable as a full back, centre back or in midfield.

CODISPOTI, Maurizio
(Foggia, Ita)
• 04.07.64 • Defender

After a couple of seasons with Juvenes Enna and Siracusa, Maurizio joined Foggia in 1986. Has played over 150 games for the club since.

COELHO, Jose da Silva
(Boavista, Por)
• 05.08.61 • Striker
• Portugal full caps

Originally made his debut for Boavista in 1981 and spent seven seasons with the Porto based club before returning to his home town side, Penafiel. Moved on to Chaves in 1990 before going back to Boavista a year later.

COIS, Sandro
(Torino, Ita)
• 09.06.72 • Defender

Born in Fossano and joined Torino in 1989. Made his Serie A debut for the club during the 1990/91 season.

COLIN, Jacky
(Rennes, Fra)
• 18.08.63 • Midfield
• France U21

Forms an experienced central midfield partnership with Blaz Sliskovic, having played all his pro football in France. Began with Sochaux in July 1981. He moved on to Lyon before signing for Rennes in 1991

COLL, James
(Dundalk, Eir)
• 28.7.62 • Defender

Born in Glasgow, Scotland, he signed from Limerick City in July 1989. Previously with Athlone Town and St Pat's Athletic. Determined and difficult to beat.

COLL, Michael
(Omagh Town, N.Ir)
• Defender

Began with Omagh while still a schoolboy. Born in Londonderry, he played more than 20 senior games during 1991/92.

Italy and member of 1982 World Cup winning squad.

COLLETER, Patrick
(Paris St Germain, Fra)

• 06.11.65 • Defender

One of several players to join the club during the summer of 1991. Began with home-town club Brest, who he joined from local football in 1986. Had a successful spell with Montpellier where he honed the art of attacking down the flanks from his position at left-back. Together with fellow full back Laurent Fournier he forms a potent threat for Paris-SG.

COLLINS, Roddy
(Crusaders, N.Ir)

• Striker

Could win an award for Most Travelled Player, as Crusaders is his 11th senior club. A former apprentice with Arsenal, he's also had spells with Bohemians, Athlone Town, Drogheda, Dundalk, Mansfield Town, Newport County, Swansea City, Shamrock Rovers and Sligo Rovers. Joined Crusaders in November 1991, and scored five times in his first seven games.

COLLOVATI, Fulvio
(Genoa, Ita)

• 09.05.57 • Defender
• Italy 50 full caps

Played for both Inter and Milan before joining Genoa in 1989 via short spells at Udinese and Roma. Capped 50 times by

COMI, Antonio
(Roma, Ita)

• 26.07.64 • Defender

Made his debut for Torino during the 1982/83 season and spent seven seasons at the club before joining Roma in 1989.

CONEJO, Luis Gabelo
(Albacete, Spa)

• 01.01.60 • Goalkeeper
• Costa Rica full caps

Impressed Albacete with his performance for Costa Rica in the 1990 World Cup finals and moved to Spain that summer.

CONINCK, Wim
(Eendracht Aalst, Bel)

• 23.06.59 • Goalkeeper

First choice 'keeper at the club, which he joined from Waregem. Also previously with Baarle Drongen, he is approaching 400 senior games.

CONNOLLY, Roger
(Sligo Rovers, Eir)

• 28.10.71 • Defender

Fine young prospect who signed for his home town club from local League football in July 1990. His first senior match came against Limerick City on April Fool's Day, 1991.

CONNOLLY, Timmy (Ballymena United, N.Ir)

• Defender

Ballymena-born player who is equally happy in defence or midfield. Signed from local minor League football, at the beginning of 1991/92, an ankle injury sidelined him for much of that season.

CONROY, Mick (Cork City, Eir)

• 31.07.57 • Defender

Hugely experienced stopper who served under Jock Stein and Billy McNeill with Celtic. Won two Scottish Premier Division titles and one Scottish Cup. Also served with Hibernian, Blackpool, Wrexham, Leyton Orient and Norwich, from whom he transferred to Shamrock Rovers in July 1988.

CONTE, Antonio (Juventus, Ita)

• 02.08.70 • Midfield

Made his League debut for Lecce while still only 16 years old - a rare achievement in Italian football. Joined Juventus for £3m in 1992.

CONVILLE, Stevie (Glenavon, N.Ir)

• Midfield

Signed from Ballymena United in December. 1988. Normally a right-sided midfielder, he's also played left-back for Glenavon! Non-stop running and good ball skills characterise his play.

CONWAY, Tom (Sligo Rovers, Eir)

• 07.03.59 • Striker

Former Athlone Town player who joined the club from Bohemians in August 1989. Ironically, his League of Ireland debut came against his present club, for Athlone, on 23rd October 1977. The goals have dried up a little over the last couple of seasons for this hugely experienced forward.

COOMAN, Peter (Cercle Brugge, Bel)

• 08.08.68 • Defender

Began with local club SK Erembodegem before hitting the big time when he signed pro with Eendracht Aalst. Cercle signed him in the summer of 1989.

COONEY, Wayne (Shamrock Rovers, Eir)

• 23.03.68 • Defender

Birmingham-born player who began with Norwich City, but failed to make the grade with the Carrow Road club and moved to Shamrock Rovers in July 1988. His League of Ireland debut came against Athlone Town in September of that year.

COOREMAN, Davy (Gent, Bel)

• 27.01.71 • Defender

Prolific attacking midfielder who has came up through the ranks at the club. Made only a handful of first team appearances, but made a huge impact in 1990/91, scoring four goals in five starts.

CORCORAN, Derek (Bray Wanderers, Eir)

• 10.11.70 • Striker

One of several Wanderers players to have signed from junior club St Joseph's Boys. Was a member of the club's promotion winning side of 1990/91.

CORINI, Eugenio (Juventus, Ita)

• 30.07.70 • Midfield
• Italy U21

Captain of the U21 team, he began his career with Brescia and made his debut in 1987/88. Signed by Juventus in 1990.

CORRADINI, Giancarlo (Napoli, Ita)

• 24.02.61 • Defender

Stopper who began his career with his home-town club Sassuolo in the Fourth Division. Signed by Second Division Genoa in 1978. two years later he swopped divisions again, joining Reggiana. Torino were the next port of call in 1982 before finally arriving at Naples in 1988.

CORROYER, Dominique (St Etienne, Fra)

• 25.08.64 • Striker

Formerly with Valenciennes he signed for the club in June 1990. Averaged a goal every four games in his first two seasons at St Etienne. First Division debut came v Rennes in July 1990, but he had to wait until October for his first goal, v Marseille.

CORTIJO, Alfonso (Cadiz, Spa)

• 14.09.66 • Defender

Broke into the Cadiz first team in 1987 and has been a regular in the side ever since.

COSGRAVE, Brian
(Bray Wanderers, Eir)

• 18.06.63 • Defender

Strong tackling stopper who signed from junior club Palmerstown Rangers in 1988. His League of Ireland debut came against Longford Town on 11th December 1988 (lost 1-0).

COSTACURTA,
Alessandro
(Milan, Ita)

• 24.04.66 • Defender

• Italy 4 full caps

Loaned to Third Division Monza in September 1986 and made his League debut there. Returned to Milan the following year and finally got his chance in the first team.

COSTELLO, Greg
(Shelbourne, Eir)

• 05.04.70 • Midfield

Spent four years with Queens Park Rangers, but failed to make the grade in England. Returned home to his native Dublin and signed for Shelbourne in January 1991. Made his debut for the Tolka Park side, v St Pat's Athletic, on 11th January 1991. Creative midfield ball-player.

COTA, Jesus Diego
(Rayo Vallecano, Spa)

• 28.07.67 • Defender

• Spain youth

Exciting full back who is very strong on the overlap.

COWAN, Steve
(Portadown, N.Ir)

• 17.12.63 • Striker

• Scotland Youth

Made an immediate impression when he joined the club in the run-up to the 1990 League Championship. Formerly with St Mirren, Aberdeen, Hibs and Motherwell he scored 20 goals during the glorious 1990/91 season, including both in the 2-1 Irish Cup Final victory over Glenavon. Forms a sound partnership with countryman Sandy Fraser and established himself as a great favourite with the fans.

COYLE, Peter
(Shelbourne, Eir)

• 24.09.63 • Defender

Began with Limerick United, and made his League of Ireland debut away to Home Farm in January 1983. Joined Limerick City before moving on to Shelbourne in January 1991. Likes to get forward and support his attack.

CRAIG, Robert (Ballymena United, N.Ir)

• Striker

Became Ballymena manager Jim Hagan's first major signing when he joined from League Champions Glentoran in the back half of season 1991/92. He made an immediate impact, scoring six goals in his first 11 games.

CRAIG, Stephen (Shamrock Rovers, Eir)

• 14.11.57 • Defender

Experienced stopper who joined the club from Bray Wanderers in August 1988.

CRASSON, Bertrand (Anderlecht, Bel)

• 05.10.71 • Defender
• Belgium 2 full cap

Highly respected young full back who joined the club from Evere in September 1990. Made his international debut against Germany in 1991.

CRAVERO, Roberto (Torino, Ita)

• 13.01.64 • Defender

Libero who made his Serie A debut for Torino during the 1981/82 season. Spent two years with Second Division side Cesena before moving back to his original club in 1985.

CRAWFORD, Colin (Glenavon, N.Ir)

• Midfield

Joined from Carrick Rangers in December. 1991 for £5,500. Formerly with Sunderland before joining Linfield, where he played more than 230 senior games, in October. 1981.

CREVE, Peter (Club Brugge, Bel)

• 17.08.61 • Midfield
• Belgium 3 full caps, 1 goal

Forms an experienced midfield axis with Jan Ceulemans and Luc Beyens. Signed from Beveren he was also previously with Bredene and AS Oostende. League title winner in 1992. Scored on his international debut after coming on as substitute against Luxembourg in November 1987.

CRIENS, Hans-Jorg (Borussia Moenchengladbach, Ger)

• 18.12.60 • Striker

Joined Gladbach from VfR Neuss in 1981. More than 250 Bundesliga appearances for the club.

CRILLY, John
(Omagh Town, N.Ir)
• Midfield

Like team-mate Harry McCourt, a trainee solicitor. Formerly with Culdaff. He forms a solid base in the midfield with his player/manager Roy McCreadie. Likes nothing more than getting forward to help out his attackers.

CRISTOBAL Parralo Aguilera
(Barcelona, Spa)
• 21.08.67 • Defender
• Spain 3 full caps

A £1m transfer from Logrones to Barcelona in 1991 also brought Cristobal to the public's notice and won him promotion to the full Spanish national squad.

CROCI, Laurent
(Sochaux, Fra)
• 08.12.64 • Defender
• France B

Attacking full back who came through the ranks at the club and has now played more than 200 Division One games. Made his debut as a 17-year- old, v Bordeaux, way back in 1982.

CROOKS, David
(Ards, N.Ir)
• Goalkeeper
• N.Ireland Youth

From Maghera. Signed for the club from minor League side Tobermore at the beginning of the 1991/92 season, having spent part of the previous season on loan at Ards. Previously with Coleraine, Distillery and Ballymoney.

CRUZ, Andre
(Standard Liege, Bel)
• 20.09.68 • Defender
• Brazil 15 full caps

Can perform at left-back or sweeper, and, like most Brazilians, likes to play his way out of trouble, and, occasionally, achieves the opposite. Formerly with three clubs in his native country - Ponte Petra, Chiasso and the famous Flamengo, from where he joined Standard in June 1990.

CUCCHI, Enrico
(Bari, Ita)
• 02.08.65 • Midfield

A left-sided midfielder who began his career in Serie C2 with Savona. His potential was quickly spotted by Inter who signed the youngster in 1982. Gained further top level experience with Empoli and Fiorentina before joing Bari in 1990.

CUCIUFFO, Jose Luis (Nimes, Fra)

• 01.02.61 • Defender
• Argentina full caps

Began at Argentina's great breeding ground Boca Juniors, before being tempted across to Europe with Nimes in 1990. Talented defender who loves to get forward and help his midfield.

CUNNINGHAM, Denis (Drogheda United, Eir)

• 13.04.62 • Striker

Signed from Finn Harps. His goals helped Drogheda in the battle for promotion from Division One in the 1990/91 campaign.

CUNNINGHAM, Joey (Portadown, N.Ir)

• Midfield

The real dangerman in the Portadown midfield he was devastating in the club's all-conquering 1990/91 season, scoring two of the club's four Cup Final goals, as well as eight in the League. Superb ball-control and great speed combine to make him a difficult customer.

CUNNINGHAM, John (Cliftonville, N.Ir)

• Midfield

Former Omagh Town wide-man who was signed by Billy Sinclair in May 1992 and has now become a firm favourite at the club.

CUNNINGHAM, John (Omagh Town, N.Ir)

• Forward

Began as a pro in England with Mansfield Town. Troublesome winger who also played for Bangor and Derry City before joining Omagh in 1991.

CUOGHI, Stefano (Parma, Ita)

• 08.08.59 • Midfield

Joined his local side Modena as a teenager and moved on to Milan in 1980. returned to Modena in 1983 and had spells with Perugia and Pisa before signing for Parma in 1990.

CURRAN, Paul (Derry City, Eir)

• 05.10.66 • Defender

Combative centre back who would die for his club. Signed from Finn Harps.

CURRY, Lindsay (Linfield, N.Ir)

• Midfield

The type of player to have managers

tearing their hair out. Superbly talented, he can win a game with one flash of brilliance, but can be equally frustrating. Signed from Ballymena United in 1991 he revels in the big game atmosphere, and won an Irish Cup winners' medal with United in 1989. An accomplished goalscorer from midfield.

the first time back in 1979. Transferred to Anderlecht and then Standard Liege before returning to Antwerp. Scored on his international debut, against France, in September 1981.

CUXART Vaquer, Enric (Espanol, Spa)

• 23.03.67 • Striker

Joined Espanol from Valencia and at 1.92m he is the tallest player in the Spanish League.

CYPRIEN, Jean-Pierre (St Etienne, Fra)

• 12.02.69 • Defender
• France U21

Joined the club in 1990 after spending three years with Le Havre, who had signed him straight from school in Guadeloupe. Solid centre back who made his debut in November 1987 v Toulouse.

CZERNIATYNSKI, Alex (Antwerp, Bel)

• 28.07.60 • Striker
• Belgium 21 full caps, 5 goals

Has played his entire career at the top level, and now has more than 340 Division One games under his belt. Began with Charleroi, before moving to Antwerp for

DADIE, Luis Fernando (Celta, Spa)

• 17.05.66 • Defender
• Spain U21

Full back who joined Celta from Real Sociedad.

DAERDEN, Jos (Germinal Ekeren, Bel)

• 26.11.54 • Defender
• Belgium 5 full caps

Experienced campaigner with Hedra Herderen, Cercle Liege, Tongeren, Standard Liege and Roda JC. He was signed from Beerschot and has now made more than 300 senior appearances. His international debut came in May 1982, when he substituted Jan Ceulemans against Denmark.

DAHLIN, Martin (Borussia Moenchengladbach, Ger)

• 16.04.68 • Striker
• Sweden 13 full caps, 7 goals

Big powerful front-runner who plays his club football in the German Bundesliga. A member of Sweden's 1992 European Championship squad, he earned his call-up with a remarkable record of scoring seven times in his first eight internationals.

Enjoyed a tremendous tournament and forged a dangerous partnership with Parma's Thomas Brolin.

DALTON, Tim (Derry City, Eir)

• 14.10.65 • Goalkeeper

One of the safest pair of hands in the League of Ireland. Began with Cork City, for whom he made his League debut v Bray Wanderers in February 1988. Derry snapped him up in the summer of 1988, and went on to help guide the club to the League and Cup double in 1989.

DALY, Declan (Cork City, Eir)

• 01.06.66 • Defender
• Eire Youth

Previously with Limerick City, from whom he joined Cork in August 1990. Won three junior international caps for Eire - two v England (1986) and one v Scotland (1985).

DAMASCHIN, Marian (Feyenoord, Hol)

• 01.05.61 • Striker
• Romania 5 full caps

Signed from Dinamo Bucharest, of Romania, prior to the 1991/92 season. Started career in Dutch League with flurry of goals, but injury in latter part of season restricted his appearances.

DAMMEIER, Detlev (SV Hamburg, Ger)

• 18.10.68 • Midfield

Signed from Hannover 96 in 1989.

DANEK, Vaclav (Le Havre, Fra)

• 22.12.60 • Striker
• Czechoslovakia 20 full caps; 9 goals3

Big and strong, this goal-grabber supreme was signed from Austrian side Swarovski-Tirol in July 1991. Scored 29 goals in 31 starts in season 1990/91 for Tirol. Without a doubt one of the most prolific strikers in France, and a real capture for Le Havre.

DANEN, Frans (Den Haag, Hol)

• 12.09.66 • Striker
• Holland U21

Joined his local side Den Haag in July 1985 and made his first team debut that season. Has now played over 230 first team games for the club.

DANGBETO, Hippolyte (Caen, Fra)

• 02.11.69 • Defender
• France U21

Joined the club in 1990, having previously been with Racing Paris. Made his First Division debut for Racing against Laval on 11th February 1989 and has now made more than 100 senior appearances.

DANIEL, Jean-Francois (Cannes, Fra)

• 14.06.64 • Midfield
• France U21

Experienced former St Etienne and Lille player who's been at Cannes since 1988. Now approaching 200 senior appearances, he was somewhat overlooked during season 1991/92.

DANIO, Didier (Nancy, Fra)

• 10.05.62 • Midfield

Goalscoring midfielder who joined the club in August 1990. Began with Auxerre, making his debut v Brest in September 1981. Also previously with Rennes and Reims.

DARRAS, Frederic (Auxerre, Fra)

• 19.8.66 • Defender

Has played more than 120 senior games since joining the club as a schoolboy in 1981. His senior debut came in 1986, v Toulouse.

DASCHNER, Reinhold (Cologne, Ger)

• 16.10.69 • Midfield

Joined Bayern Munich from local Bavarian football as a youngster but failed to make the grade. Moved on to Cologne in 1990.

DAUWEN, Frank (Gent, Bel)

• 03.11.67 • Defender
• Belgium 2 full caps

Equally happy as a conventional full back, at sweeper, or in the midfield, where he likes to get forward and score goals. Formerly with Westerlo VC and Lierse. Made his international debut in 1991, when he substituted Marc Wilmots in the game v Italy.

DAVIDSON, Greg (Portadown, N.Ir)

• Midfield

A member of the famous McCreery Irish footballing family, he is a great favourite with the Portadown fans - mainly because he scored the goal past Linfield that clinched the 1991 League title. An expert at timing a late run into the area at dead-ball situations.

DEBATY, Phillipe (Nimes, Fra)

• Goalkeeper

Belgian born 'keeper who has been with the club since 1981.

DEBEVE, Michael (Toulouse, Fra)

• 01.12.70 • Midfield
• France U21

Moved to the club in the wake of their best season in recent years (3rd, 1986/87). Happy on either flank he signed from Abbeville, making his debut v Brest in October 1989.

DEBROSSE, Laurent (Lyon, Fra)

• 02.10.69 • Midfield

Formerly with Montceau, he joined the club in 1989. An attacking midfielder who loves to get forward, he was handed his First Divsion debut in May 1990, against Mulhouse.

DECROIX, Eric (Lille, Fra)

• 07.03.69 • Defender

Has progressed through the junior ranks at the club, which he joined in 1987. Has made more than 50 senior appearances since his debut, against Caen, in July 1989.

DEGEN, Jurgen (Kaiserslautern, Ger)

• 07.11.67 • Striker

Inexperiened forward who joined Kaiserslautern at the start of the 1991/92 season. Played his junior football with VfL Hamburg, Bramfelder SV and Alstertal.

DEGRYSE, Marc (Anderlecht, Bel)

• 04.09.65 • Striker
• Belgium 33 full caps, 11 goals

One of Belgium's leading strikers he really arrived on the international scene at World Cup Italia '90. Began with minor League club Ardooie, but has spent most of his pro career at the very top in Belgium with Brugge and Anderlecht. Joined the club in July 1989. Voted Belgium's Footballer of the Year or 1991, he signed a new five-year contract with Anderlecht in January 1992.

DEGUERVILLE, Christophe (St Etienne, Fra)

• 27.06.70 • Defender
• France U21

Came up through the ranks at the club, where he's been since he was 15-years-old. First Division debut came in June 1988 v Laval. Attacking full back.

DEHU, Frederic (Lens, Fra)

• 24.10.72 • Defender

Exciting young player who is comfortable playing at full back or wide midfield. Came up through the ranks at Lens.

DEKENNE, Franky (Waregem, Bel)

• 07.07.60 • Defender
• Belgium 3 full caps

Experienced professional who was brought in to lend an old head at the back for the club. Now in his second spell with the club, having had a successful period at Antwerp in the interim.

DELAMONTAGNE, Laurent (Rennes, Fra)

• 09.10.65 • Midfield

One of a pair of footballing brothers who thrilled Rennes fans with their goalscoring from midfield during the club's first season back in the top flight (1990/91). Brother Patrick was forced to retire because of injury at the beginning of 1991/92, but Laurent carried on scoring and creating from the left wing. Home grown player who also tasted Division One glory with the club back in 1986/87. A great favourite with the fans.

DELANGRE, Etienne (Standard Liege, Bel)

• 12.03.63 • Defender
• Belgium U21

Now in his 11th season at Standard this versatile defender, who canplay anywhere across the back four or in midfield, is a firm favourite with the fans.

DELAUNAY, Jean-Pierre (Le Havre, Fra)

• 17.01.66 • Defender

Home-grown central defender who is very powerful in the air. One of several inexperienced players in the Le Havre defence, he did not make his League debut until the 1991/92 season.

DELMOTTE, Christophe (Lens, Fra)

• 09.06.69 • Striker

Huge striker (6ft 3in) who has come up through the ranks at Lens.

DELPECH, Jean-Phillipe (Toulouse, Fra)

• 01.09.67 • Midfield
• France U21

Creative, two-footed, central midfield playmaker. Local boy who is a product of the club's admirable youth policy. Has established himself as a regular in the side since first coming to the fore in February 1986, v Bastia.

DEMAN, Patrick (Gent, Bel)

• 31.07.68 • Goalkeeper

Has lost his first team spot since the arrival of Hungarian international Zsolt Petry in the summer of 1991. Formerly with Kortrijk.

DEMANDT, Sven (Fortuna Dusseldorf, Ger)

• 13.02.65 • Striker

Returned to Dusseldorf club from Bayer Leverkusen in 1990.

DENIER, Pierre (Genk, Bel)

• 09.11.56 • Midfield

Home grown player who has been with the club since it was formed in 1988. Experienced the low of relegation in 1988/89, but showed the character and determination to turn the club round and captain the side straight back into Division One.

DENIS, Francois (Rennes, Fra)

• 14.05.64 • Defender

A vital member of the side which was promoted from Division Two in 1990. Had spent his entire career in the lower divisions prior to season 1990/91. Started with St Nazaire, moving to Brest and Redon before Rennes snapped him up in 1986.

DENVER, Alex (Crusaders, N.Ir)

• Midfield

Joined the Crues in August 1990, having previously played more than 250 senior games for Glenavon. Ever present in 1990/91, until injury forced him out of the final five games of the season. Contractual difficulties meant he had a slow start to 1991/92, and he struggled to regain his place.

DERAEVE, Daniel (Lokeren, Bel)

• 26.06.61 • Midfield

Battling central midfielder who re-joined the club from Westerlo in 1990. Also previously with Winterslag (twice) and Bilzerse.

DEROUCK, Michel (Kortrijk, Bel)

• 30.08.63 • Midfield

Could not find a club in his native Belgium and had to move to Spain for his big break, signing for CD Espanola in 1981. Kortrijk signed him from Hautrage and he has now played more than 250 First Division games in Belgium and is one of the club's longest serving players.

DERTYCIA Alvarez, Oscar (Tenerife, Spa)

• 03.03.65 • Striker

Completely bald and very physical Argentinian forward.

DER ZAKARIAN, Michel (Montpellier, Fra)

• 18.02.63 • Defender
• France U21

Soviet-born central defender who began with Mazargues, before moving to Nantes, where he made his top flight debut, v Monaco, in September 1981. Joined Montpellier in 1988 and is now approaching 250 senior appearances. Won the French Cup with Montpellier in 1990.

DESAILLY, Marcel (Nantes, Fra)

• 07.09.68 • Defender
• France U21

Born in Accra, Ghana, this central defender has been affiliated to the club since he was 12-years-old. Made his senior debut back in 1986 against Bordeaux. Has made more than 150 First Division appearances.

DESCAMPS, Nick (Waregem, Bel)

• 24.03.66 • Defender

Central midfield ball-winner who joined the club from Kortrijk and has now played more than 140 senior games.

DESCHAMPS, Didier (Marseille, Fra)

• 15.10.68 • Midfield
• France 22 full caps, 3 goals

Highly experienced young player who began with Bayonne. Moved to Nantes in 1986, for whom he made his First Division debut, v Lille, in August of that year. Spent a period on loan at doomed Bordeaux, before moving to Marseille in 1990. Played his part in Marseille's 1991/92 Championship success, scoring four League goals during the successful campaign.

DESIDERI, Stephano (Internazionale, Ita)

• 03.07.65 • Midfield

Joined his home-town club Roma as a teenager, but had to go to third Division Piacenza to make his League debut. Returned to Rome and had six seasons as a first team player before moving to Internazionale of Milan prior to the 1991/92 season.

DESLOOVER, Yvan (Waregem, Bel)

• 29.07.63 • Defender

Solid, dependable stopper who was signed from Nederename back in 1981 and is the club's longest serving player. Has made more than 250 senior appearances in his eleven years at the top.

DESMET, Filip (Eendracht Aalst, Bel)

• 29.11.58 • Midfield
• Belgium 14 full caps, 1 goal

Widely travelled winger-cum-striker who signed from Charleroi in the summer of 1991. Previously with Desselgem, Waregem, Lille (Fra) and Kortrijk. Made his international debut in November 1985, and went on to play in the 1986 Mexico World Cup.

DESPEYROUX, Pascal (Toulouse, Fra)

- 17.11.65 • Midfield
- France 2 full caps

Home-grown, battling midfielder who's been with the club since their Second Division days of the early 1980s. His debut came against Laval in October 1985 and he has now made more than 200 senior appearances. Not a regular goalscorer, he failed to find the net once during 1991/92.

DESSY, Christophe (Charleroi, Bel)

- 08.03.66 • Defender

Attacking full back who signed from minor League club RJ Jet. Previously with Molenbeek and Wavre Sports.

DETARI, Lajos (Bologna, Ita)

- 24.04.63 • Midfield
- Hungary 43 full caps, 10 goals

Played with Honved in Hungary and was the country's top scorer in 1985 and 1986. International debut v Switzerland August 1984. Hungarian Footballer of the Year in 1985. Joined Eintracht Frankfurt in summer 1987 for East European record fee of £1.2m. Won German Cup in 1988, scoring winner in final v Bochum. Sold to Olympiakos for £4.7 after final, making

him most expensive ever East European player. Sold to Bologna for £3m to ease financial crisis at Greek club.

DEVINE, John (Glentoran, N.Ir)

- Defender
- N.Ireland 1 full cap

Made his full international debut in 1990, while still only 19-years-old. Commanding central defender he completed a century of senior games for the club during 1991/92.

DEVLIN, Christy (St Patrick's Athletic, Eir)

- 17.08.59 • Goalkeeper

Vastly experienced 'keeper who is understudy to Dave Henderson at Harold's Cross. Signed from Bray Wanderers. Nicknamed Chippy.

DEVRIESE, Dirk (RWD Molenbeek, Bel)

- 03.12.58 • Defender
- Belgium 1 full cap

One of a trio of vastly experienced players to join after the club were crowned Division Two Champions in 1989/90 - the other two being Ipermans and Vercauteren. His one international appearance came v Albania in a World Cup Qualifier in October 1984. Has now played more than 400 senior games with Knokke, CS Brugge, La Louviere, Anderlecht and Lokeren. In his second spell at Molenbeek.

DEWILDE, Filip (Anderlecht, Bel)
• 05.07.64 • Goalkeeper
• Belgium 2 full caps

Began with Eendracht Zele before hitting the big-time with Beveren in 1982. Moved to Anderlecht in 1988, making his debut in September of that year. His shot-stopping helped the club to the 1991 League Championship and also the Belgian Cup in 1989.

DEWILDER, Eric (Sochaux, Fra)
• 10.04.64 • Midfield

Signed a new four-year contract with the club recently, having signed from Caen in 1990. Also previously with Lens and Bordeaux. Has played more than 200 Division One games, scoring more than 20 goals in the process.

DEZOTTI, Gustavo Abel (Cremonese, Ita)
• 14.02.64 • Striker

Began his career in Argentina with Newell's and was brought to Italy by Lazio in 1988. Joined Cremonese a year later

and, despite the club's relegation, scored 13 Serie A goals in his first campaign, attracting interest from several of the League's bigger clubs, although at present he appears happy at Cremonese.

D'HONDT, Danny (Lokeren, Bel)
• 21.09.63 • Goalkeeper

First choice 'keeper at the club since signing from minor League club AV Dendermonde in the summer of 1987.

DIB, Marcel (Monaco, Fra)
• 10.08.60 • Midfield
• France 6 full caps

In the best traditions of the club's creative style, Dib is a tough ball-winner who combines strength with tremendous ability on the ball. Formerly with Toulon, he made his First Division debut against Rennes in August 1983. Joined Monaco in 1985.

DIEGO Diaz Garrido (Atletico Madrid, Spa)
• 30.12.68 • Goalkeeper

Discovered in local football and made his first team debut during the 1991/92 season when Abel was injured.

DINIS Silva Gomes Resende
(Beira-Mar, Por)
• 15.04.67 • Defender

Massive central defender who began his career with Pacos de Brandao, his home town club. Got his chance in the First Division with Beira-Mar in the 1988/89 season.

DINO
(Beira-Mar, Por)
• 04.05.61 • Striker

Brazilian born Raimundo Novato Barreto began his career in the Portuguese First Division with Nacional in 1988. Signed by Beira-Mar prior to the start of the 1990/91 season.

DISZTL, Laslo
(Club Brugge, Bel)
• 04.06.62 • Defender
• Hungary 21 full caps, 1 goal

Centre back who joined from Honved at the beginning of season 1989/90. Formerly with Videoton, to whom he was first affilliated as a ten-year-old.

DITTWAR, Jorg
(Nuremburg, Ger)
• 01.08.63 • Midfield

A right-sided midfield player who joined Nuremburg from SpVgg Bayreuth in September 1987.

DIVERT, Fabrice
(Montpellier, Fra)
• 09.02.67 • Striker
• France 2 full caps

With 40 goals in 107 games in his first three seasons of pro football, Fabrice became one of the hottest properties on the market. Formerly with Caen, he was snapped up on a five-year contract in July 1991. At 6ft 3in, he uses his height to good effect in the area and is a constant handful for defenders. A late replacement for Amara Simba, of Paris St Germain, in France's disappointing 1992 European Championship squad. He was easily Montpellier's top scorer in 1991/92, with 15 League goals to his credit.

le DIZET, Serge
(Rennes, Fra)
• 27.06.64 • Defender

Full back who had spent his entire career in the lower divisions before winning promotion with Rennes in 1990. Formerly with Stella Maris and Quimper. Like several of his team- mates he got his first taste of top flight football against St Etienne on 21st July 1990 - Rennes' first game back in Division One after an absence of three years.

DJOINCEVIC, Sedomir (Salgueiros, Por)

• 05.05.61 • Defender

Belgrade born defender who, along with fellow Slavs Milovac and Nikolic, was bough to Salgueiros by Yugoslavian coach Zoran Filipovic.

DOBROVOLSKI, Igor (Genoa, Ita)

• 27.08.57 • Striker
• USSR 28 full caps, 8 goals

Ukrainian-born winger who began his career with Moscow Dynamo. Won an Olympic gold medal at Seoul in 1988 and was also the tournament's top scorer that year. Included in the national squad for the 1990 World Cup finals. Signed by Genoa after the finals, but was loaned out to Castellon in Spain for first season. Spent 1991/92 season on loan to Servette in Switzerland. Scored the CIS's only goal, from the penalty spot, at the 1992 European Championship in Sweden.

DOCHEV, Pavel (Hamburg, Ger)

• Defender

Highly influential player who helped CSKA Sofia to win the Bulgarian League in 1992. Left his homeland in June of that same year when signed by Hamburg for £350,000.

DOHERTY, Lee (Linfield, N.Ir)

• Midfield
• N.Ireland 2 full caps; Irish League

An experienced player who fills the key playmaker role at Linfield - his only senior club. A series of injuries have restricted his appearances over the past couple of seasons, but he has still played more than 300 games for the Belfast club. Made his international debut v Israel in 1984.

DOLAN, Pat (Shamrock Rovers, Eir)

• 20.09.67 • Midfield

Dagenham-born midfielder who joined the Rovers from Galway United in June 1990. His League of Ireland debut came while he was with St Patrick's Athletic, against Waterford United, in February 1988.

DOLL, Thomas (Lazio, Ita)

• 09.04.66 • Midfield
• East Germany youth, U21, Olympic 29 full caps 7 goals/Germany 12 caps, 1 goal

Attacking midfielder who began his career in East Germany with Hansa Rostock and made his Oberliga debut during the 1983/84 season. Later moved on to Dynamo Berlin where he picked up two

League and two Cup winners' medals. In 1990 he moved West to Hamburg for £500,000 and was also selected for the united German side. After just one season in the Bundesliga he was signed by Lazio for £5.5, becoming the first East German ever to play in the Italian Serie A. Along with Karl-Heinz Riedle he is nicknamed 'Romulus and Remus' after the two founders of Rome.

DOMINGOS, Jose Paciencia Oliveira (Porto, Por)

• 02.01.69 • striker
• Portugal 2 full caps, 1 goal

Has spent his entire career at Porto, making his League debut during the 1987/88 season while still a teenager. Scored an impressive 24 goals in 34 League games for Porto during the 1990/91 season.

DONADONI, Roberto (Milan, Ita)

• 09.09.63 • Midfield
• Italy 39 full caps, 4 goals

Spent five seasons with Atalanta, helping the club to rise from the Third Division to the First, before signing for Milan in 1986. Roberto also made his international debut in October that year against Greece. He was a member of the Italian European Championship squad of 1988 and now has more than 30 caps.

DONATO (Atletico Madrid, Spa)

• 30.12.62 • Midfield

Solid Brazilian midfielder who was bought to Spain by Madrid from Vasco da Gama in his homeland in 1988.

DONNELLY, Jimmy (Drogheda United, Eir)

• Midfield

Began with Waterford United, for whom he made his League of Ireland debut against St Patrick's Athletic in September 1984. Moved to Shamrock Rovers, but couldn't settle at the RDS and, after a spell on loan at Kilkenny, moved to Drogheda in February 1991. His arrival helped the club sustain the push for the First Division Championship and promotion to the Premier League.

DONNELLY, Michael (Cliftonville, N.Ir)

• Defender

Club captain at Solitude Park who has been targeted by several Football League clubs. Fearsome tackler in the Stuart Pearce mould who is equally at home at the back or in midfield.

DONOVAN, Brian
(St Patrick's Athletic, Eir)

• 17.01.65 • Defender

Comparative latecomer into senior football, he made his League of Ireland debut, for St Patrick's Athletic, at Waterford United in September 1990.

DOOHAN, Mick
(Bray Wanderers, Eir)

• 13.07.67 • Defender

Birmingham-born full back who scored on his League of Ireland debut, for Bray against Drogheda United on 4th September 1988. Likes to get forward and help out his midfield.

DOOLEY, Thomas
(Kaiserslautern, Ger)

• 12.05.61 • Defender
• USA 1 full cap

A former member of the FK Pirmasens club, Thomas joined Kaiserslautern from Homburg in 1983. Has made well over 100 First Division appearances. Made his international debut at USA '92, against the Republic of Ireland in May 1992.

DORFNER, Hans
(Nuremburg, Ger)

• 03.07.65 • Midfield
• West Germany 7 full caps

Former international who won all his caps before the re-unification of Germany. Now in his second spell at the club, he returned to Nuremberg from Bayern Munich in 1991, after leaving originally in 1986. He was controversially omitted for West Germany's 1990 World Cup squad.

DORNAN, Alan
(Linfield, N.Ir)

• Defender
• Irish League Representative

Since signing from Ards in 1987, Dornan has played more than 250 senior games for Linfield, and is a firm favourite at Windsor Park. Not the most naturally gifted player, but his 100 per cent effort make him invaluable.

DORNAN, Reg
(Bangor, N.Ir)

• 09.12.58 • Defender

Consistent full back who can play on either flank. He is now in his second spell at Bangor, having re-joined the club from Ards in 1988. Won the 1991/92 Lombard Ulster Cup with the club.

DOSSENA, Giuseppe (Perugia, Ita)

• 02.05.58 • Midfield
• Italy 38 full caps

Joined Torino as youth and, after being rejected by both Milan clubs, was farmed out to Pistoiese, Cesena and Bologna for experience. Giuseppe made his international debut against East Germany in April 1981. Joined Udinese in 1987 and a year later moved to Sampdoria where he won a League Champions' medal in 1990/91. Signed by Perugia in 1992.

DOUGLAS, Ian (Bohemians, Eir)

• 13.02.71 • Striker

Joined the club from Drogheda United in Jun 1990. His League of Ireland debut came for Drogheda, v Cork, in September 1989. Was an immediate success at Dalymount Park, as he scored 11 goals in 31 outings during his first season.

DOUGLAS, Stephen (Glentoran, N.Ir)

• Striker

After a slow start at Glentoran, Stephen hit a rich vein of form during 1991/92, scoring six goals in four games in one memorable run. His partnerhsip with Gary Macartney helped the club to their 12-point winning margin in the League.

DOUGLAS, William (Sporting Lisbon, Por)

• 01.03.63 • Midfield

Brazilian-born midfielder who made his Sporting Lisbon debut during the 1988/89 season and immeadiatley became a first team regular.

DRAKE, Billy (Cliftonville, N.Ir)

• Striker

Like fellow forward Sean O'Kane he had a fine season in 1990/91 (20 goals), but suffered a goal drought in the last campaign. Big and strong he always gives 100% and makes up for what he lacks in finesse with total commitment.

DRAKE, Johnny (Distillery, N.Ir)

• Defender

Right-back who missed much of the second half of 91/92 through injury. Spent seven months with Cliftonville - where he played alongside brother Billy - before returning to Distillery in March 1991.

DREOSSI, Pierre (Cannes, Fra)

• 12.10.59 • Defender

Much-travelled central defender who's

career has taken him to Lille, Sochaux, Nice and Paris St Germain, from whom he joined Cannes in 1989. Rapidly approaching the 500th top flight game of his career, which began against Nancy in July 1978.

DRESSEL, Olaf (Bochum, Ger)
• 19.09.68 • Defender

Although Olaf first joined Bochum as an 11-year-old his first team chances have been very limited in the First Division.

DRESSEN, Hans-Georg (Cologne, Ger)
• 30.12.64 • Defender

Began his career with Cologne before moving on to Borussia Moenchengladbach. Moved back to his original club in 1991.

DREWS, Gunter (Nuremburg, Ger)
• 09.07.67 • Midfield

Signed from Hannover 96 in 1989. Previously with Bayer Leverkusen.

DROUGUET, Pierre (Kortrijk, Bel)
• 02.06.62 • Goalkeeper

Gained much experience in the lower divisions with CS Juslenvillois and Battice before hitting the big time with Cercle Liege.

DUARTE, Paulo (Salgueiros, Por)
• 06.04.69 • Defender

Began his career with Boavista and finally got his chance in First Division football when signed by Salgueiros from Leiria during the summer of 1991.

DUBOIS, Didier (Lens, Fra)
• 11.04.67 • Midfield

First affiliated to the club as an 11-year-old in 1978, he made his first senior appearance at Laval in August 1988.

DUFF, Brian (Home Farm, Eir)
• 21.03.60 • Striker

Began with Dundalk, where he scored on his debut against St Patrick's Athletic on 29th January 1978 (won 2- 1). Had a very brief spell at Sligo Rovers (two games), but couldn't settle at The Showgrounds, and signed for Home Farm in October 1990.

DUFFY, Martin (Bohemians, Eir)
• 26.02.59 • Defender

Experienced central defender who followed a popular route when he moved from Athlone Town to Bohemians in 1987. Superb header of the ball.

DUFFY, Ray
(Shelbourne, Eir)

• 05.02.64 • Midfield

Was spotted playing local football for Cherry Orchard and snapped up by Shelbourne in 1982.

DUFOURNET, Eric
(Sochaux, Fra)

• 02.05.69 • Defender
• France U21

Signed from Annecy in 1984, he has made more than 60 appearances since making his debut, v Nantes, in September 1988.

DULLY, Padraig
(Shelbourne, Eir)

• 20.04.65 • Striker

Born in Athlone, he signed for his local club, Athlone Town, straight from school. His League of Ireland debut came some four years later, in October 1985, against Cork City. Signed for Shelbourne in July 1990.

DUMAS, Franck
(Caen, Fra)

• 09.01.68 • Defender
• France U21

Commanding central defender who likes to get forward and help out at corners and free-kicks. Strong in the air, he has played more than 120 first team games, chipping in with some vital goals.

DUNGA, Verri Carlos
(Fiorentina, Ita)

• 31.10.63 • Midfield
• Brazil full caps

Played for Internacional, Corinthians, Santos and Vasco da Gama in Brazil before leaving South America for Europe in 1987. Signed by Pisa, but joined Fiorentina after just one season.

DUNNION, Paul
(Omagh Town, N.Ir)

• Midfield

University student who joined Omagh from Strabane - a source for many players now at St Julian's Road. Likes to get forward

DURAN Pages, Juan
(Figueres, Spa)

• 10.07.59 • Midfield

Tall midfielder who moved to Figueres

from Barcelona in 1985 after failing to establish himself with Barca.

DURAND, Jean-Phillipe
(Marseille, Fra)

• 11.11.69 • Midfield
• France 21 full caps

Former Toulouse and Bordeaux star who joined Marseille at beginning of 1990/91. Since his debut, for Toulouse v Auxerre, in January 1983 he has made close to 300 senior appearances.

DURIX, Franck
(Cannes, Fra)

20.10.65 • Midfield

Former Lyon player who joined the club in 1988. He took his bow in the French First Division in February of the following year against Lille.

van DURME, Donald
(Kortrijk, Bel)

• 23.08.67 • Defender

Attacking full back who chips in with the occasional goal. He was signed from Anderlecht.

DUSSUYER, Michel
(Cannes, Fra)

• 23.05.59 • Goalkeeper
• France Olympic

Local boy who began his career with Division Two club Ales, before moving to Cannes in 1983. Has now played more than 200 Division One games since making his debut, for Bastia, v Nice in 1981.

DWYER, David
(Bohemians, Eir)

• 14.08.61 • Defender

Signed from Kilkenny City in July 1990.

DYKES, Gavin
(Sligo Rovers, Eir)

• 02.10.67 • Defender

Home grown talent who was spotted playing local football by the Rovers in October 1987. Made his debut at home to Cork City later that same month and has gone on to establish himself as a firm favourite at The Showgrounds. He is strong in the air, and likes to get forward for free kicks and corners.

DZIUBINSKI, Thomas
(Club Brugge, Bel)

• 08.08.68 • Striker
• Poland 1 full cap

Deadly goal-grabber who made his international debut v N.Ireland in February 1991. 21 goals in 29 games for Wisla Krakow during season 1990/91 tempted Brugge to sign Thomas prior to season 1991/92. Also formerly with Bron Radom.

EACHUS, Stephen (Bangor, N.Ir)

• 15.12.64 • Goalkeeper
• Irish League Representative

At 6ft 5in he is the tallest 'keeper in the Irish League. Joined Bangor in August 1988 from amateur side Comber Rec, and has been almost ever-present since. Was selected for the Irish League squad against the English League during 1990/91. He created a new club record when he went eight full matches without conceding a goal during season 1989/90, and was a member of the 1991/92 Lombard Ulster Cup winning side. Previously with Linfield and Ballymena United.

EASTON, John (Linfield, N.Ir)

• Defender

Despite missing a large chunk of the 1990/91 season through injury, John has gone on to establish himself as a first team regular. Graduating through the youth ranks at Windsor Park, manager Eric Bowyer has predicted a golden future.

ECCLES, Peter (Shamrock Rovers, Eir)

• 24.08.63 • Defender

Experienced centre back who likes to get forward at set pieces, and is now in his second spell at the club. Re-signed from Dundalk in October 1989. Made his League of Ireland debut, with the Rovers, back in October 1981, v UCD (won 1-0).

ECK, Armin (SV Hamburg, Ger)

• 08.12.68 • Midfield

Signed from Bayern Munich in 1989.

ECKEL, Uwe (SV Hamburg, Ger)

• 06.07.66 • Striker

Signed from Hannover 96 in 1991. Previously with Kaiserslautern.

ECKSTEIN, Dieter (Nuremburg, Ger)

• 12.03.64 • Striker
• Germany 7 full caps

Big favourite with the Nuremburg fans. Rejoined the club from Eintracht Frankfurt in 1991.

EDDIS, David (Ards, N.Ir)

• Striker

Formerly leading scorer with his home-town club Bangor, from where he transferred prior to the 1990/91 season. Also a very keen rugby union player.

EDELMANN, Reiner
(Kortrijk, Bel)
• 19.03.65 • Striker

Journeyman forward who was signed at
the beginning of season 1991/92 to give
the club's young forward line some
much needed experience. German-born
player who has experience with Phonix
Bellheim, SVW Mannheim, SV
Schwetzingen, Schalke 04 and Preussen
Munster

EDEL
(Salgueiros, Por)
• 05.03.66 • Striker

Angolan born forward who joined
Salgueiros from Sporting Lisbon during
the summer of 1991. His real name is
Edelfrides Viveiros Lima.

EDMILSON Dias
Lucena
(Maritimo, Por)
• 29.05.68 • Striker

One of two Brazilians in the Maritimo
side, and a proven goal-scorer. Hit 22 in
three glorious years at Nacional before
moving to Maritimo for the 1991/92
season.

EFFENBERG, Stefan
(Fiorentina, Ita)
• 02.08.68 • Midfield
• Germany 11 full caps, 1 goal

Outspoken attacking midfielder signed
from Borussia Moenchengladbach for
£1.4m in summer 1990. Previously with
junior clubs Victoria Hamburg and
Bramfelder SV. Made full debut v Wales
June 1991. Joined Fiorentina at start of
1992/93 season.

EGU, Augustine
(Kortrijk, Bel)
• 19.08.65 • Defender

Nigerian-born defender who arrived at
the club from Gent midway through
season 1990/91. Made a name for
himself in his home country playing for
a succession of company sides such as
Igobosa Babes, Samco Stars and Bendel
Insurance. Gent brought him to Europe
in 1987.

EHRMANN, Gerald
(Kaiserslautern, Ger)
• 18.02.59 • Goalkeeper

A 1984 signing from Cologne, Gerald
has made over 200 appearances in the
German First Division. Originally
started in junior football with TSV
Tauberbischofsheim.

EICHIN, Thomas (Borussia Moenchengladbach, Ger)

• 09.10.66 • Defender

Joined Gladbach from Freiburger FC in 1985. Has made more than 100 German First Division appearances.

EIGENRAUCH, Yves (Schalke, Ger)

• 24.04.71 • Defender

Young defender who joined Schalke from Arminia Bielefeld in 1990.

EIJKELKAMP, Rene (Mechelen, Bel)

• 06.04.64 • Striker
• Holland 3 full caps

Previously with Go Ahead and FC Groningen he joined the club prior to season 1990/91. Scored six goals in 29 games in his first season - hardly a prolific return but enough to put him back on the fringes of the Dutch international set-up.

van EIJKEREN, Emiel (Den Haag, Hol)

• 27.07.67 • Striker

Den Haag born forward who joined his local side in July 1990. Quickly established himself as a first choice as has now made over 60 appearances for the club he supported as a boy.

EILENBERGER, Ralf (Wattenscheid, Ger)

• 16.11.65 • Goalkeeper

Signed from Hasper SV in 1984.

EKSTROM, Johnny (Gothenburg, Swe)

• 05.03.65 • Striker
• Sweden 39 full caps, 11 goals

Began career with IFK, breaking into the Gothenburg first team and full national side in 1986. Performances at international level earned move to Italian side Emploi in October 1986. Sold to Bayern Munich in 1988 but family could not settle in Germany. Moved on to France with Cannes and won place in Swedish 1990 World Cup squad. Returned to IFK in summer 1991.

ELDUAYEN, Augustin de Carlos (Burgos, Spa)

• 04.08.64 • Goalkeeper
• Spain U21

Tall 'keeper who was previously with Real Sociedad and Atletico Madrid.

EL HADAOUI, Mustapha (Lens, Fra)

• 28.07.61 • Midfield
• Morocco full caps

French-Moroccon left winger who started his career with home-town club Raja Casablanca, before moving to Lausanne. It was not until he joined St Etienne that he started making a name for himself, his first senior game in France coming, away to Laval, in July 1987. Always liable to score goals, he was snapped up by Lens in 1990.

ELLERMAN, Juul (PSV Eindhoven, Hol)

• 07.10.65 • Striker
• Holland 1 full cap

Signed from Sparta Rotterdam in July 1988. Scored more than 50 goals in Dutch First Division.

ELLIOTT, Eamonn (Distillery, N.Ir)

• Midfield

Hard-working midfielder who inspires the players around him. Formerly with Carlisle United, he joined Distillery after a spell playing and coaching in the US. Signed in January 1992.

ELOY, Olaya Prendes (Valencia, Spa)

• 10.07.64 • Striker
• Spain 15 full caps, 4 goals

Diminutive, lively forward who joined Valencia from Sporting Gijon.

ELOY Perez Garcia (Espanol, Spa)

• 25.03.65 • Defender

Full back signed by Espanol from regional Second Division side Hospitalet in 1988.

van der ELST, Franky (Club Brugge, Bel)

• 30.04.61 • Midfield
• Belgium 50 full caps

Belgian Footballer of the Year for 1990, and a Belgian Cup winner with Brugge that same year. Determined ball-winner who started with Blau-Wit Lombeek before moving to Molenbeek, from where Brugge signed him. Played a central role in Belgium's 1990 World Cup side. Has now played more than 400 senior games in Belgium.

van der ELST, Leo (Genk, Bel)

• 07.01.62 • Midfield
• Belgium 13 full caps

Midfield playmaker and goalscorer who has played more than 350 First Divsion games. Previously with Eendracht Mazenzele, HO Merchtem, Antwerp, Club Brugge, Metz, RKC and Charleroi, from where he signed for Genk. International debut came against Poland in April 1984 (lost 1-0).

EMENALO, Michael
(RWD Molenbeek, Bel)

• 14.07.65 • Defender

Nigerian-born central defender who won a sports scholarship to Boston University in the US. Came to Europe in the summer of 1991, and signed for Molenbeek. Scored once in 16 games during his first season with the club.

EMMERECHTS, Geert
(Antwerp, Bel)

• 05.05.68 • Defender
• Belgium 1 full cap

With more than 130 senior games to his credit, this versatile defender was signed from Molenbeek. Likes to get forward for corners and free-kicks.

EMMERLING, Stefan
(Wattenscheid, Ger)

• 10.02.66 • Midfield

Signed from 1.FC Kaiserslautern in 1988.

EMMERS, Marc
(Anderlecht, Bel)

• 25.02.66 • Midfield
• Belgium 27 full caps, 2 goals

International debut came v Israel in January 1988. Solid central defender who loves to get forward, particularly at dead ball situations. Previously with Hamontlo and Thor Waterschei he has now played more than 200 senior games. Transferred to Anderlecht in June 1992.

ENGIN, Ipekoglu
(Fenerbahce, Tur)

• 07.06.61 • Goalkeeper
• Turkey 15 full caps

Joined the club from Besiktas for £350,000 in July 1991, where he replaced German veteran Toni Schumacher as number one 'keeper. Up until March 1991 he was Turkey's first choice, but crucial mistakes in a European Championship qualifier v Poland cost him his place in the national side. Began with Sakaryaspor.

ENNIS, Mark
(St Patrick's Athletic, Eir)

• 12.02.64 • Striker

Lethal finisher who averages a goal every other game for St Pat's.

EPP, Thomas
(Bochum, Ger)

• 07.04.68 • Striker

Thomas played for VfB Stuttgart before making his first move to Bochum. Left to join Saarbrucken for a spell, but returned home to Bochum in 1990.

ERANIO, Stefano
(Genoa, Ita)

• 29.12.66 • Midfield
• Italy 8 full caps

Local youth product, now played over 150 League games for Genoa. Full international debut came against Cyprus in December 1990.

ERDAL, Keser
(Galatasaray, Tur)

• 20.06.61 • Midfield
• Turkey 24 full caps; 3 goals

Migrant player who was born in Turkey, but grew up in West Germany, after his father, Erol, an ex- footballer himself, moved in search of work. Began with SSV Hagen, before hitting the big time with Borussia Dortmund. Galatasaray paid £200,000 to tempt him back to Turkey in 1984, but he couldn't settle and returned to Dortmund for £130,000. Yet another change of heart saw this creative midfielder sign for Sariyer, in the Turkish First Division. His international debut came in September 1982, v Hungary, and he'd been out of favour at national level for three years until he was recalled for the 1-1 draw with the US in September 1991. He celebrated his return by scoring Turkey's goal.

ERIKSSON, Jan
(IFK Norkopping, Swe)

• 24.08.67 • Defender
• Sweden 23 full caps, 3 goals

Big, solid central defender who caught the eye during the 1992 European Championships with his heading ability at set-pieces, which unhinged both England and France. Began his career with AIK Stockholm and had trails with Newcastle United before opting to move on to Norkopping.

ERIKSSON, Lars
(IFK Norkopping, Swe)

• 21.09.65 • Goalkeeper
• Sweden 8 full caps

Sweden's second choice 'keeper behind Thomas Ravelli, Lars had a nightmare debut at international level as Sweden lost 6-0 to Denmark in 1989. Before joining Norkopping he played his football with Hammarby.

ERIKSSON, Peter
(Gothenburg, Swe)

• 18.05.69 • Midfield

Joined Gothenburg youth team from Skepplamds BTK in 1984. Helped the club to win a Swedish League and Cup double in 1991.

ERLINGMARK, Magnus
(Orebro, Swe)

• 08.07.68 • Midfield
• Sweden 17 full caps, 1 goal

Versatile midfielder who can also operate at the heart of the defence. Was unlucky to be left out of the Swedish squad that went to Italy for the 1990 World Cup finals, but got the nod from national coach Tommy Svensson for the 1992 European Championship squad.

ERNES, Luc
(RC Liege, Bel)

• 24.02.65 • Striker
• Belgium 5 U21 caps

Midfielder turned attacker who is always dangerous around the six-yard area. Signed from Villersoise he has now played more than 250 First Division games.

ERNST, Rainer
(Kaiserslautern, Ger)

• 31.12.61 • Midfield
• East Germany 56 full caps

Joined Kaiserslautern from Berlin at the start of the 1990/91 season and made 18

League appearances during their title winning campaign.

ERSKINE, Darren
(Ards, N.Ir)

• Striker

Was voted the "Amateur League Player of the Season" in 1990/91, when he played for Ards Rangers. Joined the club in July 1991.

ESCAICH Ferrer, Xavier
(Espanol, Spa)

• 08.09.68 • Striker

Exciting youngster who was Espanol's top scorer during the 1991/92 season.

ESKELINEN, Kaj
(Gothenburg, Swe)

• 21.02.69 • Striker
• Sweden youth, U21

A former youth international who joined Gothenburg from Vastra Frolunda. Won the Swedish League and Cup double with the club in 1991.

ESKURZA Garcia, Xabier
(Atletico Bilbao, Spa)

• 17.01.70 • Midfield

Came up through Bilbao's youth ranks and finally broke into the first team squad during the 1991/92 season.

ETIM ESIN, John (Lierse, Bel)

• 15.11.69 • Striker

Nigerian-born forward who has now played more than 100 senior games in Belgium with Gent, Lokeren and Lierse. Began in his home country with Flash Flamingoes and also played for Calabar Rovers.

ETTORI, Jean-Luc (Monaco, Fra)

• 29.07.55 • Goalkeeper
• France 17 full caps

Despite a lack of height (5ft 10in) he has proved himself one of the greatest 'keepers in France. Was discovered playing local parks football by INF Vichy, and moved to Monaco in 1975 - and he's been there ever since. Has now played more than 500 First Divsion games since making his debut, v Bordeaux, in December 1975.

ETTORRE, Michel (Metz, Fra)

• 14.10.57 • Goalkeeper
• France U21

Highly experienced 'keeper who is now in his second spell with the club, having had periods at Quimper and Toulon. Made his

debut back in October 1974, v Sochaux, and has now made well over 300 First Division appearances. At 6ft 2in he is surprisingly agile, as well as expert on crosses.

EUGENIO Rui Pedro Rodrigues (Farense, Por)

• 21.07.66 • Defender

Joined the club in 1988 and has been the stalwart of the defence ever-since playing over a hundred games.

EUSEBIO, Sacristan Mena (Barcelona, Spa)

• 13.04.64 • Midfield

• Spain U21; 10 full caps

Began his career with his home town team, Valladolid, and was a member of the Spain side that won the 1986 European U21 title. Joined Atletico Madrid in 1987 and then moved on to Barcelona a year later.

EVANI, Robert (Milan, Ita)

• 01.01.63 • Midfield

Robert joined Milan as 15 year-old and made his debut 3 years later against Bologna. He scored the winning goals in both the 1990 European Super Cup and the 1990 World Club Cup.

EVERTON Machado Jaenisch (Maritimo, Por)

• 26.12.57 • Goalkeeper

Didn't join the club until 1987/88 season but has been ever present since, making nearly 200 appearances.

EVISTON, Terry (Dundalk, Eir)

• 17.7.57 • Winger

A member of Dundalk's 1988 double-winning side, and a firm favourite with the Oriel Park fans. Previously with Athlone Town, Bohemians and Shamrock Rovers. Happy on either wing, he is a regular goalscorer.

EYLDELIE, Jean-Jacques (Nantes, Fra)

• 03.02.66 • Midfield

Apart from a brief spell on loan at Tours, Nantes is his only club. Joined straight from school, making his debut v Auxerre in September 1984. Equally at home as full back or wide midfielder he has now made more than 100 senior appearances for the club. Scored one goal in the 1991/92 campaign.

EYRAUD, Patrice (Marseille, Fra)

• 18.12.67 • Midfield
• France U21

Currently in his second spell at the club where he began his professional career. Made his First Division debut against Laval in April 1988 before enjoying spells with Nantes and Toulouse. Returned to Marseille in June 1991.

FACCENDA, Mario
(Fiorentina, Ita)

• 23.11.60 • Defender

Signed by Genoa from junior club
Latina in 1981 and immediately became
a first team regular. Moved on to Pisa in
1986, helping the club to win
promotion from the Second Division in
his first season. He was signed by
Fiorentina in 1989.

FACH, Holger
(Borussia
Moenchengladbach,
Ger)

• 06.09.62 • Midfield
• Germany 5 full caps

Signed from Bayer Uerdingen in 1991.
Previously with Fortuna Dusseldorf and
Wuppertal.

FALKENMAYER, Ralf
(Eintracht Frankfurt,
Ger)

• 11.02.63 • Midfield
• Germany 4 full caps

Returned to Frankfurt from Bayer
Leverkusen in 1989. He has now made
substantially more than 270 First
Division appearances.

FAMULLA, Alexander
(Karlsruher, Ger)

• 20.09.60 • Goalkeeper

Signed from SG Kirchheim in 1986.
Previously with Gornik Zabrze.

FAVALLI, Giuseppe
(Cremonese, Ita)

• 08.02.72 • Defender

Made his debut for Cremonese during the
1989 promotion season and then
established himself as a first team regular
the following year as the club attempted to
consolidate its place in Serie A.
Unfortunately they were relegated, but
Giuseppe helped Cremonese return once
again in 1991.

FEINBIER, Marcus
(Bayer Leverkusen,
Ger)

• 30.11.69 • Midfield

Joined Bayer Leverkusen as a teenager in
1986. Played for both Hertha Zehlendorf
and Berlin SV92 as a youth.

FENGLER, Dirk
(Nuremburg, Ger)

• 03.03.70 • Midfield

Signed from Stuttgarter Kickers in 1991.

FENLON, Pat
(St Patrick's Athletic, Eir)

• 15.03.69 • Striker

Former Chelsea apprentice who signed for St Pat's at the beginning of the 1991/92 season - and scored 12 goals in his first 32 games for the club.

FERHAOUI, Kader
(Montpellier, Fra)

• 29.03.65 • Midfield
• Algeria full caps3

Attacker turned wide midfielder, who was signed by the club straight from school in 1981. Had to wait six years for his debut, which eventually came against Toulouse in July 1987. Has now played more than 120 senior games.

FERGUSON, Glenn
(Glenavon, N.Ir)

• Forward
• Irish League Representative

Civil Servant who is an ace goal poacher. Chose Glenavon from a host of Irish League clubs interested in him in August 1990. From Ballybeen. Scored 37 goals in 64 games in 1990/91. Injury restricted him in 91/92.

FERNANDEZ, Alfonso
(Lyon, Fra)

• 20.04.63 • Midfield

Experienced ball-winner brought in to bolster a lightweight midfield at Lyon. Began with Standard Liege before signing for his home town club Castellon in Spain. Lyon signed him in July 1991.

FERNANDEZ, Luis
(Cannes, Fra)

• 02.10.59 • Defender
• France 58 full caps, 5 goals

One of the world's leading sweeper's, signed from Matra Racing Paris in 1989. Formerly with Paris St Germain. Approaching his 400th top level game, he has been the mainstay of the French national team's defence for several seasons. Was an integral member of France's 1984 European Championship winning side.

FERNANDEZ, Thomas
(Toulouse, Fra)

• 03.08.70 • Defender
• France U21

Came up through the ranks at the club to form a solid central defensive partnership with 'sound-alike' Hernandez. Signed on as a 15-year-old in 1985, making his debut four years later against Marseille.

FERNANDO COUTO
(Porto, Por)
• 02.08.69 • Defender
• Portugal 1 full caps

Formerly with Lourosa, he made his
League debut for Porto as a teenager
during the 1987/88 season. Spent a couple
of seasons playing outside Portugal before
returning to Porto in 1990 and claiming a
regular first team place.

FERNANDO CRUZ
Mendes
(Uniao, Por)
• 29.04.62 • Striker

A proven goal-scorer who has hit the target
regularly for a variety of clubs over the past
decade. Started with Vitoria Setubal in
1980/81, moved to Sporting Lisbon three
years later, and then returned. Joined
Farense for a couple of seasons in 1987/88
and is now Uniao's star front man.

FERNANDO Gomez
Colomer
(Valencia, Spa)
• 11.09.65 • Midfield

Long serving player who graduated to the
Valencia first team squad from the reserves
in 1983.

FERNANDO MENDES
(Boavista, Por)
• 05.11.66 • Defender
• Portugal full caps

Began his career with little Montijo before
getting his chance in the top flight with
Sporting Lisbon in 1984. Moved across
the city to Benfica four years later, but
failed to hold down a regular first team
place. Signed by Boavista during the
summer of 1991.

FERNANDO PIRES
(Sporting Braga, Por)
• 18.01.69 • Midfield

Born in Angola and has spent all of his
career in the Portuguese with Braga. Broke
in to the first team during 1986/87

FERRARA, Ciro
(Napoli, Ita)
• 11.02.67 • Defender

Born in Naples and joined his local serie A
side Napoli in 1983.
Made his League debut the following
season, but did not establish himself as a
regular in the side until 1986/87.

FERRAND, Stephane
(Sochaux, Fra)
• 02.10.68 • Goalkeeper

Young reserve 'keeper who's been at the club since 1984. Has made only a handful of appearances, due to the presence of number one Christophe Gardie.

FERRARONI, Ettore (Cremonese, Ita)

• 17.01.68 • Midfield

Joined his local side Cremonese in 1985 and made his debut for the club that season. Had a season apiece with Novara and Derthona before coming back to Cremonese in 1989 and establishing himself as a regular.

FERRI, Jean-Michel (Nantes, Fra)

• 07.02.69 • Midfield

Local discovery who has been with the club since leaving school at 16. Equally at home at full back or in a wide midfield role.

FERRI, Ricardo (Internazionale, Ita)

• 20.08.63 • Defender
• Italy 43 full caps, 4 goals

Loyal servant of the club that he first joined as teenager. Made his League debut during the 1981/82 season. Has now made more than 250 Serie A appearances for the club.

FERRIS, Tony (Distillery, N.Ir)

• Striker

Former Distillery player who emigrated to New Zealand in 1987. Plays for Mount Maungarni in NZ, but spends a couple of months each year back 'on loan' with the Belfast club. Brother Paul played for Newcastle United and Northern Ireland.

FERRON, Fabrizio (Atalanta, Ita)

• 05.09.65 • Goalkeeper

Joined Milan in 1984 but did not make a League appearance until moving to Second Division Sambenedettese two years later. Got his chance in Serie A when signed by Atalanta in 1988.

FERRONI, Armando (Genoa, Ita)

• 03.04.61 • Defender

Experienced full back. Previously with Fiorentina and Avellino.

FESTA, Gianluca (Cagliari, Ita)

• 12.03.69 • Defender

Born in Cagliari and joined the club in 1986, making his League debut later that season. Spent the following year with

Fersulcis, before returning to Cagliari in 1988. Helped the club to promotion from Serie C to Serie A in successive seasons.

FEUER, Ian
(RWD Molenbeek, Bel)

• 20.05.71 • Goalkeeper
• USA 1 full cap

One of several North American players currently plying their trade in Europe. Began with Brugge, before moving to Molenbeek in the summer of 1991. Understudy to Peter Thijs. His international debut came against Morocco in March 1992.

FEYS, Yves
(Cercle Brugge, Bel)

• 16.01.69 • Goalkeeper

Has come through the junior ranks at the club and established himself as first choice 'keeper over the last two seasons.

FEYYAZ, Ucar
(Besiktas, Tur)

• 27.10.63 • Striker
• 17 full caps, 4 goals

Free-scoring club player who made his international debut as sub v England in the 0-0 draw in Izmir in 1987. Was the Turkish League's leading scorer with 28 goals as Besiktas romped to the 1990 Championship, and he followed up by scoring 16 in 1990/91 as the title was retained. His goals again made the difference as Besiktas made it a hat-trick of League wins in 1991/92.

FIARD, Alain
(Lille, Fra)

• 17.09.58 • Midfield

Born in Phnom-Penh, Cambodia, he has played all his senior football in France, where he is a naturalized citizen. Began with Bastia in August 1979, making his debut at Nice later that month, before spending several successful seasons with Auxerre. Signed for Lille in 1987, and has now made more than 400 senior appearances in France.

FICHAUX, Claude
(Lille, Fra)

• 24.03.69 • Midfield

Ball-winner in the middle, and 'protector' of playmaker Per Frandsen. Former defender with Mulhouse and Metz before Lille coach Jacques Santini signed him in July 1990 and handed him the crucial role in midfield.

FIEBER, Peter
(Genk, Bel)

• 16.05.64 • Striker

Czech-born player who was signed solely as a winger, but is equally at home anywhere across the midfield or up front. Formerly with Internacional Bratislava and

DAC Dunajska Streda. He first moved to Belgium with Beerschot, where he played just 15 games before transferring to Genk in July 1991.

FIERENS, Marc
(Lierse, Bel)

• 12.06.63 • Midfield

One of several players to have graduated through the ranks at the club. Solid defender who is strong in the air he celebrated his 100th senior game during 1991/92.

FIGO, Luis Filipe Madeira
(Sporting Lisbon, Por)

• 04.11.72 • Midfield

Locally born midfielder who is a fringe member of the Sporting squad. Made his debut during the 1989/90 season, but has struggled to gain a regular place.

FINK, Thorsten
(Wattenscheid, Ger)

• 29.10.67 • Midfield

Signed from Borussia Dortmund in 1989.

FINNEGAN, John
(Bray Wanderers, Eir)

• 08.12.63 • Midfield

Signed from Wicklow Rovers in the summer of 1998, he made his League of Ireland debut the following season, on 4th September 1988, away to Drogheda United (lost 2-1). Equally happy playing midfield or up front, he scored twice in five starts in 1990/91 as the club won promotion to the Premier Division.

FIORI, Valerio
(Lazio, Ita)

• 27.04.69 • Goalkeeper

Signed by Lazio from Lodigiani in 1986. Has benefitted tremendously from having former Italian national 'keeper Dino Zoff as his club manager.

FIRICANO, Aldo
(Cagliari, Ita)

• 12.03.67 • Defender

After two seasons at Cavesse, he was signed by Udinese in 1985 and then later loaned out to Nocerina. Broke into the Udinese first team in 1987 and then sold to Cagliari in 1989.

FISCHER, Andreas
(Bayer Leverkusen, Ger)

• 20.10.64 • Midfield

Former Preussen Munster midfielder who arrived at Bayer Leverkusen from Remscheid in 1989.

FLAD, Egon
(Schalke, Ger)
• 05.03.64 • Midfield

Much travelled midfielder who has had spells with Vfb Stuttgart, Stutgarter Kickers and Blau-Weiss Berlin before joining Schalke from St Pauli in 1989.

FLANAGAN, Frank
(Drogheda United, Eir)
• 17.06.61 • Defender

Signed from Home Farm. Big centre back who likes to get forward and is especially dangerous in the air from free kicks and other dead ball situations.

FLICK, Hans-Dieter
(Cologne, Ger)
• 24.02.65 • Midfield

Made his name with Bayern Munich after joining the club from SV Sandhausen. Signed by Cologne in 1990 and has now made well over 130 First Division appearances.

FLUCKINGER, Philippe
(Metz, Fra)
• 24.05.63 • Goalkeeper

Signed from Montpellier as back up for first choice stopper Michel Ettorre in the summer of 1991. Born in Metz, but overlooked by his home town club, he began his career with Merlebach. Moved to Strasbourg in 1988, where he made his senior debut, against Sochaux, in July of that year. Had further spells with Abbeville and Montpellier before joining Metz.

FODA, Franco
(Bayer Leverkusen, Ger)
• 23.04.66 • Defender
• Germany 2 full caps

Plays as a sweeper and is a vital member of the Leverkusen set-up. Transferred to the club from Kaiserslautern for £1 million in 1990. Prior to that Franco had played his professional football with Saarbrucken.

FOFANA, Youssouf
(Monaco, Fra)
• 26.07.66 • Striker
• Ivory Coast full caps

Came to France with Cannes, who signed him from ASEC Abidjan in his native Ivory Coast. Failed to establish himself at Stade Pierre-de-Coubertin, however, and quickly moved onto Monaco in 1985. Key member of the 1992 African Nations' Cup winning Ivory Coast side.

FONSECA Antonio Manuel Tavares (Vitoria Guimaraes, Por)

• 30.01.65 • Defender
• Portugal 4 full caps

A tough-tackling defender who has scaled the heights in the Portuguese League, having spent three seasons at Benfica. Went to the Stadium of Light in 1987/88 and made 39 appearances for the Lisbon giants before moving to Vitoria at the start of the 1990/91 season.

FONSECA Recio, Gregorio (Valladolid, Spa)

• 26.10.65 • Striker
• Spain 2 full caps

Prolific goal scorer with an ever-growing reputation in Spain. He returned to Valladolid in 1987 after originally leaving the club for a spell with Malaga.

FORET, Jean-Phillipe (Lyon, Fra)

• 04.08.68 • Goalkeeper

Understudy to French national 'keeper Gilles Rousset. Signed from Montceau in summer 1989.

FORTES, Jose Luis Santos (Salgueiros, Por)

• 03.04.66 • Striker

Began his career with Salgueiros and then returned to the club from Mirandela during the summer of 1991.

FORTUNATO, Andrae (Genoa, Ita)

• 26.07.71 • Defender

Signed from Como summer 1991.

FORTUNATO, Daniele (Bari, Ita)

• 08.01.63 • Midfield

After seven years with Legnano and Vicenza in the lower Italian divisions, Daniele finally got his chance in Serie A with Atalanta as they won promotion to the top flight in 1988. Joined Juventus a year later and arrived at Bari last summer as part of the club's £12m spending spree.

FOURNIER, Hubert (Caen, Fra)

• 03.09.67 • Defender

Accomplished right-back, who uses his height to good effect in the air. Formerly with INF Vichy and

Maubeuge. Signed for Caen in 1989, making his First Division bow v Monaco in August of that year.

FOURNIER, Laurent (Paris St Germain, Fra)

• 14.09.64 • Defender
• France U21

Whether Fournier is a defender or a midfielder depends on your point of view. He is an attacking full back, and is normally to be found haring down the right flank in support of the midfield and attack. Signed from Marseille, where he had made a handful of appearances, in June 1991. Previously with Lyon and St Etienne. Scored three goals during the 1991/92 season.

FRAILE Sanchez, Alfonso (Zaragoza, Spa)

• 15.01.60 • Defender

Signed by Zaragoza from Real Madrid in 1984. An accomplished defender who is earning an ever growing reputation in his home country.

FRAN (Coruna, Spa)

• 14.07.69 • Midfield

Midfield ball-winner whose real name is Francisco Javier Gonzalez Perez.

FRANCESCOLI, Enzo (Cagliari, Ita)

• 12.11.61 • Striker
• Uruguay full caps

Exciting midfielder-cum-striker who made his name in Uruguay with the Wanderers club. Originally left his homeland for River Plate of Argentina in 1984. Moved to Europe in 1986 when signed by Racing Club Paris. Had further spells in France with Matra and Marseilles before being brought to Italy by Cagliari in 1990. He is widely regarded as one of the country's leading hit men.

FRANCISCO SILVA (Sporting Braga, Por)

• 16.03.67 • Defender

Began his career with the Vianense club and joined Sporting Braga in 1988.

FRANCINI, Giovanni (Napoli, Ita)

• 03.08.63 • Defender

Began his career at Torino, but struggled to establish himself in the first team and spent the 1982/83 season with Reggiana. Returned to Turin the following year and then signed by Napoli in 1987.

FRANCIS
(Tenerife, Spa)
• 18.12.62 • Defender
• Spain U21

Former U21 cap who move to Tenerife from Espanol in 1989.

FRANCISCO Lopez Alfaro
(Espanol, Spa)
• 01.11.62 • Midfield
• Spain 20 full caps, 1 goal

Free-kick specialist who spent nine seasons with Seville before signing for Espanol in 1990.

FRANCK, Thomas
(Borussia Dortmund, Ger)
• 24.02.71 • Midfield

Formerly with FC Heppenheim, Thomas joined Dortmund in 1990 from Waldhof Mannheim.

FRANDSEN, Per
(Lille, Fra)
• 06.02.70 • Midfield

Goalscoring central midfielder, who is expert at timing his runs into the area to pick up half-cleared balls. Signed on the advice of former BK 1903 Copenhagen team-mate Jacob Friis Hansen in September 1990. Scored five goals in 19 starts in his first season.

FRASER, Henk
(Feyenoord, Hol)
• 07.07.66 • Defender
• Holland full caps

Quick Dutch West Indian who began his career as a striker with Sparta Rotterdam. Moved on to Utrecht and Roda Kerkrade before returning to Rotterdam with Feyenoord who converted him into a central defender.

FRASER, Sandy
(Portadown, N.Ir)
• 31.08.67 • Striker

Began in his native Scotland with Glasgow Celtic, but joined Hamilton Accies in July 1987 without having made a first team appearance. After just ten Premier Division matches in two years he moved to Shamrock Park where he's formed a tremendous partnership with fellow countryman Steve Cowan. Holds the ball up superbly, although ought to score more goals.

FRAWLEY, Conor
(Athlone Town, Eir)
• 20.03.72 • Midfield

Highly regarded youngster, and one of the top attractions in the League of Ireland .

Local boy who joined his home town club from minor League side Willow Park. Made his debut against Derry City in January 1991, and finished the season with a flourish scoring in three successive games.

FREDERICO Nobre Rosa (Vitoria Guimaraes, Por)

• 06.04.57 • Defender
• Portugal full caps

One of three internationals in the Vitoria defence, and one of two to have played for Benfica. Now nearing the end of an impressive career, he joined Vitoria at the end of the 1991 season. Before that he had spent eight years at Boavista after a three year spell at Benfica which started in 1980/81.

FRENAY, Didier (Cercle Brugge, Bel)

• 09.04.66 • Defender

Former Jeunesse Vivegnis player who signed from Seresien and is now approaching his 200th senior appearance for Cercle.

FREUND, Stefan (Schalke, Ger)

• 19.01.70 • Defender

Yet another former East German League player on Schalke's staff, Stefan moved West from Stahl Brandenburg in 1991.

FRIEDMANN, Kay (Nuremburg, Ger)

• 15.05.63 • Defender

Kay won the Bundesliga title with 1.FC Kaiserslautern in 1991. Signed by Nurnberg that following summer. Previously with FC Homburg.

FRIDRIKAS, Robertas (FK Austria, Aus)

• Striker
• Lithuania full caps

Signed from Torpedo Moscow during the Austrian winter break last season.

FRONTZECK, Michael (VfB Stuttgart, Ger)

• 26.03. 64 • Defender
• Germany 17 full caps

Very experienced central defender who moved to Stuttgart from Borussia Moenchengladbach in 1989. Prior to that he was with junior side Odenkirchen.

FUCHS, Uwe (Cologne, Ger)

• 23.07.66 • Striker

Signed from Fortuna Dusseldorf in 1990. He was previously with Fortuna Koln, Stuttgarter Kickers, FC Homburg, FK Pirmasens, Stuttgart and Kaiserslautern.

FUENTES Aspiroz, Miguel Angel
(Real Sociedad,Spa)

• 06.08.64 • Striker

Nippy front runner who arrived at Sociedad from Eibar in 1987.

FUGIER, Pascal
(Lyon, Fra)

• 22.09.68 • Defender
• France U21

Home-grown full back who has been with the club since 1987. Strong tackler who likes to get forward and help out his midfield.

FUNKEL, Wolfgang
(Kaiserslautern, Ger)

• 10.08.58 • Defender
• Germany 2 full caps

Previously with Viktoria Goch and RW Oberhausen, Wolfgang was signed from Bayer Uerdingen in 1991. A veteran of over 200 Bundesliga games.

FURTOK, Jan
(SV Hamburg, Ger)

• 09.03.62 • Striker
• Poland 28 full caps, 8 goals

Made his international debut against Czechoslovakia in September 1985 and was a member of the Polish 1986 World Cup squad. Won the Polish Cup with GKS Katowice in 1986 and was tempted to Germany by Hamburg for £800,000 in 1988.

FUSCO, Salvatore
(Ascoli, Ita)

• 12.04.71 • Defender

Joined Ascoli in 1988 and has made just three appearances in three years

FUSI, Luca
(Torino, Ita)

• 07.06.63 • Defender

Began his career with Como and made his League debut during 1981/82 season. Helped the club win promotion to Serie A in 1984 and joined Sampdoria two years later. Moved on to Napoli in 1988 and signed by Torino in 1990.

FUTRE, Paulo
(Atletico Madrid, Spa)

• 28.02.66 • Striker
• Portugal 25 full caps, 4 goals

Pacy striker who has now been with Atletico Madrid for five seasons. Was a big money signing from Portuguese side Porto.

GAFFNEY, Robbie (St Patrick's Athletic, Eir)

• 17.12.57 • Midfield

Battling midfielder who is a valuable squad member at Harold's Cross. Signed from Shelbourne in June 1988. Brought in to lend some experience.

GAILLOT, Phillipe (Metz, Fra)

• 28.02.65 • Defender

Came up through the ranks at Metz to make his First Division debut, v Nancy, in March 1987. More than 130 senior games, but has been overlooked over the last couple of seasons thanks to the solidity of Cartier and Pauk in central defence.

GAJATE Vidriales, Agustin (Real Sociedad, Spa)

• 22.03.58 • Defender

Joined Sociedad in 1977 and has gone on to form a fine central defensive partnership with Gorriz.

GALIA, Roberto (Juventus, Ita)

• 16.02.63 • Midfield

Versatile player who can also operate in

defence. Began his career with Como and spent three seasons with the club before signing for Sampdoria in 1983. Moved to Verona in 1986 and was then signed by Juventus in 1988.

GALJE, Hans
(Club Brugge, Bel)

• 21.02.57 • Goalkeeper

Dutch-born understudy to Danny Verlinden who was signed from Kortrijk. Began with Den Haag, in his native Holland, and moved to Ajax. Spent just half a season with the Amsterdam club before transferring to Utrecht. Brugge signed him at the beginning of season 1990/91.

GALLEGO Redondo, Ricardo
(Rayo Vallecano, Spa)

• 08.02.59 • Striker
• Spain full caps

Lanky winger who had a highly successful 12 years with Real Madrid before joing Rayo in 1992.

GALLI, Filippo
(Milan, Ita)

• 19.05.63 • Defender

Apart from spending the 1982/83 season in Serie C with Pescara, Filippo has been at Milan all of his career. A tough stopper, he has now played more than 170 League games for the club.

GALLI, Giovanni
(Napoli, Ita)

• 29.04.58 •Goalkeeper

Born in Pisa but began his career with Fiorentina, making his League debut during the 1977/78 season. Signed by Milan in 1986 and signed by Napoli four years later.

GALTIER, Christophe
(Toulouse, Fra)

• 28.06.66 • Defender
• France U21

First appeared on the scene as a 19- year-old, when he played full back for Marseille against Brest on July 1985. Moved on to Lille before signing for Toulouse in June 1990.

GARABA, Imre
(Charleroi, Bel)

• 29.07.58 • Defender
• Hungary 84 full caps; 3 goals

Former Vasas Budapest stopper, and Charleroi club captain, who has been the mainstay of the club's defence for the last three seasons. Aiming to overtake Jozef Bozsik's Hungarian record of 100 full caps. Signed from St Rennes.

GARCIA, Clement
(Montpellier, Fra)

• 26.06.68 • Striker

Signed from Grenoble, he joined the club in the summer of 1990. His First Division debut came against St Etienne in January 1991.

GARCIA, Jean-Louis (Nantes, Fra)

• 20.09.62 • Goalkeeper

Signed at the beginning of 1991/92 as cover for first choice 'keeper David Marraud. Previously played for Chatellerault and Nancy.

GARCIN, Eric (Nimes, Fra)

• 06.12.65 • Midfield
• France U21

Home-grown midfield playmaker who has been with the club since 1986 and helped them to promotion from Division Two A in season 1990/91.

GARDE, Remy (Lyon, Fra)

• 03.04.66 • Defender
• France 6 full caps

One of Lyon's trio of home-grown defenders to have established themselves as among the best in France. Made his Division One debut v Marseille in 1989, on Lyon's return to the top flight. Has gone on to win a place in Michel Platini's international set-up. Calm on the ball, and excellent in the air despite a comparative lack of height (5ft 9in). Equally happy in midfield or as sweeper. He has been severely hampered by a string of injuries over the past couple of seasons.

GARDIE, Christophe (Sochaux, Fra)

• 22.11.64 • Goalkeeper

Agile 'keeper who began with Lens back in 1985 (debut v Auxerre, 27th April). He moved to the lower divisions with Guingamp, before signing for Sochaux in 1990. He has also played for French Army XI.

GARDINER, Jim (Crusaders, N.Ir)

• Striker

Experienced forward who was previously with Portadown (twice), Burnley, Ards and Glenavon. Scored ten goals in 24 starts in his first season at Seaview (1990/91) and has proved a fine buy.

GARITANO Urquiza, Ander (Atletico Bilbao, Spa)

• 26.02.69 • Midfield
• Spain youth

Promising youngster picked up from local regional side Derio in 1987.

GARRETT, John (Ballymena United, N.Ir)

• Defender

Born in Ballymena, he began his senior career with Linfield. Played more than 300 first team games for the Windsor Park outfit before joining his home town club. Missed a large chunk of 1991/92 with a knee injury that necessitated an operation.

GARRIDO, Jose Antonio Rocha (Boavista, Por)

• 11.07.60 • Defender

Angolan-born defender who began his career with Caminhya. Made the Chaves first team in 1986 before gaining a regular first team place at Boavista in 1989.

GARZILLI, Felice (Cremonese, Ita)

• 30.03.58 • Defender

Began his long career in 1974 with Milan but, after failing to break into the first team, he played his football with Iglesias and Teramo before joining Cremonese in 1979. The club were a Third Division side then, but Felice helped them gain promotion to Serie A on no less than three occasions.

GASCOIGNE, Paul (Lazio, Ita)

• 27.05.67 • Midfield
• England U21, B, 20 full caps, 2 goals

One of the most talked-about - and talkative - talents in the game. Shot to world wide fame during the 1990 Italian World Cup when his brilliant performances for England won him many admirers and the "Best Young Player in the Tournament" accolade. Voted England's "Young Player of the Year" in 1988, while still with Newcastle. He signed for Tottenham in July of that year for a then British record £2 million. Lazio spotted him at Italia '90 and offered £8 million for his services, but an atrocious 'tackle' on Gary Charles in the 1991 FA Cup Final put 'Gazza' out of action with knee ligament damage for more than 12 months, and the fee was cut to £5.5 million when he eventually signed in June 1992. Can be petulant and childish, but undeniably brilliant. Was missed during England's creatively barren performances at the 1992 European Championships.

GASPERCIC, Roland (Genk, Bel)

• 09.05.69 • Goalkeeper

Has come up through the ranks at the club, and is currently understudy to Jacky Mathijssen. Coach Paul Theunis considers him a fine prospect.

GAUDINO, Maurizio (VfB Stuttgart, Ger)

• 12.12.66 • Midfield

After playing for Rheinau as a youngster he was snapped up by Waldhof Mannheim. Signed by Stuttgart in 1987 and has now made more than 200 appearances for the club.

GAULD, Stuart (Derry City, Eir)

• 26.03.64 • Defender

Edinburgh-born stopper who is an absolute menace from dead ball situations. His attacking qualities came to the fore during season 1990/91 when he rattled in eight goals - as many as leading scorer Jon Speak. Began with St Pat's Athletic, but failed to make the grade and moved to The Brandywell in October 1987. His League of Ireland debut came against Monaghan United in December 1987.

GAVA, Franck (Nancy, Fra)

• 03.02.70 • Midfield
• France U21

Widely tipped for future honours. Quick and intelligent, his strong running make him equally useful in defence and attack. Emerged as a fine young talent after finishing his military service in 1990. Joined club as trainee in 1986. Debut, v Paris St Germain, 21st July 1990.

GAVIN, Eamonn (Athlone Town, Eir)

• 21.11.65 • Midfield

Ball-winner in the midfield, who supplies much of the ammunition for the more creative Conor Frawley. Began with Longford Town, for whom he made his League of Ireland debut, against Drogheda, in September 1987. Moved to Athlone, his home town club, in August 1990.

GAY Lopez, Jose Aurelio (Zaragoza, Spa)

• 10.12.65 • Midfield

Had two seperate spells with Real Madrid, but failed to make the grade. Signed for Zaragoza in 1991.

GENAUX, Thierry (Standard Lieg, Bel)

• 31.08.73 • Defender
• Belgium 1 full cap

Promising youngster who has come up through the junior ranks at Standard. He had made just four League appearances before the start of the 1991/92 season but by the end of it he had won his first international cap, in a friendly against Tunisia. Unfortunately he put the ball into his own net 14 minutes from time to present the home side with a 2-1 victory.

GENESIO, Bruno (Lyon, Fra)

• 01.09.66 • Midfield

Discovered by the club playing local junior football and snapped up in June 1988. His raids down the right wing are a good supply of ammunition for sharpshooters Bouderbala and Bouafia.

GENTILE, Marco (Den Haag, Hol)

• 24.08.68 • Defender

Joined his local side, Den Haag, as a 17 year old and got his chance in the first team during the 1987/88 season. Has since made over 100 appearances for the club.

GEOGHEGAN, Declan (Drogheda United, Eir)

• 20.08.64 • Defender

Older brother of Stephen Geoghegan, who is also on Drogheda's books. Hard working left back who likes to get forward and help out in midfield. Played during the promotion season of 1990/91.

GEOGHEGAN, Stephen (Drogheda United, Eir)

• 03.06.70 • Striker

One of the brightest young forwards in the League of Ireland. Made a name for himself during the promotion season of 1990/91, when he scored nine goals in 27 games to help fire the club into the Premier Division.

GERALDAO (Paris St Germain, Fra)

• 24.04.63 • Defender
• Brazil full caps

Could be described as the Phillius Fogg of the French League - his career has so far taken in five clubs in four countries and three continents! Began with Belo Horizonte in his native Brazil, quickly moving on to S.American giants Flamengo. His travels really began when he moved to Qatar-based club Doha, where he spent one season before packing his bags again and heading off to Porto, where he averaged a goal every other game... from central defence! Joined Paris-SG at the beginning of the 1990/91 season to team up with fellow Brazilian Ricardo.

GERARD, Roch (Charleroi, Bel)

• 04.11.72 • Defender

Home grown full back or central defender who signed straight from school. Likes to get forward down the flanks and support his midfield.

GERETS, Eric
(Cercle Liege, Bel)
• 18.05.54 • Defender
• Belgium 86 full caps, 3 goals

Began his career as a centre-forward with
Standard Liege, but soon switched to
right-back. Runner-up with country in
1980 European Championships and club
in 1982 Cup-Winners' Cup. Joined Milan
in 1983, but after being implicated in
match-fixing scandal when at Standard,
was sacked by Milan in 1984 and banned
for year. Returned with MVV Maastricht
in Holland, joining PSV in summer 1986.
Won League title follow year and
captained club to treble in 1988. Played in
1986 World Cup finals. Announced his
retirement from full time playing in the
1992 close season, and was appointed
player/manager at Cercle Liege, bitter
rivals of his former club Standard.

GERMAIN, Bruno
(Paris St Germain, Fra)
• 28.04.60 • Midfield
• France 1 full cap

Had almost 300 League games, and five
clubs, under his belt by the time he arrived
in Paris in June 1991. Failed to make the
breakthrough at first club Orleans and
moved on to Nancy, where he took his
First Division bow in 1982. From Nancy
his travels took him to Racing Paris and
Toulon before landing him at Marseille,
where he won the 1991 Championship.

GERMAIN, Joel
(Caen, Fra)
• 07.12.64 • Striker

Signed from Orleans in the summer of
1990, he made his top level debut in
August of that year, against Sochaux, and
has now completed more than 50 senior
games.

GERMANO Joaquim
Estevao Santos
(Vitoria Guimaraes,
Por)
• 27.11.65 • Defender

Started his career well with Sporting
Lisbon but never really made the top
grade. A steady but unspectacular defender
he spent the 1984/5 season at Sporting
then had three years on the move from
Covilha to Farense and back again. Joined
Vitoria in 1988 and had made more than a
hundred appearances.

GESTHUIZEN,
Francois
(PSV Eindhoven, Hol)
• 18.09.72 • Midfield
• Holland Youth

Home-grown midfielder.

GHISLAIN, Patrick (Germinal Ekeren, Bel)

• 29.08.65 • Defender

Former SCUP, RC Jet and STVV player who joined the club in July 1991.

GIAMPAOLO, Frederico (Bari, Ita)

• 03.03.70 • Midfield

Promising youngster signed from Spezia in Serie C, the Italian Third Division, during the summer of 1991. Took just three games to score his first Serie A goal, away to Foggia in November 1991.

GIANDEBIAGGI, Marco (Cremonese, Ita)

• 01.02.69 • Midfield

Apart from one season at Pro Patria in 1987, Marco spent five years with Parma before joining Cremonese in 1990. Helped the club to promotion during his first season.

GIANNINI, Giuseppe (Roma, Ita)

• 20.08.64 • Midfield
• Italy youth, 47 full caps, 6 goals

Rome born and bred and one of the few locals to have succeeded at Roma. Made his League debut in 1982 and has now made more than 200 Serie A appearances for the club.

GIBSON, George (Bangor, N.Ir)

• 10.10.58 • Defender

The club captain, who signed from Linfield in 1986. Has won pretty much everything Irish football has to offer, including several League and Cup winners' medals, with Linfield. Scored five goals from central defence in 1990/91, despite missing the last seven games of the season with a broken arm. Was a member of Bangor's 1991/92 Lombard Ulster Cup winning side. Also previously with Ards.

GIELCHEN, Andreas (MSV Duisburg, Ger)

• 27.10.64 • Defender

After playing for Alemannia Aachen, Andreas was given his chance to join the First Division with Cologne. Played 131 League games for the club before moving to newly promoted Duisburg prior to the 1991/92 season.

GIJBELS, Robert (RWD Molenbeek, Bel)

• 19.02.62 • Defender

Veteran of nearly 200 First Division games he was signed from Gent.

GIJSBRECHTS, Davy
(Mechelen, Bel)

• 20.09.72 • Defender

Highly regarded youngster who was signed from Beringen. Made his League debut in season 1990/91.

GILLESPIE, Mark
(Bangor, N.Ir)

• 25.03.64 • Goalkeeper
• N.Ireland Youth

A committed Christian who plays the game for fun - and says he will retire as soon as he stops enjoying himself. Now in his second spell with the club, he rejoined during the 1991/92 season, having had a lengthy period with 'B' Division Brantwood. He has quite a reputation as a penalty stopper, which he earned during the 1982/83 season when he saved six spot kicks. His Youth international cap came against Eire during the 1981/82 season.

GILL, Mark
(Shelbourne, Eir)

• 06.06.66 • Striker

Devastating goalscorer who began with Home Farm before crossing the Irish Sea to try his luck with Newcastle United. Spent three years at St James' Park, but failed to make the grade and returned home to sign for Shelbourne in January 1991. League of Ireland debut came for Home Farm, v Cobh Ramblers, in September 1987.

GILLOT, Francis
(Lens, Fra)

• 09.02.60 • Defender

Lens' most experienced player, and club captain. Lead the club to runners-up spot in Division Two B in 1990/91, and promotion to the top flight. Began with Valenciennes, making his debut v Nancy in September 1978. Now in his second spell with the club, having played for them in 1980 before moving to Strasbourg. Returned to Stade Felix-Bollaert in 1982, and has been there ever since.

GILMORE, Jason
(Ballymena United, N.Ir)

• Midfield

Local lad who signed from minor League football midway though the 1991/92 season. An excellent passer of the ball he is expected to play a big part in the side during 1992/93.

GINER Gil, Francisco
(Valencia, Spa)

• 31.12.64 • Defender

Tall central defender who is always likely to score his fair share of goals from set pieces.

GINOLA, David
(Paris St Germain, Fra)
• Midfield
• France U21; B; 1 full cap

Young midfield star who signed for the club after Brest were declared bankrupt in 1991. Outstanding for the 'B' team against England in February 1992, and widely tipped as a future star of the international stage. Originally turned down by Nice he played for Toulon and the (also doomed!) Matra Racing before moving, via Brest, to Paris-SG. His full international debut came v Albania in November 1990.

GIRVAN, Mark
(Drogheda United, Eir)
• 24.09.68 • Midfield

Signed from Kilkenny City. An inspiring central midfielder who was ever present during the glorious 1990/91 season , when the club clinched promotion to the Premier Division by winning the First Division Championship.

GISKE, Anders
(Cologne, Ger)
• 22.11.59 • Midfield
• Norway 38 full caps

Brought to Germany from Brann Bergen by Bayer Leverkusen. Moved on to Nuremburg before joining Cologne in 1989.

GIUSTO, Moreno
(RC Liege, Bel)
• 03.11.61 • Defender

Italian-born central defender who holds dual Italian-Belgian citizenship. Joined the club from local football in 1981, and has remained with them ever since. Played a big part in the 1990 Belgian Cup win. More than 220 senior games to his credit.

GLENDINNING, Mark
(Bangor, N.Ir)
• 02.04.70 • Defender

Won the Irish League's "Young Player of the Season" poll in 1987/88 and is widely regarded as one of the country's top attacking full backs. Was called up to the N.Ireland U23 squad in 1990/91, but missed a large chunk of 1991/92 following a knee operation.

GLESIUS, Arno
(Karlsruher, Ger)
• 22.09.65 • Striker

Joined Karlsruher from FV Bad Honnef in 1986. Previously with Eisbachtal, Mayen and Koblenz.

GLYNN, Johnny
(Cork City, Eir)
• 10.10.66 • Striker

Signed from Galway United, whom he capatained to FAI Cup Final victory in 1990/91. Was called into full Eire squad while holidaying in Boston, USA, in 1991 - and was sub for the game v the US. Also played with Sligo Rovers and Shamrock Rovers.

G'NAKO, Jerome
(Monaco, Fra)
• 17.02.68 • Striker

Former Bordeaux and Angers player who joined the club in July 1991. His First Division debut came for Bordeaux, against Laval, in November 1986.

van GOBBEL, Ulrich
(Feyenoord, Hol)
• 16.01.71 • Defender

Right-back nicknamed "Speedy Gonzalez" by Feyenoord fans because of his pace. Signed from Willem II Tilburg in exchange for Martin van Geel plus cash in 1989.

de GOEY, Ed
(Feyenoord, Hol)
• 20.12.66 • Goalkeeper

Began career with amateur side Olympia of Gouda before joining Sparta Rotterdam as a junior, making League debut during 1985/86 season. Signed by Feyenoord, summer 1990, as replacement for Dutch full 'keeper Joop Hiele. Has been selected for full Holland squad.

GOICOECHEA, Jon Andoni
(Barcelona, Spa)
• 21.10.65 • Midfield
• Spain 7 full caps

Winger who came to prominence with Osasuna and was a member of Spain's triumphant European U21 Championship side in 1986. Signed by Barcelona in 1988, but was loaned to John Toshack's Real Sociedad for two seasons. His international debut came against Brazil in September 1990 (won 3-0). He was voted Spain's "Footballer of the Year" in 1991, as he helped Barcelona to their 11th League title.

GOKHAN, Keskin
(Besiktas, Tur)
• 24.11.68 • Defender
• Turkey 21 full caps

Discovered by former Leicester City boss Gordon Milne at Besiktas. He has become a vital part of the all- conquering Besiktas side that romped to the title in both 1990/91 and 1991/92. One of the best headers of the ball in the Turkish game, he became a firm favourite of national boss Sepp Piontek.

GOLDBAEK, Bjarne
(Kaiserslautern, Ger)
• 06.10.68 • Midfield
• Denmark 3 full caps

Originally bought to Germany from Naestved IF by Schalke. Moved to Kaiserslautern in 1989.

GOLKE, Andre
(VfB Stuttgart, Ger)

• 15.08.64 • Striker

Andre joined Nuremberg from St Pauli in 1991 and prior to that he played for Hamburg's 'other' club, SV. Joined the German Bundesliga Champions in the summer of 1992.

GOLZ, Richard
(SV Hamburg, Ger)

• 05.06.68 • Goalkeeper

Joined Hamburg from SC Tegel as a teenager and has now made over 100 first team appearances for the club.

GONZALEZ Vasquez, Jose Luis
(Real Sociedad, Spa)

• 27.08.64 • Goalkeeper

Tall 'keeper who replaced the legendary Luis Arconada in the Sociedad goal in 1989.

GOOSSEN, Steven
(Lierse, Bel)

• 12.11.68 • Defender

Dutch-born player who joined the club at the end of the 1989/90 season from Ajax.

GOOTS, Patrick
(Genk, Bel)

• 10.04.66 • Striker

Fifteen goals in 28 games for Kortrijk in 1990/91 was enough to tempt Genk to plump for Patrick's signature in July 1991. Previously with Dessel, Lommel and Beerschot.

GORDILLO, Rafael
(Real Madrid, Spa)

• 24.02.57 •Midfield
• Spain Olympic, U21, U23, 75 full caps, 3 goal

Vastly experienced midfielder who joined Real from Real Betis in July 1985.

GORLUKOWITSCH, Sergei
(Borussia Dortmund, Ger)

• 18.11.61 • Defender
• USSR 21 full caps, 1 goal; Olympic

Played for Dinamo Minsk and Lokomotive Moscow in the Soviet League before moving to Germany and signing for Dortmund in 1989. A surprise inclusion in the Soviet Union's squad for the 1988 Seoul Olympics. His form was so good at the Games that he forced himself into the full international reckoning.

GORMAN, Dessie
(Derry City, Eir)

• 13.12.64 • Striker

Born in Dundalk, he began with his home town club, taking his bow in the League of Ireland against Shelbourne in March 1985. Originally came to Derry on loan from French Second Division side Bourges, making the move permanent at the end of season 1990/91, when he scored seven goals in 21 starts for the club.

GORRIZ Echarte, Alberto
(Real Sociedad, Spa)

• 16.02.58 • Defender
• Spain full caps

Experienced central defender who, along with partner Gajate, is a mainstay of the Sociedad side.

GORTER, Wilhelmus
(Caen, Fra)

• 06.07.63 • Defender
• Holland full caps

Another member of Caen's multi-cultural midfield. This Dutch born ball-winner was signed from Lugano at the beginning of the 1991/92 season. His hard running is the perfect foil to Jesper Olsen's creative, but lightweight, midfield play.

GOSECA, Dragan
(Uniao, Por)

• 12.10.65 • Defender

Brought from the Yugoslavian league to strengthen Uniao's shaky defence during their second season in the top flight in 1990/91.

GOTZ, Falko
(Cologne, Ger)

• 26.03.62 • Striker

Signed from Bayer Leverkusen in 1988. Previously with Dynamo Berlin.

GOUDET, Thierry
(Le Havre, Fra)

• 11.11.61 • Midfield
• France U21

Experienced midfield playmaker who was formerly with Laval, Brest and Rennes. Debut came for Laval, v Sochaux, back in July 1987.

GOUGH, Derek
(Bray Wanderers, Eir)

• 14.01.67 • Striker

Began his senior career with Bray, making his League of Ireland debut against Cork City on 19th October 1986 (won 1-0). Spent a brief period on loan at Athlone Town at the beginning of the 1990/91 season, before returning to score eight goals in 16 starts as Bray clinched runners-up spot in the First Division, and promotion to the Premier League.

GRACE, Jim
(Athlone Town, Eir)

• 17.07.54 • Goalkeeper

Veteran 'keeper who has been playing at the top level for more than 20 years. Began with Home Farm/Drumcondra, making his debut v Athlone in December 1972. Signed from St Pat's Athletic.

GRAHAMMER, Roland
(Bayern Munich, Ger)

• 03.11.63 • Defender

• Germany U21, Olympic, B

Signed from 1.FC Nuremburg along with Stefan Reuter for then German domestic record fee of £1.4m in 1988.

GRANT, Damian
(Ballymena United, N.Ir)

• Goalkeeper

Signed from Port Vale in 1987.

GRAVELAINE, Xavier
(Caen, Fra)

• 05.10.68 • Midfield

Highly-rated midfielder who spent a couple of periods on loan - at St Seurin and Laval - in 1990/91 to gain some valuable experience. Signed a four-year contract in 1991.

GREGUCCI, Angelo
(Lazio, Ita)

• 10.06.64 • Defender

Big central defender who started his career with Taranto. Joined Alessandria in 1982 and moved to Lazio four years later.

GREINER, Frank
(Cologne, Ger)

• 03.07.66 • Midfield

Signed from Nuremburg in 1988. Previously with VfB Coburg.

GREN, Mats
(Grasshoppers, Swi)

• 20.12.63 • Defender

• Sweden 16 full caps

Versatile player who joined Grasshoppers from Hammarby of Sweden in 1985.

GRETARSSON, Sigurdur
(Grasshoppers, Swi)

• 02.05.62 • Striker

• Iceland 37 full caps, 7 goals

After winning the Swiss League with Lucerne in 1989, Sigurdur moved to Grasshoppers in 1990, and won a second Championship medal with his with new club in 1991.

GRIGA, Stanislav (Feyenoord, Hol)

• 04.11.61 • Striker
• Czech 33 full caps

Began career in Czechoslovakia with Zilina, but later joined army side Dukla Prague. Signed from Sparta Prague for £450,000 during 1989/90 season. Made two appearances as a sub for Czechoslovakia in 1990 World Cup finals

GROENENDIJK, Fons (Ajax, Hol)

• 17.04.64 • Midfield

Began his career with Den Haag before moving to Roda JC in 1987. Signed by Ajax prior to the start of the 1991/92 season.

van GRONSVELD, Dirk (Gent, Bel)

• 16.08.67 • Midfield

Ball-winner who is equally happy at the centre of defence or midfield. Signed from Genk at the beginning of the 1991/92 season.

de GROOTE, Michel (Gent, Bel)

• 18.10.55 • Defender
• Belgium 4 full caps

Signed from Anderlecht, this uncompromising and hugely experienced central defender has established himself as captain at the Ottenstadion. Began with Anderlecht back in 1971, and had a brief spell at Cercle Liege before returning to his first club. His international debut came against East Germany in March 1983

GROS, Thierry (St Etienne, Fra)

• 10.09.66 • Defender
• France U21

Experienced centre back who has come up through the ranks at the club. Was an important member of the side which won promotion from Division Two in 1986 to end the lean years at Stade Geoffroy-Guichard. Has now made more than 150 senior appearances.

GRUNDEL, Heinz (Eintracht Frankfurt, Ger)

• 13.02.57 • Midfield
• West Germany 4 full caps

Vastly experienced midfielder who began his career with Hertha Berlin. Signed by Frankfurt from Bayer Leverkusen 1988.

GRUN, Georges (Parma, Ita)

• 25.01.62 • Defender

Made his League debut for Anderlect during the 1982/83 season and spent a further seven seasons with the Belgian side before being tempted to Parma in 1990. Due to return to his homeland for the 1992/93 season for family reasons.

GRUNHOLZ, Edwin (Den Haag, Hol)

• 15.08.69 • Striker

Joined Den Haag as a 17 year old and made his first team debut two years later. Has struggled to hold down a regular place.

GUARDIOLA, Jose (Barcelona, Spa)

• 18.01.71 • Midfield

Born in the suburbs of Barcelona, Jose was bought into the first team squad in 1990 and made himself a regular in 1992.

GUEDES Jose Joao Moura (Pacos De Ferreira, Por)

• 19.02.62 • Striker

Snatched from Maritimo after a superb 1990/91 season when he bagged eight goals in 32 games. Seen as the man to spearhead the Pacos De Ferreira strike force.

la GUEN, Paul (Paris St Germain, Fra)

• 01.03.64 • Midfield
• France U21; Olympic

Giant central midfielder (6ft 2in) who is very much the ball-winner and centre-point of the Paris-SG side. Previously with Brest and Nantes, he is one of several players to have joined the club at the beginning of 1991/92.

GUENTCHEV, Bentcho (Sporting Lisbon, Por)

• 07.07.64 • Striker
• Bulgaria full caps

Followed in the footsteps of former team mate Krassimire Balakov when he moved from Etar in Bulgaria to join Sporting in 1991.

GUERIT, Eric (Cannes, Fra)

• 21.07.64 • Midfield

Naturally right-sided midfielder, who was previously with Angouleme, Nice and Monaco. Signed for Cannes in 1990. Has played more than 150 senior matches.

GUILLOUD, Steve
(Grasshoppers, Swi)
• 27.12.68 • Striker

Joined Grasshoppers from junior club Beauregard in 1991.

GUILLOU, Patrick
(Bochum, Ger)
• 16.04.70 • Defender

Made his First Division debut for Bochum during the 1998-91 season after joining the club from Freiburger that summer.

GULLIT, Ruud
(Milan, Ita)
• 01.09.62 • Midfield
• Holland 60 full caps, 15 goals

Played for Meerboys and DWS as youth before making League breakthrough in Holland with Haarlem. Moved onto Feyenoord and then PSV Eindhoven. Signed by Milan for world record £6m in 1987. Scored twice in 1989 European Cup Final victory. Made Holland debut v Switzerland September 1981. Captained country to European Championship triumph in 1988, but failed to make the same impression four years later in Sweden. A string of knee injuries have plagued him since 1989.

GUTSCHOW, Torsten
(Dynamo Dresden, Ger)
• 28.07.62 • Striker
• East Germany 3 full caps

One of many players who have now admitted spying on former team mates for the East German secret police. As top scorer in the 1991 East German League it was his goals that took Dresden to the last Oberliga Championship title. This was his third successive season as the Oberliga's top scorer, but he has been unable to reproduce his domestic form at international level.

GUTTLER, Gunter
(Schalke, Ger)
• 31.05.61 • Defender

Ex-Bayern Munich, Mechelen and Nuremberg. Joined Schalke from Waldhof Mannheim in 1990.

GYAU, Philip
(Genk, Bel)
• 07.02.65 • Striker
• USA 6 full caps

Born in Maryland, USA, he is the son of Former Ghana international Joseph Gyau, known as 'Nana'. Made his national team debut in the 1989 Marlboro Cup of New York, scoring in a 2-1 defeat of Benfica. His full international bow came the following day, when he played in the 3-0 win over Peru. Left-winger with tremendous pace. Has a degree in athletic training from Howard University, Washington DC.

GYIMESI, Laszlo (Genk, Bel)

• 08.09.57 • Defender
• Hungary 12 full caps

Former Rabo Eto Gyor and Honved star who joined the club during the battle for promotion from Division Two. Helped them up in 1989/90 and has become a firm favourite at the Thyl Geyselinck Stadion. Likes to get forward.

HABER, Marco (Kaiserslautern, Ger)

• 21.09.71 • Midfield

Midfielder who scores his fair share of goals. Joined Kaiserslautern in 1985. Previously with VfR Frankenthal.

HABRANT, Bernard (SC Liege, Bel)

• 23.09.60 • Defender
• Belgium U21

Signed from minor local club Gold Star Liege and has gone on to make more than 300 First Division appearances with his only senior professional club.

HADJITHANASIOU, Lakovos (Panathinaikos, Gre)

• Defender
• Greece 17 full caps

Centre back who joined the club in 1987.

HADZIBEGIC, Faruk (Sochaux, Fra)

• 07.10.57 • Defender
• Yugoslavia 60 full caps, 6 goals

Began with home-town club Sarajevo, before moving to Spanish League side Betis, of Seville. Sochaux signed him, along with fellow countryman Mehmed

Bazdarevic, in 1987. Veteran of more than 140 French Division One games, he made his debut v Strasbourg in July 1987.

HAGI, Gheorghe (Brescia, Ita)

• 05.02.65 • Midfield
• Romania youth, 65 full caps

Highly talented playmaker who began his career with Sportul Studentesc in Bucharest after being selected for the national youth team aged 15. Made full debut at 18 v Norway in 1983. Member of 1984 European Championship squad. He was the Romanian League's top scorer in 1985 and 1986. Moved to Steaua Bucharest in 1988. Signed by Real for £2m in June 1990 after playing in World Cup finals. Brescia snapped him up in July 1992.

HAJRY Radouane (Farense, Por)

• 05.03.64 • Striker

Born in Casablanca in Morocco he is now a naturalised Portuguese. Started with Benfica in 1987/88 then had a year each at Farense and Uniao before rejoining Farense. Yet to find a regular place.

HAJSZAN, Gyula (MSV Duisburg, Ger)

• 09.10.61 • Midfield

Left ETO Raba Gyor in his native Hungary to join Duisburg in 1989.

HALLAERT, Peter (Lokeren, Bel)

• 25.01.66 • Defender

Sturdy defender who signed from Gent during the 1991/92 close season. Strong in the air at free-kicks and corners. Previously with White Star and SC Sint-Amandsberg.

HALL, Allan (Distillery, N.Ir)

• Midfield
• N.Ireland Schools; Youth

Set-piece specialist who was previously on the books of Wigan Athletic. Loves to get forward and has become a regular goalscorer in the last couple of seasons after a shaky start at Ballyskeagh Road.

HALLEUX, Frederic (Mechelen, Bel)

• 07.12.69 • Goalkeeper

Understudy to Belgian number one Michel Preud'homme at Mechelen. From Seresien.

HALTER, Andre (Grasshoppers, Swi)

• 21.04.66 • Striker
• Switzerland full caps

Signed from Lucerne in 1988.

HALVORSEN, Jan-Halvor
(AGF Aarhus, Den)

• 08.03.63 • Defender
• Norway 6 full caps

After playing for Brann Bergen and Start Kristiansand, the big Norweigan left Scandanavia in 1989 and signed for Hertha Berlin. Had two and a half years in Germany before being signed by Aarhus of Denmark in February 1992.

HAMILTON, Billy
(Distillery, N.Ir)

• Striker
• N.Ireland 50 full caps; 4 goals

Player/manager and top scorer at Distillery. Very experienced striker with Linfield, Ipswich, Everton, Millwall and Swindon. He retired from the international scene in 1980.

HAMILTON, Ian
(Ballymena United, N.Ir)

• Defender

Joined the club as a midfielder, but has been successfully converted into one of the Irish League's most accomplished full backs.

van HAM, Maurice
(Beveren, Bel)

• 25.04.66 • Midfield

Dutch-born striker who signed from AZ67 in 1989 - and almost immediately regretted the decision as Beveren crashed out of the Belgian First Division that same season. Quality ball-player who creates a stream of chances for his front-runners Bataille, van Vossen and Soudan.

HAMI, Mandirali
(Trabzonspor, Tur)

• 06.06.68 • Striker
• Turkey 8 full caps, 1 goal

Tends to be kept on the bench and used as a 'supersub'. More than half of his international appearances have been as substitute, and he is often thrown in to chase lost causes in the last quarter of the game.

HANKE, Stefan
(Bayer Leverkusen, Ger)

• 19.10.72 • Midfield

Young midfielder who joined Leverkusen from junior club Schwetzingen prior to the 1991/92 season and proved he could adapt to the difference in class.

HANNA, Wesley
(Larne, N.Ir)

• Defender

Signed from Tobermore United in the ealry part of the 1991/92 season, he was quickly appointed club captain by manager Gary Erwin. Very dangerous at set-pieces. Also previously with Cliftonville.

HANRAHAN, Joe
(Derry City, Eir)

• 21.03.64 • Striker

Elder brother of Dundalk's Peter Hanrahan, who was top scorer in the League of Ireland in 1990/91. Began with UCD, for whom he made his League debut as a 17-year-old, against Dundalk, in September 1981. Moved to his home town club Limerick before signing for Derry at the beginning of the 1990/91 campaign.

HANRAHAN, Peter
(Dundalk, Eir)

• 23.2.68 • Striker

Voted League of Ireland's "Player of the Year" in 1990/91, after finishing season as top scorer with 18 League goals. Hugely popular with the fans. Struck up fruitful partnership with winger Mick Kavanagh. Wanted by several English clubs.

friis HANSEN, Jacob
(Lille, Fra)

• 06.03.67 • Defender
• Denmark 2 full caps

One of Lille's two towering centre backs (6ft 4in), who has been successfully moved back from midfield. Formerly with top Danish club BK 1903 Copenhagen, where he was part of the club's 1986 domestic Cup winning side. Signed a seven- year contract when he joined in July 1989. Made his international debut against Sweden in September 1990.

HAON, Pierre
(St Etienne, Fra)

• 10.10.66 • Defender

Discovered playing local football by the club, and given his senior debut in July 1987, v Laval. Spent the 1990/91 season on loan at Metz, where he scored twice in 24 starts, but returned to St Etienne in May 1991. Attacking centre back who is dangerous at set-pieces.

HAPPE, Marcus
(Bayer Leverkusen, Ger)

• 11.02.72 • Midfield

Until the 1991/92 season Marcus had played all his football in the German Third Division with Preussen Munster. Signed by Leverkusen for £70,000 in

1991 and made a big impact in his first season in the top flight.

HARFORTH, Michael (Karlsruher, Ger)
• 09.02.59 • Midfield

Formerly a junior with the club, Michael returned to Karlsruher from SV Wiesbaden in 1983. Has now made over 150 First Division appearances.

HARTMANN, Jurgen (SV Hamburg, Ger)
• 27.10.62 • Midfield

Signed from VfB Stuttgart in 1991. Previously played for Offenburger FV, FV Lahr and Seebach.

HARRINGTON, Phil (Cork City, Eir)
• 23.11.64 • Goalkeeper
• Wales Youth, U21

Extensive experience in England with Preston, Burnley, Oxford United, Blackpool and Chester City. Signed in July 1988.

HARRISON, Fergal (Sligo Rovers, Eir)
• 14.07.67 • Defender

Local boy who joined the club in 1990, making his League of Ireland debut in the 1990/91 season.

HARTMANN, Frank (Wattenscheid, Ger)
• 27.09.60 • Midfield

Ex-1.FC Cologne and FC Schalke 04. Signed from 1.FC Kaiserslautern in 1989.

HASSAN, Hossam (Neuchatel Xamax, Swi)
• 10.08.66 • Striker
• Egypt full caps

Made international debut v Norway in September 1985. Brother of Ibrahim Hassam, Egypt's 1990 World Cup full back. Member of Egypt squad at 1992 African Nations Cup.

HASSLER, Thomas (Roma, Ita)
• 30.05.66 • Midfield
• Germany 33 full caps, 5 goals

Born in Berlin but signed up as a teenager by Cologne. Made more than 150 appearances for the German club before being lured to Italy by Juventus for £5.5m in 1990. Struggled in his first season and was sold to Roma during the summer of 1991. Made his international debut v Finland in 1988 and played in the 1990 World Cup finals and the 1992 European Championships. Devastating at dead-ball situations, his free-kicks were a highlight of Sweden 1992.

HAUPTMANN, Ralf
(Dynamo Dresden, Ger)

• 20.09.68 • Midfield
• East Germany 4 full caps

Like so many of the Dresden squad, Ralf joined the club at a very tender age and developed through the youth ranks to finally break into the first team and then the international team.

HAYES, Terry
(Distillery, N.Ir)

• Midfield

Former Linfield player who made a comeback to the game with Distillery in 90/91. Injury restricted his appearances to a mere handful during last season.

HAYLOCK, Garry
(Shelbourne, Eir)

• 31.12.70 • Striker

Bradford-born player who began with Huddersfield Town before moving to Shelbourne on loan in 1990. Made his League of Ireland debut v Cork City in January that year. Scored nine goals in 11 games.

HAYRETTIN, Demirbas
(Galatasaray, Tur)

• 26.06.63 • Goalkeeper
• Turkey 4 full caps; Olympic

Made his international debut against England in April 1991. He had an outstanding game as England won 1- 0, and he's missed just one game since. Replaced veteran Yugoslav 'keeper Zoran Simovic as first choice at Galatasaray.

HEALY, Felix
(Derry City, Eir)

• 27.09.55 • Midfield

Signed from Coleraine in June 1987 and helped the club to their historic League and Cup double in 1988/89.

HEATH, Seamus
(Glentoran, N.Ir)

• Defender

Originally signed as a midfield player, he was converted to full back by manager Tommy Jackson, and has enjoyed some success in that position. After ten years plying his trade in Finland he returned to his home land with Glentoran in 1990. A major reason behind the club's runaway League success in 1991/92.

von HEESEN, Thomas
(SV Hamburg, Ger)

• 01.10.61 • Midfield

Joined club more than 10 years ago. More than 275 League appearances for Hamburg.

HEFULLZE, Jan
(PSV Eindhoven, Hol)
- 17.08.63 • Defender
- Denmark 24 full caps, 1 goal

Began career with Kastrup in Denmark and signed by PSV in November 1982. Now made more than 250 appearances for Eindhoven.

HEIDENREICH, Hans-Jurgen
(Nuremburg, Ger)
- 17.08.67 • Defender

Returned to Nuremburg from Hessen Kassel in 1990.

HEINEMANN, Frank
(Bochum, Ger)
- 08.01.65 • Midfield

Vastly experienced midfielder who has been with Bochum for 15 years now. First joined the club as schoolboy.

HEINEN, Dirk
(Bayer Leverkusen, Ger)
- 03.12.70 • Goalkeeper

Has constantly been in the shadow of Bayer's first choice 'keeper, Rudi Vollborn. First joined the club as a schoolboy more than a decade ago.

HEITOR Camarin Junior
(Maritimo, Por)
- 14.02.64 • Defender

Brasilian-born, he came to the Portugeuse League in 1986 when he joined Vitoria Guimaraes. An attacking full back, he has scored more than a dozen goals in the League, all for his second club, Nacional, who he joined in 1988. has been with Maritimo since the start of the 1991/92 season.

HELLERS, Guy
(Standard Liege, Bel)
- 10.10.64 • Midfield
- Luxembourg 32 full caps, 1 goal; U21

Defensive midfielder who has occasionally been drafted in as sweeper. He is the faithful assistant to the magical Frans van Rooy. Has played more than 200 senior games since joining from Metz. Also previously with CS Hollerich in his home country.

HELDER Joaquim Maximo Catalao
(Beira-Mar, Por)
- 01.01.55 • Goalkeeper

Very experienced keeper who made his First Division debut with Viseu back in 1980. Moved on to Sporting Braga two years later before joining Beira-Mar at the start of the 1990/91 season.

HELMER, Thomas (Bayern Munich, Ger)
• 21.04.65 • Defender
• Germany 7 full caps

Plays as sweeper for Dortmund and has made over 170 appearances for the club since his arrival from Arminia Bielefeld in 1986. His international debut came against Sweden in October 1990. He signed for the giant Munich club for £2.8 million shortly after the 1992 European Championships in Sweden.

HELMIG, Dirk (Bochum, Ger)
• 03.05.65 • Midfield

Signed by Bochum from Rot-Weiss Essen in 1990, but initially struggled to make his mark in the First Division.

HENDERSON, Dave (St Patrick's Athletic, Eir)
• 11.06.60 • Goalkeeper

First choice stopper at Harold's Cross, he has kept the hugely experienced Chippy Devlin on the bench for the past couple of seasons.

HENDERSON, Stephen (Distillery, N.Ir)
• Goalkeeper

Signed from Limerick at the beginning of 1990/91. Agile 'keeper with tremendous reflexes. Regarded as one of the finest shot-stoppers in the Irish League. Born in Dublin.

HENNEMAN, Wim (Cercle Brugge, Bel)
• 01.09.72 • Goalkeeper

One of two young 'keepers currently at the club who have progressed from the youth set-up at Olympiastadion. Understudy to Yves Feys.

HENRY, Fabrice (Sochaux, Fra)
• 13.02.68 • Midfield
• France U21

Signed from Paris UC back in 1982, he did not make his First Division debut until some five years later, v Toulouse. Likes to get forward and help out in attack.

HENRY, Joel (Nantes, Fra)
• 19.04.62 • Midfield
• France U21

Widely travelled, goalscoring midfield

player. With more than 50 goals in over 230 games at six top clubs he has seen it all. Formerly with Lille, Bastille, Brest, Nice and Toulon. Signed for Nantes in June 1988.

HERMANN, Christian (Bochum, Ger)
• 16.01.66 • Defender

After playing junior football in Berlin, Christian joined Schalke, before moving on to Homburg. Arrived at Bochum in 1990.

HERMANN, Gunter (Werder Bremen, Ger)
• 05.12.60 • Midfield
• Germany 2 full caps

Experienced midfielder who joined Bremen in 1980. Previously with TSV Rehburg/Loccum. Has now played well over 200 First Division games for Werder.

HERMANS, Alain (Genk, Bel)
• 04.09.65 • Midfield

Began with minor League club Hasselt SC, before Genk gave him the chance of success. Signed in 1989/90 and helped the club to promotion from the Second Division.

HERNANDEZ, Jean-Francois (Toulouse, Fra)
• 23.04.69 • Defender

Giant (6ft 4in) home-grown centre back who's been with the club since 1984. Made his debut v Brest in October 1989 and is now approaching 100 senior appearances.

HERRERA, Jose (Cagliari, Ita)
• 17.06.65 • Midfield

Uruguayan-born midfielder who began his professional football career with Penarol in his homeland until being bought to Europe in 1989 by Figueras of Spain. Moved on to Italy and Cagliari a year later.

HERRLICH, Heiko (Bayer Leverkusen, Ger)
• 03.12.71 • Striker

Joined Leverkusen from Freiburg in 1989 and came to the club with the reputation of being something of a playboy. Heiko was taken to bible classes by club skipper Jorginho and has apparently seen the error of his ways.

HERZOG, Hendrix
(Schalke, Ger)

• 02.04.69 • Defender
• East Germany 7 caps

Formerly with Dynamo Eisleben, Hendrix joined Schalke from Berlin in 1991.

HEUS, Ruud
(Feyenoord, Hol)

• 24.02.61 • Defender

Left-back who began his career at AZ67 Alkmaar. Joined Feyenoord in 1986. Career has suffered through recurrent injury problems.

HEYNE, Dirk
(Borussia Moenchengladbach, Ger)

• 10.10.57 • Goalkeeper
• East Germany 9 full caps

Experienced 'keeper who left East German side Magdeburg to join Gladbach in the West at the start of the 1991/92 season.

HIARD, Pierrick
(Rennes, Fra)

• 27.04.55 • Goalkeeper
• France 1 full cap

Long-serving stopper who is in the twilight of his career. Joined Bastia straight from school, but moved to home-town club Rennes in 1973, and stayed there. Division One debut came v Strasbourg in November that year and he's now made more than 300 top flight appearances.

HIERRO, Fernando Luiz
(Real Madrid, Spa)

• 23.03.68 • Midfield
• Spain U21, 9 full caps, 1 goal

Began his career as a defender with older brother Manolo at Velez Malaga and both were later signed by Real Valladolid. Fernando was signed by Real Madrid for £1m in July 1989 and converted into a goalscoring midfielder. Made his international debut against Poland in September 1989 and was a member of Spain's 1990 World Cup squad.

HIGL, Alfons
(Cologne, Ger)

• 17.12.64 • Midfield

Formerly with TSV Rehling, Alfons joined Cologne from Freiburg in 1989. He has now made more than seventy first team appearances for the club.

HIGUERA Fernandez, Francisco
(Zaragoza, Spa)
• 03.01.65 • Striker
• Spain Olympic

Signed by Zaragoza from Mallorca in 1988.

HILL, Ian
(Shelbourne, Eir)
• 09.05.65 • Defender

'Mr Reliable' who signed from Leicester City in 1988, having failed to break into the first team at Filbert Street. Very solid central defender

HILL, Raymond
(Bangor, N.Ir)
• 05.12.61 • Midfield

A schoolteacher by profession, he began with Glasgow Rangers, but failed to make the grade at Ibrox and returned to Ireland. Had spells with Ards and Portadown before joining Bangor in 1988. Solid and reliable he rarely misses a game and was a vital member of the Bangor side that won the 1991/92 Lombard Ulster Cup. Can also fill-in at full back in an emergency.

HILLIS, Gary
(Glentoran, N.Ir)
• Striker

Injuries and a run of indifferent form hampered him after returning to The Oval from Crusaders for a five figure fee prior to the 1990/91 season. He rediscovered his scoring touch in 1991/92 and his explosive shooting from outside the area was rewarded with some spectacular strikes.

HILLRINGHAUS, Gerald
(Bayern Munich, Ger)
• 22.06.62 • Goalkeeper

Amatuer previously with Türk Gücü Munich, SpVgg Bayreuth and TSV 1860 Munich. Made first team debut during 1991/92 season due to Bayern goalkeeping injury crisis.

HINSCHBERGER, Phillipe
(Metz, Fra)
• 19.11.59 • Midfield

One club man who has made more than 400 senior appearances since his debut back in April 1978. His experience and composure in central midfield make him the perfect foil for exciting young team-mate Nicolas Huysman.

HITCHCOCK, Fran
(Sligo Rovers, Eir)
• 02.12.60 • Striker

Modest striker who is an excellent target man, and holds the ball up superbly.

Previously with Shelbourne, for whom he made his League of Ireland debut in September 1980, against Thurles Town.

HOCHSTATTER, Christian (Borussia Moenchengladbach, Ger)

• 19.10.63 • Midfield
• Germany 2 full caps

Signed by Borussia from FC Augsburg in 1982. Has now made more than 200 appearances for Gladbach.

HODGSON, David (Metz, Fra)

• 01.11.60 • Striker
• England U21

Much-travelled hit-man who made 212 League appearances in England, scoring 28 goals with Middlesbrough, Liverpool, Sunderland, Norwich City and Sheffield Wednesday. Had a period at Spanish club Xerez and Mazda of Japan before moving to Metz in 1990.

HOFFMAN, Guido (Kaiserslautern, Ger)

• 20.12.65 • Midfield

Formerly with Borussia Monchengladbach, Guido joined Kaiserslautern from Homburg in 1990.

HOFKENS, Wim (Kortrijk, Bel)

• 27.03.58 • Defender
• Holland 5 full caps

Experienced pro who missed much of 1990/91 through injury and then decided to leave Mechelen and make a fresh start with Kortrijk. Has more than 400 senior games under his belt and has played with Madese Boys, Willem II, SK Beveren, Anderlecht, Beerschot and Mechelen.

HOFMANS, Gunter (Ekeren, Bel)

• 03.01.67 • Midfield
• Belgium 1 full cap

Newcomer to the international scene having been called up by Belgian coach Paul van Himst for the first time last season. Made his debut at home to Cyprus in April 1992. Joined Ekeren from FC Ranst.

HOMP, Tobias (Dynamo Dresden, Ger)

• 31.10.63 • Defender

Joined Dresden at the start of the 1991/92 season to help tighten up the defence. One of only a handful of the club's squad who had any previous Bundesliga experience. Played in the First Division for Hamburg and Homburg before his move East.

HORACIO Fernandes Rodrigues
(Uniao, Por)

• 06.03.62 • Midfield

At thirty years old he is the veteran of his side not just in age but also in experience. Played for Olimpia Elvas for two seasons and swapped to Uniao in 1990/91.

HORGAN, Robbie
(Drogheda United, Eir)

• 07.06.68 • Goalkeeper

Former Shamrock Rovers 'keeper who was ever-present in the Drogheda side that won the First Division title, and promotion to the Premier League, in 1990/91.

HOTIC, Demir
(Kaiserslautern, Ger)

• 09.07.62 • Striker

Joined Kaiserslautern from VfB Stuttgart in 1989. Previously with Fortuna Dusseldorf, Union Solingen and Stuttgarter Kickers.

HOUTMAN, Peter
(Den Haag, Hol)

• 04.06.57 • Striker
• Holland Olympic, full caps

Vastly experienced player with impressive scoring record everywhere he has played. Born in Rotterdam, he played for local side Feyenoord, Groningen and Brugge in Belgium. Also had a spell in Portugal in 1987. In 1989 he moved to Sparta Rotterdam and then signed for Den Haag in December 1991.

HUC, Robin
(Toulouse, Fra)

• 20.03.65 • Goalkeeper
• France U21

Signed for Motpellier from local football, but failed to make the grade and moved on to Toulouse in 1985. He first donned his gloves for a Division One game at Laval on August 15th the following year. Has now made more than 150 senior appearances for the club.

HUGHES, Michael
(Strasbourg, Fra)

• 02.08.71 • Striker
• N.Ireland U23, 4 full caps, 1 goal

Was one of the sensations of the English First Division in 1991/92, when playing with Manchester City. Tremendous pace and skill on the ball, coupled with a rocket shot made him a hot property. City signed him from Irish League club Carrick Rangers in 1989. Moved to Strasbourg on trial in July 1992, after rejecting offers of a new contract at Maine Road.

HUGO Jose Duarte (Sporting Braga, Por)

• 20.06.64 • Goalkeeper

Brazilian born keeper who began his career in Portugal with Olimpica Elvas and made his First Division debut for the club during the 1987/88 season. Joined Amadora the following season and moved to Sporting Braga in 1991.

HUGUES, Angelo (Monaco, Fra)

• 03.09.66 • Goalkeeper

Signed from Dunkerque in 1986 as cover for the evergreen Jean-Luc Ettori. Has played only a handful of games in six years.

HUNTER, Barry (Crusaders, N.Ir)

• Defender

Signed in 1988 from Coleraine. Previously on the books at Newcastle United, but he failed to make the grade at St James' Park and moved back to Ireland. His consistency at the heart of the defence attracted the attention of several English League clubs in 1991/92.

HUNTER, Glenn (Linfield, N.Ir)

• Striker

Young striker who is particularly dangerous in the six-yard box. Signed from Crusaders in April 1991.

HUNTER, Kirk (Crusaders, N.Ir)

• Striker
• Irish League Representative

Missed a large chunk of 1991/92 with an ankle injury. Prefers to play as a wide midfielder, but can also fill in as an out-and-out striker.

HUSCHBECK, Thomas (Borussia Moenchengladbach, Ger)

• 17.12.67 • Defender

Joined Gladbach from TuS Hohenhaus in 1987.

HUSTON, Tommy (Larne, N.Ir)

• Defender
• N. Ireland Schools, Youth, Irish League Representative

Has been first choice left back at the club since signing from Ballymena in 1984. Was granted a testimonial season in 1991/92. He has made more than 350 senior appearances for the club.

HUYSMANS, Dirk
(Lierse, Bel)

• 03.09.73 • Striker

Highly regarded young striker who came up through the youth ranks at the club, making his debut during the 1990/91 season.

HUYSMANS, Marc
(Waregem, Bel)

• 05.04.61 • Goalkeeper

First choice 'keeper who was signed from Ekeren during the 1990/91 season. Also previously with Mechelen and Stade Leuven.

HUYSMAN, Nicolas
(Metz, Fra)

• 09.02.68 • Midfield

Began as a striker with Dunkerque, before being snapped up by Metz on 21st June 1990. He had a baptism of fire weeks later with his debut v Marseille, and has now become one of the country's leading young midfield stars.

HYRAVY, Viliam
(Toulouse, Fra)

• 26.11.62 • Striker

Czech-born midfielder turned forward who signed from Banik Ostrava, where he had scored twice in the club's 6-1 Czech Cup victory of 1991. Has a tremendous shot, as well as the happy knack of being in the right place at the right time.

IACHINI, Giuseppe (Fiorentina, Ita)

• 07.05.64 • Midfield

Born in Ascoli and joined the local Serie A side as a 16-year-old. Spent seven years with the club before signing for Verona in 1987. Joined Fiorentina prior to the start of the 1989/90 season.

IACOBELLI, Agostino (Cremonese, Ita)

• 22.08.63 • Midfield

Made his League debut with Napoli in 1982 and played 12 games in Serie A before moving on to Catanzaro, via Pistoiese, in 1984. Later had spells with Empoli, Avellino and Udinese before arriving at Cremonese in 1990.

IBRAHIM, Ali (Wattenscheid, Ger)

• 01.09.69 • Striker
• Ghana full caps

Signed from Accra Great Olympic in 1990. Member of Ghana squad at 1992 African Nations Cup.

IELPO, Mario (Cagliari, Ita)

• 08.06.63 • Goalkeeper

Born in Rome and joined local Serie A side Lazio in 1983. Had a season with Siena and then returned to Lazio who were by then in Serie B. Dropped down even further when he joined Cagliari of Division Three in 1987, but Mario soon established himself as their number one choice and helped the club reach Serie A in 1990.

IKPEBA, Victor (RC Liege, Bel)

• 12.06.73 • Striker

Dazzling young Nigerian who made a sensational start, scoring three times in his first seven games for the club in 1990/91. Spotted playing for New Nigerian Bank he was snapped up in 1989 while still only 16-years-old and has proved a popular signing.

ILLGNER, Bodo (Cologne, Ger)

• 07.04.67 • Goalkeeper
• Germany 38 full caps

Experienced 'keeper who joined Cologne from Hardtberg in 1985. Was the German reserve number one at the 1988 European Championships and helped his country to victory at the 1990 World Cup. Came under fire for his performances in the 1992 European Championships in Sweden.

IMANOL Alguacio Barrenechea (Real Sociedad, Spa)

• 04.07.71 • Defender

Promising youngster who broke into the Sociedad first team during the 1991/92 season.

IMMEL, Eike (VfB Stuttgart, Ger)

• 27.11.60 • Goalkeeper
• Germany 19 full caps

Highly experienced 'keeper who has now made more than 400 Bundesliga appearances. Began his career as a junior with TSV Eintracht Stadtallendorf before getting his chance in the top flight with Borussia Dortmund. Joined Stuttgart in 1986 and helped the club to win the German Championship in 1992.

INGESSON, Klas (Mechelen, Bel)

• 20.08.68 • Midfield
• Sweden 26 full caps, 6 goals

Goalscorer and midfield playmaker who joined from IFK Gothenburg at the start of the 1991/92 season. A regular in the Swedish national line up, his craft and guile form the basis for much of Mechelen's attacking play.

INVERNIZZI, Giovanni (Sampdoria, Ita)

• 22.08.63 • Midfield

Discovered by home-town club Como, but spent 2 years on loan to Reggiana. Returned to Como in 1984 and spent five years with the first team before being signed by Sampdoria in 1989.

IPERMANS, Patrick (RWD Molenbeek, Bel)

• 20.11.59 • Defender

Has now played more than 400 senior games in Belgium. Signed from Germinal in the wake of Molenbeek's promotion from Division Two in 1990. Much experience with Vitesse Stabroek, Beerschot, Antwerp and Cercle Brugge.

ISAIAS Marques, Soares (Benfica, Por)

• 17.11.63 • Striker

Brazilian-born forward whose two goals at Highbury during the 1991/92 season knocked Arsenal out of the European Cup. Made his Portuguese League debut with Rio Ave in 1987, but joined Boavista after just one season. Signed by Benfica in 1990.

IVANAUSKAS, Valdas (FK Austria, Aus)

• Striker
• Lithuania full caps/USSR 5 full caps

Lithuanian, also capped five times by the USSR at full international level. Began his career with Zhagiris Vilnius, but left for a short spell with CSKA Moscow. Returned to Zhagiris before leaving once again in 1990 for FK Austria. Helped his new club to win the League title in his first season. Lithuania's Footballer Of The Year in 1991.

IVKOVIC, Tomislav (Sporting Lisbon, Por)

• 11.08.60 • Goalkeeper
• Yugoslavia 37 full caps

Born in Zagreb and joined Sporting prior to the 1989/90 season. Helped the club win a UEFA Cup place during his first term.

JACOB, Gunter (RWD Molenbeek, Bel)

• 10.05.68 • Midfield
• Belgium U21

Two-footed player who can perform anywhere in the midfield. Previously with Rummen and St Trond he spent two years at Standard Liege, playing 33 senior games, before moving to Molenbeek midway through season 1991/92.

JACOBS, Pascal (RWD Molenbeek, Bel)

• 27.11.67 • Midfield

Ball-winning central midfielder who was signed from Gent in 1990.

JACOBS, Patrick (Lokeren, Bel)

• 29.11.66 • Defender

Highly regarded full back who joined the club from minor League side Westerlo in the run-up to the 1991/92 season.

JAHNIG, Uwe (Dynamo Dresden, Ger)

• 26.08.69 • Striker
• East Germany youth

As a youth he also had a spell with Magdeburg. Uwe was a member of the East German side that finished third in

1987 World Youth Cup, but he never made it to the full international arena with his country.

JAIME Alves Magalhaes (Vitoria Guimaraes, Por)

• 28.03.65 • Striker

Started his career with his home town club of Espinho in 1983 then moved to Boavista in the 1985/86 season. Scored sixteen times for the club in six years before signing for Vitoria in 1992.

JAIME CERQUEIRA (Boavista, Por)

• 24.12.67 • Midfield

Made his League debut for Amadora during the 1988/89 season, but made only 17 appearances before moving to Boavista two years later.

JAIME MAGALHAES (Porto, Por)

• 10.07.62 • Midfield
• Portugal full caps

Has spent his entire career with Porto, his home town club. Made his League debut during the 1980/81 season and scored 2 goals in his 2 games that term. Has now made over 200 League appearances.

JAIME PACHECO Moreira (Pacos De Ferreira, Por)

• 22.07.58 • Midfield
• Portugal 25 full caps

A player seeing out his final competitive games after more than a decade at the top in which he played for Porto and Sporting Lisbon as well as the Portuguese national side. Joined Pacos De Ferreira for their first season in the top flight in 1991/92.

JAIRO Francisco (Uniao, Por)

• 16.05. 63 • Midfield

One of two Uniao players born in Rio de Janeiro he first made his mark in Portugal with Rio Ave in 1987/88. Signed for Uniao in 1989/90 and has made his mark in the side as an attacking midfielder.

JANONIS, Arvidas (St Polten, Aus)

• Defender
• Lithuania full caps

Made his debut for Zhalgiris Vilnius in the Soviet Second Division in 1978. Made over 200 appearances for the club in the Premier Division before joining St Polen in Austria. Played eight games for the USSR at Olympic level.

JANSSEN, Anton
(Kortrijk, Bel)

• 10.08.63 • Midfield

Dutch-born attacking midfielder who was tempted to Belgium from his home land in 1989. Previously with Beneden-Leeuwen, NEC Breda, Fortuna and PSV Eindhoven. Is now approaching 100 senior games in the Belgian First Division.

JANSSEN, Pierre
(Genk, Bel)

• 09.09.56 • Defender
• Belgium 3 full caps

Former Anderlecht favourite who joined the club from Lokeren midway through the 1991/92 season. Also formerly with minor League clubs FC Opitter and Thor Waterschei. His international career was short-lived, but began against Bulgaria in November 1986.

JANSSENS, Rudy
(Gent, Bel)

• 05.08.63 • Midfield

Playmaker and goalscorer from the midfield. Has played more than 150 senior games. Began with Meerhout, moving to Genk and then signing for Gent in the wake of the club's promotion in 1989.

JARBAS, Aguiar
(Beira-Mar, Por)

• 07.10.60 • Striker

Brazilian born forward who made his Portuguese First Division debut during the 1988/89 season. Has spent all his career in Portugal with the Beira-Mar club.

JARNI, Robert
(Sampdoria, Ita)

• 26.10.68 • Defender
• Yugoslavia 7 full caps, 1 goal

Creative left-back who can also play on the left side of midfield. Robert spent the 1991/92 season on loan to Bari. A Croatian, he represented Yugoslavia at the 1990 World Cup finals.

JARO, Pedro-Luis
(Real Madrid, Spa)

• 22.02.63 • Goalkeeper

Reserve 'keeper who joined Real from Malaga in June 1990.

JEFFREY, David
(Ards, N.Ir)

• Defender
• Irish League Representative

Transferred to Windsor Park in 1982, having spent three years with Manchester United. The Linfield captain and driving force in central defence he has won everything Irish football has to offer, except the Irish Cup. A veteran of more than 350 games, 1991/92 was his testimonial season with the club. Moved to Ards in a part exchange deal involving Robert Campbell in June 1992.

JENSEN, Jan
(Cologne, Ger)
• 22.02.69 • Midfield

Danish midfielder who originally joined Cologne from Odense in 1987, but found it hard to establish himself in the side.

JENSEN, John
(Brondby, Den)
• 03.05.65 • Midfield
• Denmark 48 full caps, 2 goals

Won soccer immortality at home in Denmark by scoring the opening goal in the 2-0 European Championship final win over Germany in June 1992. Strong, hard-running midfielder with a tremendous right foot shot.

JESUS Antonio Pereira
(Vitoria Guimaraes, Por)
• 11.02.55 • Goalkeeper

Veteran of the Vitoria side who joined the club in 1981 and helped them to the final of the Portuguese Cup in the 1987/88 season and to the quarter finals of the UEFA Cup the year before. he left Vitoria in 1988 for brief spells at Leixoes and Desp Chaves but was re-signed for the 1990/91 campaign.

JIMINEZ, Manuel
(Seville, Spa)
• 26.01.64 • Defender

Full back who has been a first team regular for Seville for the past eight years.

JOAO BATISTA de Melo
(Vitoria Guimaraes)
• 20.12.62 • Midfield

Born in Sao Paulo in Brazil, this classy playmaker was signed up by Vitoria for his attacking prowess in 1988. He repaid the club's faith in him by scoring six times that season and five the following year. A dual national he has made over 100 appearances for the club.

JOAO LUI Gouveia Martins
(Maritimo, Por)
• 24.04.67 • Midfield

One of six locally born players who have graduated to the Maritimo side. Has played for the club since the 1986 season.

JOAO MARIO
(Sporting Braga, Por)
• 28.12.66 • Midfield

Born in Porto and began his career with
his local First Division club, but failed to
break into the first team. Joined Sporting
Braga in 1987 and has now made over 100
appearances for the club.

JOAO PAULO, Sergio
Luis
(Bari, Ita)
• 07.09.64 • Striker
• Brazil full caps

Exciting striker who joined Bari from
Guarani in his native Brazil in 1989. Top
scorer for the club in 1990/91, he missed
almost all of last season after breaking his
leg against Sampdoria. Was a member of
Brazil's 1991 South American
Championship squad.

JOAO PINTO,
Domingos Silva
(Porto, Por)
• 21.11.61 • Defender
• Portugal 42 full caps, 1 goal

Originally with the Oliveira do Douro
club as a youngster, he made his League
debut for Porto during the 1981/82
season. Has won the Portuguese League
championship three times and has now
made over 250 appearances for the club.

JOAO PINTO, Manuel
Vieira
(Benfica, Por)
• 19.08.71 • Striker

Porto born player who left Boavista in
1990 after just 17 League games, but
returned to his home city and former club
from Real Madrid a year later. Won the
Portuguese Cup with Boavista in 1992
before transferring to Benfica in June of
that year.

JOAQUIM SOARES
(Salgueiros, Por)
• 20.03.61 • Midfield

Began his career with Lourosa, but
eventually joined Salgueiros from
Varzim.

JOAQUIN Alonso
Gonzalez
(Sporting Gijon, Spa)
• 09.06.56 • Midfield

Veteran star of the Gijon side who has
been with the club for 15 seasons.

JOHANSSON, Magnus
(Gothenburg, Swe)
• 10.11.71 • Midfield
• Sweden youth, Olympic

Strong in the tackle and with a desire to go

forward at every opportunity, Magnus is a right back who joined Gothenburg from IFK Olme in 1989.

JOHNSTON, John
(Ards, N.Ir)
• Midfield
• N.Ireland Schools, Youth, U18

Equally happy at full back or in a wide midfield role, John returned to Northern Ireland during 1990/91 having spent three seasons as an apprentice with Port Vale.

JOHNSTON, Ritchie
(Linfield, N.Ir)
• 15.10.69 • Striker
• N.Ireland Youth

Joined Tottenham straight from school, but was unable to force his way into the first team and, after a brief spell on loan at Dunfermline, joined Linfield in 1990. Former Youth international.

de JONG, Jerry
(PSV Eindhoven, Hol)
• 29.08.64 • Defender
• Holland 3 full caps

Began career with AZ 67. Joined Telstar in 1984 before joining SC Heerenveen in 1988. Signed by PSV in July 1989. Made his international debut against Greece in November 1990.

JONK, Wim
(Ajax, Hol)
• 12.10.66 • Midfield
• Holland 3 full caps

Scored 28 goals in just 59 League games for Volendam before being signed by Ajax in 1988. Made his debut for the Amsterdam club in a 2-1 defeat at Fortuna Sittard in August 1988.

JORGE COSTA Paulo Rocha
(Maritimo, Por)
• 08.11.66 • Defender

A solid defender and good striker of the ball, he scored three goals in his first League season when playing for Penafiel in 1990/91. The following year he signed for Maritimo

JORGE COUTO
(Porto, Por)
• 02.08.69 • Defender
• Portugal 1 full cap

Formerly with the Lourosa club as a youngster, he made his League debut for Porto during the 1989/90 season and immeadiately eastablished himself as a first team regular.

JORGE Garcia Santos
(Celta, Spa)
• 10.08.57 • Defender

Joined Celta from rivals Deportivo in 1991.

JORGE PLACIDO
(Salgueiros, Por)
• 19.06.64 • Striker

Angolan born forward who made his First Division debut with Amora back in the 1981/82 season. Moved on to Vitoria Setubal two years later and then signed by Chaves in 1985. Had further seasons at Porto, Sporting Lisbon and Porto once again before joining Salgueiros in 1991.

JORGE SILVERIO
(Beira-Mar, Por)
• 25.06.62 • Striker

Began his career with Odivelas and made his First Division debut with Chaves during the 1987/88 season. After three years with the club in the top flight he joined Beira-Mar in 1990.

JORGINHO
(Bayern Munich, Ger)
• 17.08.64 • Midfield
• Brazil 34 full caps

His real name is Jorge de Amorim Campos. Originally a right-back with Flamengo in Brazil, Leverkusen signed their future skipper in 1989 and successfully converted him to a midfield role. Joined Bayern Munich at the start of the 1992/93 season. Was the winner of FIFA annual Fair Play award in 1992.

JORGINHO
(Sporting Lisbon, Por)
• 19.05.62 • Defender

The widely travelled Jorge Sousa Gomes joined Sporting from Mulhouse of France in 1991. He had previously had two earlier spells in Portuguese football with Viseu, agueda and Boavista.

JOSE CARLOS
(Benfica, Por)
• 02.08.66 • Defender
• Portugal 1 cap

Made his first team debut during the 1987/88 season while with Portimonense and made 72 League appearances before joining Benfica in 1989.

JOSE CARLOS
Nascimento
(Porto, Por)
• 19.03.65 • Defender

Yet another of Porto's Brazillian contingent, he first joined the club prior to the 1989/90 season. Spent the following year with Gil Vicente, but returned to Porto in 1990.

JOSE PEDRO Fernandes Mota (Maritimo, Por)

• 06.07. 65 • Striker

Reliable front man who holds the ball up well, but does not score as many as expected. Hit only nine goals in over a hundred games with Portimonense before swithcing to Maritimo at the end of 1990.

JUAN CARLOS, Rodriguez (Barcelona, Spa)

• 19.01.65 • Defender
• Spain 1 full cap

Experienced defender who moved to Barcelona in 1991 after being transfer-listed and dropped by Atletico Madrid. His international debut came against Romania in April 1991, while still with Atletico.

JUDGE, Dermot (Shelbourne, Eir)

• Midfield

Signed from Bray Wanderers in 1990.

JUGOVIC, Vladimir (Sampdoria, Ita)

• Midfield
• Yugoslavia full caps

Bought by Sampdoria from Red Star Belgrade in June 1992, but had his transfer fee frozen by the Italian FA due to united Nations sanctions on Yugoslavia.

JULIA Fontane, Narcis (Zaragoza, Spa)

• 24.05.63 • Defender
• Spain U21

Joined Zaragoza in 1985 from regional junior club Giona.

JULIO CESAR DA SILVA (Juventus, Ita)

• 08.03.63 • Defender
• Brazil full caps

Began his career with Brazilian side Guarani and was a member of his country's 1986 World Cup side. Joined French side Brest after the finals before moving on to Montpellier in 1987. Signed by Juventus for £100,000 in July 1990.

JULIO PRIETO Martin (Atletico Madrid, Spa)

• 21.11.60 • Midfield

Veteran who rejoined Atletico in 1989 after a spell with Celta.

JUSUFI, Sascha (Schalke, Ger)

• 20.01.63 • Midfield

Ex-Bayer Uerdingen and Saarbrucken. Signed from SV Hamburg in 1991.

KADLEC, Miroslav (Kaiserslautern, Ger)

• 22.06.64 • Defender
• Czech 30 full caps

Played his football in Czechoslovakia with TJ Vitkovice and Red Star Cheb before moving to Germany in 1990.

KAHN, Oliver (Karlsruher, Ger)

• 15.06.69 • Goalkeeper

Has been with Karlsruher since the age of seven, but was kept waiting for his chance in the first team due to the consistency of Alexander Famulla.

KALITZAKIS, Yannis (Panathinaikos, Gre)

• Defender
• Greece 17 full caps

Tremendous young centre back who inspired the team to the League and Cup double in 1990/91. His international debut came against Belgium in 1990 (won 2-0).

KAMARK, Pontus (Gothenburg, Swe)

• 05.04.69 • Defender
• Sweden youth; U21

A former youth and U21 international,

Pontus was signed by Gothenburg from Vasteras SK in 1989.

KAMPS, Uwe (Borussia Moenchengladbach, Ger)

• 12.06.64 • Goalkeeper

Joined Gladbach from BV 04 Dusseldorf in 1982 and has now made over 175 First Division appearances for the club.

KANA-BIYIK, Andre (Le Havre, Fra)

• 01.09.65 • Midfield
• Cameroon full caps

Best remembered for a brutal body-check on Claudio Cannigia (Arg) which got him sent off in the first game of Italia '90. Tough midfield ball-winner who moved to Le Havre in 1990, having previously played for Diamant Yaounde and Metz.

KARACIC, Branko (Cercle Brugge, Bel)

• 24.09.60 • Midfield

Signed for the club at the same time as ex-Hajduk Split team-mate Jerko Tipuric - and has proved equally successful. A goalscoring midfielder he scored 13 times in 28 games during 1990/91. Yugoslavian-born.

KARAGEORGIOU, Nikos (Panathinaikos, Gre)

• Midfield
• Greece 12 full caps

Big money buy from PAOK Salonika in June 1991. A versatile player who is equally comfortable in midfield or central defence. His international debut came against Poland in September 1989 (lost 3-0).

KARAGIANNIS, Emmanuel (Waregem, Bel)

• 22.11.66 • Midfield

Signed from Second Divsion side Patro Eisden.

KARAPIALIS, Vassilios (Olympiakos, Gre)

• Midfield
• Greece 11 full caps, 1 goal

Big money signing from Larissa at the tail end of the 1990/91 season. Midfield playmaker for both club and country, he played a huge part in Larissa's Championship winning side of 1987/88.

KARL, Steffan (Borussia Dortmund, Ger)

• 03.02.70 • Defender

Bought to West Germany by Dortmund in 1990. Previously played his club football with Chemie Halle in the East.

KASTENDEUCH, Sylvian (St Etienne, Fra)

• 31.08.63 • Defender
• France 10 full caps

A sweeper in the finest tradition. Expert at reading the game and confident bringing the ball out from the back he has had two spells with Metz, broken up by a brief stay at Red Star Belgrade. Celebrated ten years at the top in September 1992, having made his senior debut on 24th September 1982, ironically against current club St Etienne.

KASTENMAIER, Thomas (Borussia Moenchengladbach, Ger)

• 31.05.66 • Midfield

Began his professional career with Bayern Munich, but struggled to make an impression. Joined Gladbach in 1990.

KASTL, Manfred (VfB Stuttgart, Ger)

• 23.09.65 • Striker

Much travelled forward who arrived at Stuttgart from Bayer Leverkusen in 1989. His other previous clubs include Nuremburg and SV Hamburg.

KATANEC, Srecko (Sampdoria, Ita)

• 16.07.63 • Midfield
• Yugoslavia 31 full caps, 5 goals

Began his career in Yugoslavia with Olimpija Lubiana. Srecko made his international debut after joining Dinamo Zagreb, and then became a regular for the national side after moving to the army team, Partizan, while doing national service. Enjoyed a spell in Germany with Stuttgart before joining Sampdoria in 1989.

KAVANAGH, Eamonn (Omagh Town, N.Ir)

• Midfield

Graduated through the junior ranks at Omagh. Versatile player who is comfortable in midfield, as a winger or up front.

KAVANAGH, Mick (Dundalk, Eir)

• Winger

Signed from UCD in the summer of 1990, Mick's viewed as one of the quickest players in the League of Ireland . His partnership with Peter Hanrahan has been lethal for Dundalk, although he missed much of 1991/92 through injury.

KAVANAGH, Paul (Shamrock Rovers, Eir)

• 14.07.67 • Goalkeeper

Signed from UCD in the long, hot summer of 1990, he has established himself as one of the top 'keepers in the League of Ireland and also as a firm favourite at Shamrock Rovers.

KEANE, Tommy (Galway United, Eir)

• 16.09.68 • Striker

Born in Dublin, had Football League experience with Bournemouth and Colchester before returning 'home' with Galway in 1988. Proven goalscorer with tremendous pace.

KEEGAN, Robbie (Sligo Rovers, Eir)

• 19.02.67 • Defender

Like several Sligo Rovers players, he began with Bohemians, for whom he took his League of Ireland bow against St Patrick's Athletic in October 1985. Sligo signed him from Shamrock Rovers in February 1990.

KEENAN, Michael (Portadown, N.Ir)

• Goalkeeper
• Irish League Representative

Portadown's longest-serving player, he has played a huge part in the club's great success of the past three years. Made a huge contribution to Portadown's tremendous defensive record of 1990/91 when they conceded just 29 goals on the way to winning the Irish League, Irish Cup and Ulster Cup. Scored from the penalty-spot during the Ulster Cup win over Glenavon. Was called up to the full international squad for the friendly against Yugoslavia in October 1991.

KEENAN, Val (Shelbourne, Eir)

• 18.02.69 • Midfield

Goalscoring central midfielder who joined the club from St Joseph's Boys' Club in July 1988.

KELCH, Pat (St Patrick's Athletic, Eir)

• 05.05.66 • Defender

Solid central defender who is dangerous at set-pieces, and usually pops up with a couple of goals a season.

KELLERMANN, Ralf
(MSV Duisburg, Ger)

• 24.09.68 • Goalkeeper

Has spent all his career at Duisburg, first joining the club at just eight years of age.

KELLY, John
(St Patrick's Athletic, Eir)

• 15.12.63 • Striker

Experienced forward who made a tremendous start to his career at Harold's Cross, scoring three goals in three starts in season 1990/91.

KELLY, Ritchie
(Drogheda United, Eir)

• Midfield

Discovered playing local League football with Drogheda Celtic and signed for United prior to the glorious 1990/91 season, when the club won the First Divison title to clinch promotion to the Premier League. Can play in midfield or at the back.

KEMPE, Thomas
(Bochum, Ger)

• 17.03.60 • Defender

Bochum's club captain and veteran of over more than 300 First Division appearances.

Signed from VfB Stuttgart in 1985. Previously with MSV Duisburg.

KENNEDY, John
(Distillery, N.Ir)

• Defender

Happy at full back or in central defence. Missed a chunk of 91/92 after a stomach infection, but returned for the end of season run-in.

KENNY, Harry
(Shamrock Rovers, Eir)

• 13.04.62 • Defender

A big favourite with the Rovers' fans, he has been unfortunate with injuries over the past couple of seasons. Joined the club from minor League side Villa United back in September 1978, making his League of Ireland debut, v Cork Celtic on April 3, 1979, shortly before his 17th birthday. Was a big influence at the club throughout the all-conquering days of the mid-1980s.

KERNOGHAN, Harry
(Larne, N.Ir)

• Midfield

Versatile performer who is equally happy playing in midfield or up front. Missed a chunk of the club's historic 1991/92 campaign - when they finished a record-breaking fourth in the League - through injury.

KERR, Joe
(Ards, N.Ir)

• Defender

Reportedly a target for English Premier League side Crystal Palace, this 6ft 3in centre back was signed from junior League supremos Donegal Celtic prior to the 1991/92 season.

de KHORS, Rod
(Shelbourne, Eir)

• Midfield

Goalscoring midfield playmaker who signed from Bohemians. Made his League of Ireland senior debut, for Bohemians against Derry City, in September 1988.

KIEFT, Wim
(PSV Eindhoven, Hol)

• 12.11.62 • Striker
• Holland 40 full caps, 11 games

Began career with Ajax and made League debut during 1979/80 season. Moved to Pisa of Italy three years later. Spent three years at Pisa and one at Torino before returning to Holland with PSV in 1987. Played for PSV between 1987 and 1990 before joining Bordeaux of France. Returned to Eindhoven in July 1991.

KIEKENS, Wim
(Antwerp, Bel)

• 26.02.68 • Defender

Ball-winner and midfield engine-room of the Antwerp side, he was signed from Molenbeek. Previously with Edixvelde.

KIKE
(Atletico Bilbao, Spa)

• 20.01.71 • Goalkeeper

Real name is Enrique Burgos Carrasco. Tall 'keeper who has now been Atletico's first choice between the posts for the past two seasons.

KIKI
(Porto, Por)

• 28.10.61 • Midfield

Alcides Rodrigues Tavares made his League debut during the 1982/83 season while at Vitoria Guimaraes, but did not gain a regaular starting place in the Portuguese League until he moved to Chaves in 1985. Joined Sporting Braga two years later and finally arrived at Porto in 1989.

KINCAID, Tom
(Ards, N.Ir)

• Midfield
• N.Ireland Youth

Very tricky winger who is nicknamed 'Tich' by the Castlereagh Park fans. Enjoyed his testimonial season in 1991/92, having joined the club from Crusaders at the beginning of 1986/87.

KING, Lee
(Bohemians, Eir)

• Striker

Fine young prospect who was snapped up from minor League side Rivermount. Made his League of Ireland debut away to Limerick in October 1988.

KING, Noel
(Shamrock Rovers, Eir)

• 13.09.56 • Midfield

Player/manager who joined the club from Waterford United. His appearances have been restricted over the last two seasons as he's been concentrating more on management, but is still a sound performer when he puts on his boots.

KINSELLA, Alan
(Athlone Town, Eir)

• 18.07.62 • Defender

Former Bohemians star who joined the club in August 1990. Solid and dependable, he is a fearsome ball-winner.

KIPRICH, Jozsef
(Feyenoord, Hol)

• 06.09.63 • Striker
• Hungary 51 full caps, 20 goals

Made name in Hungary with Tatabanya and was country's top League scorer with 18 goals during 1984/85 season. Made full debut v Austria, September 1984. Now won more than 40 caps, scoring 20 goals. Signed by Feyenoord in 1990. Scored goal that knocked Spurs out of 1992 UEFA Cup.

KIRK, James
(Ballyclare Comrades, N.Ir)

• 01.05.63 • Striker
• N.Ireland Youth

Former Carrick Rangers player who joined Ballyclare in 1990. As well as being a top soccer player, with two Smirnoff Cup winners' medals to his credit, he has also represented Ulster at badminton.

KIRSTEN, Ulf
(Bayer Leverkusen)

• 04.12.65 • Striker
• East Germany 49 full caps

Former East German Footballer of The Year and, like so many of his Eastern colleagues, a past informer for the Stasi secret police. Signed by Leverkusen from Dynamo Dresden in 1990 and rated so highly by Bayer that they turned down a bid of more than £3m from Italian club Napoli in 1992.

KLAUSS, Michael (Bochum, Ger)

- 15.09.70 • Striker

After beginning his League career with MSV Duisburg, Michael moved to Bayer Uerdingen before joining Bochum in 1991 after Bayer were relegated from Division One.

KLICHE, Ulf (Bayern Munich, Ger)

- 07.08.69 • Defender
- Germany U21

6ft 4in amateur who played for TSV Oeversee before joining Bayern in 1987.

KLINKERT, Michael (Borussia Moenchengladbach, Ger)

- 07.07.68 • Defender

Signed from Schalke 04 in 1989. Previously with 1.FC Saarbrucken.

KLINSMANN, Jurgen (Real Madrid, Spa)

- 30.06.64 • Striker
- Germany 41 full caps, 10 goals

Began career with Stuttgarter Kickers before moving to Stuttgart. UEFA Cup finalist 1989. Later signed by Inter. International debut v Brazil December 1987. Displays in 1988 European Champs won him European Football of Year title. Won World Cup in 1990 and UEFA Cup with Inter in 1991. Joined Real Madrid at the start of the 1992/93 season.

KLOS, Stefan (Borussia Dortmund, Ger)

- 16.8.71 • Goalkeeper
- Germany U21

Joined Dortmund as an amateur from Eintracht Dortmund in 1988.

KNAPP, Jean-Marc (Lyon, Fra)

- 12.01.63 • Defender
- France U21

Strasbourg-born full back who began with his home-town club in 1981, making his senior debut away to Lens in July that year. After a brief spell at Mulhouse he moved to Lyon in 1988 and was instrumental in the club's Division Two title win of 1989.

de KNEEF, Benny (Waregem, Bel)

- 12.06.65 • Defender

Former Gent player who has played more than 120 First Division games.

KOBER, Uwe
(MSV Duisburg)
• 24.04.61 • Midfield

Signed from Rot-Weiss Essen in 1986, Uwe previously had spells with Bayer Leverkusen and Fortuna Dusseldorf, but failed to make the first team with either side.

KOEMAN, Erwin
(PSV Eindhoven, Hol)
• 20.09.61 • Midfield
• Holland 29 full caps, 2 goals

Began career with Groningen but left for PSV after just one season in 1979. Returned to Groningen in 1982. Left PSV and moved to Belgium with Mechelen in 1985. Re-signed by PSV in July 1990.

KOEMAN, Ronald
(Barcelona, Spa)
• 21.03.63 • Defender
• Holland 59 full caps, 10 goals

Ronald began his career at Groningen with elder brother Erwin who is also a Dutch international. Moved on to PSV Eindhoven and was incredibly successful. In 1988 alone he won the European Cup, the Dutch League and Cup double, and helped Holland to the 1988 European Championship title. The following year he joined Barcelona for £3.5m. His bullet

free-kick won the 1992 European Cup for Barcelona, when they beat Sampdoria 1-0.

de KOEYER, Eric
(Lokeren, Bel)
• 22.02.67 • Goalkeeper

Dutch-born player with Belgian citizenship who has come up through the ranks at the club. Has played just a handful of games owing to the form of first choice 'keeper Danny D'Hondt.

KOGL, Ludwig
(VfB Stuttgart, Ger)
• 07.03.66 • Midfield
• Germany 2 full caps

Joined Stuttgart from Bayern Munich in 1990. Prior to joining Bayern he was with Munich 1860.

KOHLER, Jurgen
(Juventus, Ita)
• 06.10.65 • Defender
• Germany full caps

Very experienced central defender who joined Juventus from Bayern Munich in 1991 for £4m. World Cup winner with West Germany in 1990.

KOHN, Stefan
(Werder Bremen, Ger)
• 09.10.65 • Striker

Ex-Stuttgarter Kickers, Arminia Bielefeld, Bayer Leverkusen and Hannover 96. Joined Bremen from Bochum in 1991.

KOLLER, Marcel
(Grasshoppers, Swi)

• 11.11.60 • Defender
• Switzerland 46 full caps, 2 goals

Grasshoppers club captian who can operate either as a sweeper or in midfielder. Made his Grasshoppers first team debut in April 1979.

KOMBOUARE, Antione
(Paris St Germain, Fra)

• 16.11.63 • Defender

Born in Noumea he moved to France with Nantes in 1984, making his debut, v Nancy, in November of that year. He followed that with a spell at Toulon before signing a four-year deal at Paris St Germain in 1991.

KONTNY, Dirk
(Bochum, Ger)

• 30.11.65 • Midfield

One of six summer signings by Bochum in 1991, Dirk came to the club from Wattenscheid.

KONSEL, Michael
(Rapid Vienna, Aus)

• Goalkeeper
• Austria 14 full caps

Replaced Tirol's veteran stopper Klaus Linderberger in the Austrian national side after World Cup Italia '90, and has developed in to one of the most consistent 'keepers in the Austrian game. Superb reflexes and a tremendous command of his area make him a great favourite of national coach Alfred Riedl.

KOOIMAN, Willem
(Anderlecht, Bel)

• 09.09.60 • Defender

Dutch-born Belgian citizen who began with Ould Beijerland in his native Holland. Anderlecht signed him from Cercle Brugge in August 1988 and he has won the Belgian Cup (1989) and League title (1991) with his new club.

KOOT, Addick
(Cannes, Fra)

• 16.08.63 • Defender
• Holland full caps

Tall central defender who joined from PSV Eindhoven in 1991. Scored one League goal during the 1991/92 campaign.

KOPKE, Andreas (Nuremburg, Ger)

• 12.03.62 • Goalkeeper
• Germany 3 full caps

Currently the second choice 'keeper for the national side, he has benefitted from the loss of form and confidence of Bayern Munich's Raimond Aumann. Andreas was signed by Nuremburg from Hertha Berlin in 1986.

KOSTADINOV, Emile (Porto, Por)

• 12.08.67 • Striker
• Bulgaria 15 full caps, 5 goals

One of two Bulgarian striker at Porto. Kostadinov arrived in Portugal a year earlier than countryman Mihtarsky, signing for the club in 1990.

KOZLE, Peter (Grasshoppers, Swi)

• 18.11.67 Striker

German-born striker who began as an amateur with Bayern Munich. Joined Young Boys of Berne in 1988 before moving to Grasshoppers in 1990.

KRANZ, Markus (Kaiserslautern, Ger)

• 04.08.69 • Defender

Joined Kaiserslautern from FSV Schifferstadt, but has had few first team oppoorunities during his six years at the club.

KREE, Martin (Bayer Leverkusen, Ger)

• 27.01.65 • Defender
• Germany U21

A useful defender who also contributes his fair share of goals. Signed from Bochum in 1989, he has made well over 200 First Division appearances.

KREEK, Michel (Ajax, Hol)

• 16.01.71 • Striker

Has spent all his career with Ajax and made his first team debut in 4-0 victory at Haarlem in October 1989.

KREUZER, Oliver (Bayern Munich, Ger)

• 13.11.65 • Defender

Central defender who began career with home-town club SpVgg 05 Ketsch. Joined Bayern from Karlsruher in July 1991 for £1.9m, which was the second biggest fee between two German clubs at the time.

KRNCEVIC, Eddie
(RC Liege, Bel)

• 14.08.60 • Striker
• Australia 47 full caps

Widely-travelled forward who is one of the most capped Australians of all time. Began with Victorian club Geelong, moving to Melbourne Croatia and Marconi before travelling to Yugoslavia with Dynamo Zagreb in 1984. Since then he has paraded his goalscoring talents at Duisburg, Brugge, Anderlecht and Mulhouse. Liege snapped him up in 1990.

KROGH, Mogens
(Brondby, Den)

• Goalkeeper
• Denmark U21

Signed by Brondby from Ikast during the summer of 1991 as a replacement for Danish goalie Peter Schmeichel.

KRONINGER Michael
(Schalke, Ger)

• 12.12.66 • Midfield

Signed from Kickers Offenbach in 1990.

KRUSE, Axel
(Eintracht Frankfurt, Ger)

• 28.09.67 • Striker

Signed from Hertha Berlin in 1991. Previously with Hansa Rostock in East Germany.

KRUZEN, Hendrie
(RC Liege, Bel)

• 24.11.64 • Midfield
• Holland 6 full caps

Joined the club in the summer of 1991 from Kortrijk. Formerly with La Premiere and Heracles before hitting the big time with moves to Den Bosch and then PSV Eindhoven. By the end of season 1991/92 he had played nearly 100 senior games.

KUBIK, Lubos
(Metz, Fra)

• 20.01.64 • Midfield
• Czechoslovakia 30 full caps, 10 goals

Giant midfield playmaker who began with home-town club Sparta HK before moving on, via Slavia Praha and Inattivo, to Italian giants Fiorentina, where he grabbed five goals in 20 games from midfield. Signed in 1991. An accomplished penalty taker.

KULA, Karel
(Stuttgarter Kickers, Ger)

• 10.08.63 • Midfield
• Czechoslovakia 33 full caps, 4 goals

Right-sided midfield player who joined Kickers from Banik Ostrava in his home country in 1991.

KULKOV, Vasili (Benfica, Por)

• 11.06.66 • Defender
• USSR 20 full caps

Formerly with Kacira Dynamo, Krasnaya Presinya and Orzhonkhidze Spartak. Made international debut v Turkey, May 1989. Has been described as the "Soviet Baresi". Won a League Championship medal with Spartak Moscow before Benfica snapped him up in June 1991, along with fellow Soviet Sergei Yuran. Injury forced him to withdraw from the CIS squad for the 1992 European Championship in Sweden.

KUNTZ, Stefan (Kaiserslautern, Ger)

• 30.10.62 • Striker

The inspiration behind Kaiserslautern's 1991 Bundesliga championships season. Joined the club from Bayer Uerdingen in 1989. Previously with Bochum. Has made over 250 FIrst Division appearances.

KURBANAS, Nikos (Panathinaikos, Gre)

• Defender
• Greece 7 full caps

Took his bow on the international stage against Canada in May 1988. Signed from

Panahaiki in 1988.

KUTOWSKI, Gunter (Borussia Dortmund, Ger)

• 02.08.65 • Defender

Joined Dortmund as a teenager and has now made well over 200 first team appearances for the club. Previously with FC Paderborn and SV Sande.

KUZMANOVIC, Boro (Den Haag, Hol)

• 02.12.62 • Striker

Yugoslavian who left his native country when first signed by Den Haag from Dinamo Zagreb in January 1988. Was to later leave the club, but returned again in July 1991.

KVITKAUSKAS, Gintaras (Dynamo Kiev, CIS)

• Midfield
• Lithuania full caps

Began his career with Zhalgiris Vilnius and made his debut during the 1988 season. Moved onto Pakhtakor in 1991 and signed by Kiev in 1992.

van der LAAN, Harry
(Den Haag, Hol)
• 24.02.64 • Striker

Began his career with Den Haag in 1988, but was sold to Feyenoord two years later. Returned to Den Haag in July 1991.

LABBADIA, Bruno
(Bayern Munich, Ger)
• 08.02.66 • Striker
• Germany U21

Began senior career with SV Darmstadt 98. Moved on to Hamburger SV before joining 1.FC Kaiserslautern. Won Bundesliga title in 1991 and signed for Bayern that summer.

LACATUS, Marius
(Oviedo, Spa)
• 05.04.69 • Striker
• Romania 48 full caps, 8 goals

Highly talented player who shone at the World Cup finals in 1990 and was chased by a number of top sides. Sold by his Romanian club side, Steaua Bucharest, to Oviedo that summer.

LADA, Eric
(Marseille, Fra)
• 14.10.65 • Striker
• France U21

Signed in 1990, his career at Marseille has been somewhat overshadowed by Jean-Pierre Papin. Began with Paris FC and moved first to Chartres and then hit the big-time with Sochaux, making his Division One debut v St Etienne in 1982.

LAIGLE, Pierre
(Lens, Fra)
• 02.09.70 • Midfield

Wide midfielder who has come up through the ranks at the club, experiencing all the highs of promotion in 1990/91.

LAMA, Bernard
(Paris St Germain, Fra)
• 17.04.63 • Goalkeeper

Experienced 'keeper who spent time with Lille, Metz and Brest before moving to Lens in the summer of 1991, when Jean-Pierre Mottet left the club. Made his debut v Auxerre in November 1986, and has now made more than 200 senior appearances. Signed by Paris-SG at the end of the 1991/92 season as a replacement for Joel Bats, who announced his retirement from the game.

LAMBEETS, Ben
(Beveren, Bel)
• 31.08.71 • Goalkeeper

Vying for the number one shirt with first choice 'keeper Geert de Vlieger. Signed from Standard Liege.

LAMBERT, Loic
(St Etienne, Fra)

• 25.10.66 • Defender

Speedy attacking full back who was born
in Le Mans. Joined the club in July 1990
after five years at his only other side, Laval.
Equally at home operating as a wide
midfielder when St Etienne revert to a
'flat' back four.

LAMIERE, Bert
(Cercle Brugge, Bel)

• 28.04.71 • Midfield

Was discovered as a schoolboy by the club,
and has progressed through the ranks to
become a first team regular. His top flight
debut came during the 1989/90 season,
but it was the following year before he
really established himself in the plans of
coach Henk Houwaert.

LAMPTEY, Nii
Odartey
(Anderlecht, Bel)

• 10.12.74 • Midfield

With seven goals in 11 starts in his first
season (1990/91), this Ghana born teenager
exploded onto the Belgian First Division
scene. He was spotted playing for his local
boys club, Cornerstone United, and
immediately snapped up by Anderlecht in
November 1990. His partnership with
striker Oliveira Barroso was a runaway

success and together they inspired the club
to their 1991 League title.

LANG, Didier
(Metz, Fra)

• 15.12.70 • Defender
• France Youth

Home grown player who made his debut
away to Sochaux in November 1991. Only
a handful of games so far.

LANNA, Marco
(Sampdoria, Ita)

• 13.07.68 • Defender

Marco began his career as right back, but was
later converted to sweeper by Sampdoria.
Made his first team debut in 1988.

LARRANAGA
Gorrutxaga, Jose
Antonio
(Real Sociedad, Spa)

• 03.07.58 • Defender
• Spain 1 full cap

Highly experienced defender who has been
at Sociedad for the past 13 seasons.

LARSSON, Peter
(AIK Stockholm, Swe)

• 08.03.61 • Defender
• Sweden 42 full caps, 4 goals

Central defender who began career with Halmstad. Joined IFK Gothenburg for Swedish domestic record fee of £70,000. Won Swedish League title in 1987 before joining Ajax. Cup-Winners' Cup finalist with Ajax 1988. Brought back to Sweden by AIK in 1991.

LASA, Mikel
(Real Madrid, Spa)

• 09.09.71 • Defender
• Spain youth, Olympic, U19, U21

Signed from Real Sociedad in June 1991.

LASSAGNE, Laurent
(Lyon, Fra)

• 06.09.65 • Defender

Spent six years with his only other club, Bordeaux, before joining Lyon in 1988 and lending a vital hand in the push for promotion. Division One debut came against Nantes in August 1984.

LAUDRUP, Brian
(Fiorentina, Ita)

• 22.02.69 • Striker
• Denmark 28 full caps, 5 goals

Younger brother of Michael Laudrup. Left Denmark and Brondby to join Bayer Uerdingen for £650,000 - a Danish record at the time. Signed by Bayern during summer 1990 for a then Bundesliga record £2m. Made full international debut during Kings Cup Tournament in Bangkok in

January 1988 and has now won over 20 caps. Denmark's Footballer of the Year in 1989. Returned to the international arena in the 1992 European Championship following a bust up with national coach Richard Moller-Nielsen. He helped inspire Denmark to their historic final win over Germany. Fiorentina stepped in after the Championships to sign him for £3.5 million.

LAUDRUP, Michael
(Barcelona, Spa)

• 15.06.64 • Midfield
• Denmark 56 full caps, 27 goals

The older brother of Brian and the son of Finn Laudrup, who was also a Danish international. Was chased by a number of leading sides as a youngster, but eventually signed by Juventus from Brondby in 1983. Loaned to Lazio for two years, but the club were relegated. Helped Juventus to win the 1986 League Championship and then later signed by Johan Cruyff at Barcelona. Appeared for Denmark in 1988 European Championships, but missed his country's finest hour after refusing to patch up his differences with national coach Richard Moller-Nielsen and play in the 1992 European Championships in Sweden.

LAURETA Alfredo
Magalhaes Rodrigues
(Gil Vicente, Por)

• 18.12.61 • Defender
• Portugal full caps

Experienced full back signed from Sporting Braga, where he had made over 130 appearances before joining Gil Vicente at the start of the 1991/92 season. Spent two years at Porto before joining Braga but failed to command a first team spot.

LAUREY, Thierry (St Etienne, Fra)

• 17.02.64 • Midfield
• France 1 full cap

Tall central midfield who is lethal in the air from free-kicks and corners. With more than 30 goals in over 170 First Division games, his scoring record speaks for itself. Much experience with Marseille, Montpellier, Sochaux and Paris St Germain. Joined the club in 1990.

LAURICELLA, Jean-Pierre (Lille, Fra)

• 04.02.65 • Goalkeeper

Stand-in for first choice 'keeper Jean-Claude Nadon at Lille. Began with Lille before moving to Valenciennes. Spent a brief period on loan at Annecy before returning to Lille in 1989. First senior game in March 1990, v Lyon.

LAUWERS, Christophe (Cercle Brugge, Bel)

• 12.09.72 • Midfield

Exciting young midfield prospect who has played a handful of first team games, mainly as sub, since progressing from the youth ranks in 1991.

LAWLESS, Eugene ('Gino') (Dundalk, Eir)

• 14.1.59 • Midfield

Won a League Cup medal with Bohemians, for whom he made more than 210 appearances, back in 1979. Began his career in 1978 (debut v Cork Alberts) and was voted Dundalk's Player of the Year in 1991.

LAWLESS, Joe (St Patrick's Athletic, Eir)

• 13.02.62 • Striker

Made his League of Ireland debut for Bray Wanderers, at Emfa, back in January 1986. St Pat's signed him from Bohemians prior to the 1990/91 campaign.

LAWLOR, Robbie (Crusaders, N.Ir)

• Defender
• Eire Youth

Joined the club in November 1991 after considerable League of Ireland experience with Dundalk, Shamrock Rovers, UCD,

Sligo Rovers and Bohemians. Attacking full back who loves to get forward.

LEAL, Jose Martins (Sporting Lisbon, Por)

• 23.03.65 • Defender
• Portugal 6 full caps, 1 goal

Born in Angola he began his career with Repesenses, joining Sporting from Viseu prior to the start of the 1989/90 season.

LEAO (Salgueiros, Por)

• 22.04.71 • Midfield

Augusto Pinto Maia is a locally born player who has spent all his career with Salgueiros. Made his First Division debut for the club during the 1990/91 campaign.

LEBOURGEOIS, Yvan (Caen, Fra)

• 26.10.62 • Defender
• France U21

Hard-running full back who signed from junior club PTT Caen in 1984. Made his debut in July 1988 v Nantes. Equally happy in wide midfield, he provides support for attack by his flank play.

LECLERCQ, Dominique (Paris St Germain, Fra)

• 30.11.57 • Goalkeeper

Looks like taking the number one spot off ex-international Joel Bats, having played almost 100 senior games since joining from Lille in 1990. Another hugely experienced pro who has also enjoyed spells at Lens, Nantes and Racing Paris.

LECLERCQ, Fabien (Lille, Fra)

• 12.10.72 • Defender

Joined the club as 15-year-old and progressed through the ranks to make his senior debut against Toulon in May 1990.

LECOMTE, Jean-Francois (RC Liege, Bel)

• 17.11.68 • Goalkeeper

Understudy to the hugely experienced Jacques Munaron. Only a handful of games to date. Signed from Bas-Oha.

LEEMAN, Tommy (Ards, N.Ir)

• Defender

Known as 'Leeper', he is the club captain. Moved to Castlereagh Park from Australian side Bayswater, near Melbourne in Victoria. Had previously spent 18 months with Glasgow Rangers, where he failed to make the grade, before enjoying a four year spell with Glentoran.

LEGAT, Thorsten
(Werder Bremen, Ger)

• 07.11.68 • Midfield

Left sided midfielder or full back who
possesses a powerful shot. Joined Bremen
from VfL Bochum in 1991.

LEHMANN, Jens
(Schalke, Ger)

• 16.11.69 • Goalkeeper

Joined Schalke from Schwarz-Weiss Essen
in 1987.

LEHNHOFF, Hans-
Peter
(Antwerp, Bel)

• 12.07.63 • Midfield

German-born raiding midfielder who
signed from Cologne in 1987. Loves to get
forward, and is rewarded with some vital
goals - ten in 26 games in 1990/91.
Formerly with Baesweiler and Alemannia
Aachen.

LEIFELD, Uwe
(Schalke, Ger)

• 24.07.66 • Striker

Managed a goal every three games in the
First Division when playing for Bochum.
Signed by Schalke in 1991. Previously
with Preussen Munster.

LELLE, Frank
(Kaiserslautern, Ger)

• 04.02.65 • Midfield

Like team-mate Thomas Dooley, Frank
was a former member of the Pirmasens
club. Joined Kaiserslautern from Rodalben
in 1985.

LEMAJIC Zoran
(Farense, Por)

• 08.11.60 • Goalkeeper

Born in Niksic in Yugoslavia he played in
his native league before switching to
Portugal for the 1990/91 season. Was
ever-present in the Farense side in his first
year with the club.

LEMOINE, Dominique
(Kortrijk, Bel)

• 12.03.66 • Midfield

Creative midfielder who is now in his
second spell with the club, having re-
signed prior to the 1990/91 season.
Began with Wiersen before moving to
Valenciennes and then onto Kortrijk.
Transferred to Mulhouse, in Denmark,
before returning to the
Guldensporenstadion.

LEMOULT, Jean-Claude
(Nimes, Fra)

• 28.08.60 • Midfield
• France full caps

Plays wide on the right of midfield and is approaching his 400th senior game. Began with Paris St Germain in 1978, v Nice, and also played with Montpellier before moving to ambitious Nimes in July 1991.

LEMS, Cor
(Den Haag, Hol)

• 13.03.61 • Midfield
• Holland Olympic

Began his career with DS 79 and broke into their League side during the 1980/81 season. Had a brief spell with Ipswich Town in 1983, but quickly returned to Holland. Finally left DS 79 in July 1986 when signed by Den Haag. Made his 150th appearance for the club last season.

LENTINI, Gianluigi
(Milan, Ita)

• 27.03.69 • Midfield

Began his career with Torino and made his Serie A debut for the club during the 1986/87 season. Had one season with Ancona in 1988 before returning to Torino in 1989 and helping the club win promotion back to the top flight. Joined Milan in a surprise move in July 1992, for

a world record breaking £12 million. He was reported to have received a signing on fee of £2.5 million and guaranteed earnings in excess of £8 million over the next four years.

LEONARDO
(Valencia, Spa)

• 05.09.69 • Defender

Brazilian who moved to Europe and joined Valencia in 1991.

LESNIAK, Marek
(Bayer Leverkusen, Ger)

• 29.02.64 • Striker
• Poland Full

Left Poland from Germany in 1988 when signed by Bayer from Pogo Stettin. Had previously been with Pomorzanin.

LIANO Fernandez, Francisco
(Coruna, Spa)

• 16.11.64 • Goalkeeper

Joined Coruna from Sestao prior to the 1991/92 season and was an ever-present in his first year with his new club.

LIEBERAM, Frank
(Dynamo Dresden, Ger)

• 17.12.62 • Defender

• East Germany youth, Olympic, U21, 1 full cap

A sweeper signed from Stahl Riesa in 1985. Previously with Magdeburg, Frank has been capped at all international levels by East Germany.

LIMPENS, Luc
(Eendracht Aalst, Bel)

• 03.04.62 • Defender

Like Rene Peeters, he has returned to the club after a brief spell away. Came through the ranks at Aalst before moving to Lokeren, where he made just two appearances before returning to his first club. Helped the side to promotion in 1990/91.

van der LINDEN, Marc
(Gent, Bel)

• 04.02.64 • Striker
• Belgium 19 full caps, 9 goals

International debut came in May 1983, v Luxembourg, but he failed to impress coach Guy Thys and did not play for Belgium again until November 1987 - ironically, also against Luxembourg. After an unhappy season at Antwerp in 1990/91, when a leg injury restricted his appearances, he decided to make a fresh start with Gent. Previously with Merksem.

LINDQVIST, Stefan
(Gothenburg, Swe)

• 18.03.67 • Midfield
• Sweden full caps; U21

A former U21 international who quit Sweden in 1990 to turn professional with Xamax Nauchatel in Switzerland. Returned home with Gothenburg in 1991.

LINO Gregorio Freitas
(Maritimo, Por)

• 02.10.71 • Midfield

A newcomer to the first team at just 21 years of age, has made few appearances.

LINSKENS, Edward
(PSV Eindhoven, Hol)

• 06.11.68 • Midfield

Made League debut for PSV during 1987/88 season. Now made over 70 first team appearances for the club.

LITOS
(Sporting Lisbon, Por)

• 06.01.67 • Midfield
• Portugal full caps

Originally with the Sanjoanense club, he made his debut for Sporting during the 1984/85 season. Has now made over 150 first team appearances for the club.

LITTBARSKI, Pierre (Cologne, Ger)

- 16.04.60 • Midfield
- Germany 73 full caps, 18 goals

Former member of the Hertha Zehlendorf youth side, Pierre was offered his chance at professional level by Cologne. After breaking into the national side he had a short spell in France with Racing Paris before moving back to Cologne in 1987. Has now played more than 300 German First Division games, scoring over 100 goals.

LJUNG, Roger (Admira Wacker, Aus)

- 08.01.66 • Midfield
- Sweden 31 full caps, 2 goals

Solid midfielder who can also play in defence if required. Made his name in Sweden with Malmo, where he was club captain, before departing to join Young Boys of Berne in Switzerland. Later moved on to Zurich and was at one time linked with Arsenal, before finally signing for Austrian side Admira Wacker.

LJUTY, Wladimir (MSV Duisburg, Ger)

- 20.04.62 • Striker
- USSR 4 full caps; CIS 2 full caps

Originally brought to Germany from Dnepr by Schalke. Moved to Duisburg in 1991. Earned a late call up to the Commonwealth of Independent States squad for the 1992 European Championship in Sweden thanks to his tremendus form in the German Bundesliga.

LLORENTE, Julio (Tenerife, Spa)

- 14.6.66 • Midfield

Joined Tenerife from Real Madrid in 1990.

LLORENTE, Paco (Real Madrid, Spa)

- 21.05.65 • Striker
- Spain Olympic, U21, 1 full cap

Nephew of the Paco Llorente, a star of the great Real side of the 1960s. Signed from Atletico Madrid in July 1987. Got his chance in the Real first team during 1991/92 season when Hugo Sanchez was injured.

LODDERS, Julien (Beveren, Bel)

- 30.11.62 • Defender

Discovered playing for minor League side Looi Sport, has experienced all the ups and downs of recent years with Beveren. A member of the side that crashed out of the First Divsion in 1990, he retained his captaincy and rediscovered his form to lead the club back into the top flight at the first attempt.

van LOEN, John
(Ajax, Hol)
• 04.02.65 • Striker
• Holland 7 full caps, 1 goal

Began his career with Utrecht, before moving to Roda JC in 1988. After seven seasons of Dutch football he joined Belgian club Anderlecht in 1991, helping them to the Belgian League title with three goals in seven starts. Spent just one season abroad before returning home with Ajax in 1991.

LOINAZ Balda, Mikel
(Real Sociedad, Spa)
• 28.03.67 • Striker

Tall target man who, not surprisingly, gets most of his goals with his head from set pieces.

LOMBARDINI,
Massimo
(Cremonese, Ita)
• 23.07.71 • Midfield

A one club player, Massimo made his League debut for Cremonese during the 1990/91 Serie B promotion winning season.

LOMBARDO, Attilio
(Sampdoria, Ita)
• 06.01.66 • Striker
• Italy 5 full caps, 1 goal

Attilio began his career with Third Division Pergocrema as a 17-year-old. Moved on to Cremonese two years later and eventually joined Sampdoria in 1989. Scored on his international debut, against Cyprus in December 1990.

LONG, Philip
(Cork City, Eir)
• 03.12.61 • Defender

Signed from St Mary's in July 1986, he was the first player in the club's history to make 200 senior appearances (v Galway, 31.03.91).

LOPETEGUI Agote,
Julian
(Logrones, Spa)
• 28.08.66 • Goalkeeper
• Spain U21

Signed by Logrones from Real Madrid where he was the reserve team keeper in 1991. Previously with Las Palmas.

LOPEZ REKARTE, Luis
Maria
(Coruna, Spa)
• 23.06.62 • Defender
• Spain 4 full caps

Experienced defender who played for Real Sociedad and Barcelona before moving to Coruna.

LOREN
(Burgos, Spa)
- 07.10.66 • Striker
- Spain U21

Lorenzo Juarros Garcia made his name at Atletico Bilbao before returning to his home town and joining Bugos in 1991.

LORIERI, Fabrizio
(Ascoli, Ita)
- 11.02.64 • Goalkeeper

Began his career with Internazionale, but failed to break into the first team. After spells with Sangiovanne, Prato and Piacenzo, Fabrizio moved to Torino in 1986. Three seasons later he was signed by Ascoli.

LORINCZ, Emil
(RWD Molenbeek, Bel)
- 29.09.65 • Midfield
- Hungary 8 full caps, 3 goals

Attacking midfielder who is lethal from dead-ball situations. Signed from MTK-VM in his native Hungary at the beginning of season 1990/91.

LOSADA, Sebastian
(Atletico Madrid, Spa)
- 03.09.67 • Striker
- Spain U21

Moved across the capital city when signed from Real Madrid in the summer of 1991.

LOUGHRAN, Kieran
(Cliftonville, N.Ir)
- Defender

Traditional full back who rarely ventures over the halfway line. He is the longest serving player at Cliftonville, and is a very reliable defender.

LOWITZ, Claude
(Nantes, Fra)
- 29.05.62 • Defender

Tremendously athletic full back who's CV reads like a Who's Who of French football clubs. Before moving to Nantes in June 1985 he had laced his boots at Metz, Paris St Germain, Marseille and Montpellier. Now approaching his 200th senior game.

LUCAS, Phillipe
(Sochaux, Fra)
- 01.11.63 • Midfield
- France B

Solid defensive midfielder who has now played more than 100 Div One games for Sochaux. Signed from Guingamp, he made his First Division debut v Laval in August 1982.

LUCCHESI, Franck (Montpellier, Fra)

• 19.03.63 • Defender
• France Schools

Started his career in Division Two A, with Nimes, before signing for Montpellier in 1986. He took his bow in Division One in July of the following year, at Toulouse. Has now played well over 100 senior games for the club. French Cup winner in 1990.

LUGINGER, Jurgen (Schalke, Ger)

• 08.12.67 • Defender

Signed from Fortuna Dusseldorf in 1988 at the age of 21. Previously with Bayer Leverkusen and Munich 1860 as a youth.

LUHOVY, Milan (Sporting Gijon, Spa)

• 01.03.63 • Striker
• Czechoslovakia full caps

Joined Gijon from Sparta Prague in 1989 and has struck up a very useful partnership with Monchu.

LUISAO Luis Naguiera (Farense, Por)

• 22.05.65 • Defender

Brazilian-born but now a naturalised Portuguese he found it hard to command a first team place when he first joined the club in 1986. In recent seasons has established himself as an attacking defender capable of scoring in breakaways.

LUIS ENRIQUE (Real Madrid, Spa)

• 08.05.70 • Striker
• Spain Olympic, U21, 1 full cap

Exciting prospect who was signed by Real from Sporting Gijon in July 1991. His international debut came in the surprise 2-0 home defeat by Romania in April 1991.

LUISINHO (Sporting Lisbon, Por)

• 22.10.58 • Defender
• Brazil full caps

One of a number of Brazilians at the Sporting club, Luisinho arrived in Portugal in 1989 and has established himself as an important member of the Sporting squad.

LUIS MANUEL (Sporting Braga, Por)

• 26.03.62 • Goalkeeper

Began his career with Maritimo Rosarense and made his Portuguese First Division debut with Sporting Braga in the 1988/89 season.

LUIS MANUEL Silva Costa
(Gil Vicente, Por)
• 28.06.66 • Midfield

A skilful but inconsistant midfielder previously with Sporting Espinho and Desportivo Chaves

LUKIC, Dejan
(Lokeren, Bel)
• 28.09.65 • Striker

Signed from Yugoslav club Borac Banja Luka at the beginning of 1991/92, after scoring 10 goals in 29 games for his home-town club the previous season. Has bolstered Lokeren's lightweight attack.

LUMBRERAS Panos, Jose Maria
(Real Sociedad, Spa)
• 06.01.61 • Defender
• Spain U21

Once with Osasuna, Lumbreras joined Sociedad from Zaragoza in 1989.

LUPESCU, Ion
(Bayer Leverkusen, Ger)
• 09.12.68 • Midfield
• Romania 13 full caps, 2 goals

Highly talented central midfield player who joined Leverkusen from Dinamo Bucharest for £750,000 in 1990.

LUPPI, Gianluca
(Juventus, Ita)
• 23.08.66 • Defender

Began his career with Bologna and made his League debut during the 1984/85 season while the club were still a Second Division side. Helped the team win promotion in 1988 before joining Juventus for £2m in July 1990. Lost his first team place at Juve last season following the arrival of Kohler at the club.

LUSCH, Michael
(Borussia Dortmund, Ger)
• 16.06.64 • Midfield

Played for Germania Hamm and Lohauserholz in junior football before turning pro with Dortmund in 1981. Has now made over 150 First Division appearances for the club.

LUST, Matthais
(Karlsruher, Ger)
• 27.04.70 • Defender

Joined Karlsruher from SpVgg Ludwigsburg in 1990. Prior to that, Matthais was with Stuttgarter Kickers.

LUTZ, Roger
(Kaiserslautern, Ger)

• 15.07.64 • Defender

Joined Kaiserslautern in 1987. Previously with SV Linden and FK Clausen.

MACARTNEY, Gary
(Glentoran, N.Ir)

• Striker

Free scoring centre forward who considered retiring at the end of season 1990/91, but eventually agreed to sign a new contract at The Oval. In four seasons at Glentoran he has scored more than 120 senior goals. His power up front played a huge part in the club's 78 goal tally as they romped to the 1991/92 League title.

MACHALA, Oldrich
(Hansa Rostock, Ger)

• 04.08.63 • Midfield

Signed by Rostock from Sigma Olomouc of Czechoslovakia along with team mate Roman Sedleck in 1991.

MACHEREY, Heribert
(MSV Duisburg, Ger)

• 03.11.54 • Goalkeeper

Joined Duisburg from Hamborn 07 in 1983.

MACHIELS, Vincent
(RC Liege, Bel)

• 16.09.65 • Midfield
• Belgium U21

Experienced Euro campaigner who signed

from Seresien. Also previously with Stree. He represented the club during their UEFA Cup run of 1990 and their Cup-Winners' Cup adventures the following year, when they reached the quarter finals before being eliminated by Juventus. Belgian Cup winner 1990.

MACKEY, Dave (Dundalk, Eir)

• 4.6.60 • Defender

Born in England, this right back struggled to make an impression after signing from Shelbourne in 1988. Came into his own when Gino Lawless was switched to midfield and was an important part of the defence which conceded just 17 goals on the way to the 1990/91 League title. Equally at home at centre back.

MADUREIRA Joge Luis Freitas (Vitoria Guimaraes, Por)

• 08.02.65 • Goalkeeper

Second string to Vitoria's veteran keeper, Jesus, he has played just three games for the club since transfering from Nacional in 1989.

MADUREIRA, Jorge Manuel Veloso (Salgueiros, Por)

• 20.12.58 • Goalkeeper

Originally with the Leixoes club, he made his First Division debut with Boavista in 1981. Three years later he moved on to Salgueiros where he has been the first choice number one ever since.

MAGEE, Jonathan (Linfield, N.Ir)

• Defender

Son of former Linfield favourite Eric Magee, signed from Dungannon Swifts in 1990. Has also played for Glenavon.

MAGILL, Darren (Ballymena United, N.Ir)

• Defender

Spent two years as an apprentice at Queen's Park Rangers, but failed to make the grade at Loftus Road and returned to his native Ireland in June 1992.

MAGNIER, Cyrille (Lens, Fra)

• 24.08.69 • Midfield
• France U21

Discovered playing local football as a 15-year-old, and signed up by the club. Made his senior debut against Laval on 30th April 1988.

MAGNUSSON, Mats
(Benfica, Por)

• 10.07.63 • Striker
• Sweden 23 full caps

Big strong striker who is always dangerous in the air. Began his career in Sweden with Malmo. Made his international debut against Mexico in August 1984 and was signed by Servette of Switzerland. Returned to Malmo in 1986 for a then Swedish record of £200,000, but was soon on his way again. Joined Benfica a year later and proved his worth during the 1989/90 season, when he was the Portuguese League's top scorer with an impressive 33 goals in 32 games.

MAGUIRE, Frank
(Cliftonville, N.Ir)

• Midfield

Equally happy as a wide midfield player or an out-and-out striker. His form has suffered since breaking his leg in 1989/90, but he is now approaching his best form again.

MAHARZI, Ahmed
(Nimes, Fra)

• 08.03.70 • Striker
• France U21

A relative veteran at Nimes, having been with the club for three seasons. Highly skilful forward who loves to take on defenders, using his pace to cause problems.

MAHER, Ciaran
(Athlone Town, Eir)

• 15.11.61 • Midfield

Tenacious midfield battler who covers every inch of the pitch during a game. Formerly with Kilkenny City, he joined the club in August 1990.

MAHUT, Philippe
(Le Havre, Fra)

• 04.03.56 • Defender
• France 9 full caps

Hugely experienced centre-half who's never quite lived up to expectations. Only a handful of international caps - when he was expected to get many, and a string of semi-successful clubs - Troyes, Metz, St Etienne, Matra Racing and Quimper - before making a new start at Le Havre in 1989.

MAI, Udo
(Wattenscheid, Ger)

• 29.07.67 • Goalkeeper

Signed from FC Schweinfurt 05 in 1989.

MAJOR, Philip
(Portadown, N.Ir)

• Defender

Strong in the tackle and constructive going forward, Phil has enjoyed a marked upturn in his fortunes over the past two seasons. Now first choice right back at the club.

MAKANAKY, Cyrille
(Malaga, Spa)
• 28.06.65 •Midfield
• Cameroon full caps

Played in France with Ajaccio, Lens (on loan) and Toulon before joining Malaga in 1990, following appearance in World Cup finals with Cameroon.

MALBASA, Nebosja
(Charleroi, Bel)
• 25.06.59 • Midfield

Yugoslav-born attacking wide-man who grabbed 15 goals in 28 games for Liege during 1990/91 before signing for Charleroi in July 1991. Also formerly with Zmaj, Rijeka NK and Dynamo Zagreb.

MALDINI, Paolo
(Milan, Ita)
• 26.06.68 • Defender
• Italy 37 full caps

Son of Cesare Maldini who captained Milan to European Cup victory in 1963. Left-back who made debut for Milan v Udinese in January 1985 aged 16. His international debut came v Yugoslavia in1988. Played in 1990 World Cup finals.

MALUSCI, Alberto
(Fiorentina, Ita)
• 23.06.72 • Defender

Youngster who has spent all his career with Fiorentina. Originally joined the club in 1989 and made his League debut in Serie A the following season.

MAMPAEY, Kris
(Lierse, Bel)
• 02.11.70 • Goalkeeper

Home grown keeper who has come up through the ranks at the Het Lisp Stadion. Understudy to Patrick Rondags.

MANCINI, Francesco
(Foggia, Ita)
• 10.10.68 • Goalkeeper

Played for his home town side of Matera for three seasons before joining Foggia, via Bisceglie, in 1987.

MANCINI, Osvaldo
(Ascoli, Ita)
• 10.11.69 • Defender

Osvaldo has spent all his career with Ascoli, having first joined the club in 1986. Made his League debut the following season, but did not establish himself as a regular in the side until 1990.

MANCINI, Roberto
(Sampdoria, Ita)

• 27.11.64 • Striker
• Italy 28 full caps, 1 goal

Made his League debut for Bologna as a 17-year-old and was later signed up by Sampdoria for £2m - a record for a teenager. Made his international debut v Canada in May 1986. Regular for country at 1988 European Championships. Unused substitute in 1990 World Cup.

MANDIANGU, Jules
(Eendracht Aalst, Bel)

• 18.03.63 • Striker

Zaire-born attacker who began with Antwerp, where he failed to make the breakthrough to the first team. Signed for Hassetl, and then moved on to Aalst in 1989. Helped the club to Second Division play-off glory in 1990/91.

MANE Manuel
Ferreira Lins
(Farense, Por)

• 16.01.64 • Striker

Only five feet six inches tall, he is the perfect foil to Farense's giant striker Sergio Duarte. Is fast across the ground and has good close control, attributes that have brought him more than a dozen goals since joining the club in 1988/89.

MANGONGA
Makpoloka
(Gil Vicente, Por)

• 03.09.68 • Striker

Zaire born striker who scored five goals in his first season with Gil Vicente.

MANNINI, Moreno
(Sampdoria, Ita)

• 15.08.62 • Defender
• Italy 2 full caps

Right-back who began with home-town club, Imola, before joining Forli and Como. Arrived at Sampdoria in 1984.

MANNION, John
(Sligo Rovers, Eir)

• 29.12.60 • Midfield

Began with his home town side Athlone Town, for whom he made his League of Ireland debut on January 25, 1979, v Dundalk. Also played for Galway United and Shamrock Rovers before joining Sligo in December 1990.

MANOLO
(Atletico Madrid, Spa)

• 17.01.65 • Striker
• Spain 20 full caps, 8 goals

Real name is Manuel Sanchez Delgado. Joined Atletico in 1988 after spells with

Sabadell and Murcia. Has improved enormously since arriving in Madrid and forms a vibrant scoring partnership with Paolo Futre. Was the top scorer in the Spanish League in 1991/92, with 27 goals.

MANOLO
(Espanol, Spa)
• 23.09.70 • Striker

Mauel Baena Porcel is a locally born forward who broke into the Espanol first team during the 1991/92 season.

MARAGOS, Spiros
(Panathinaikos, Gre)
• Midfield
• Greece 11 caps

Ex-Panionios player who joined Panathinaikos in the summer of 1990, and helped guide the club to a League and Cup double the following season. Took his international bow against Portugal in January 1989 (lost 2-1).

MARCATO, Luca
(Ascoli, Ita)
• 08.02.67 • Defender

After a couple of seasons in the lower leagues with Mira and Treviso, Luca got his chance in the Second Division with Piacenza. Remained in Serie B with first Sambenedettese and then Barletta before joining Ascoli in 1990. Helped the club to win promotion to Serie A in his first season.

MARCHEGIANI, Luca
(Torino, Ita)
• 22.02.66 • Goalkeeper

Played for Jesi and Brescia before moving to Torino in 1988. Could not help prevent the club's relegation from Serie A in 1989, but was part of the team that came back up at the first attempt a year later.

MARCHIORO, Fabio
(Juventus, Ita)
• 01.04.68 • Goalkeeper

Made his League debut for his local Third Division side LR Vicenza during the 1988/89 season and made a total of 27 League appearances before transferring to Juventus in the summer of 1991.

MARCICO, Alberto
(Toulouse, Fra)
• 13.05.60 • Midfield
• Argentina full caps

A traditional winger, who loves to run at defenders and whip over dangerous crosses for his strikers. Previously with Ferrocarril Oeste and Rosario in his native Argentina he has settled well at Toulouse since signing in the summer of 1985. With over 60 goals in more than 200 senior games, he is a firm favourite at the club.

MARCO AURELIO Cunha Santos (Uniao, Por)

• 18.02.67 • Defender

Born in Rio de Janeiro in Brazil he signed for Uniao in 1990/91 and has been the ever-present in their defence since then.

MARCOLIN, Dario (Cremonese, Ita)

• 28.10.71 • Midfield

Has spent all his career with Cremonese and made his debut for the club in the Italian First Division while still only a teenager.

MARCO Paulo Pinheiro Sousa (Farense, Por)

• 01.11.67 • Defender

A capable but inconsistent player who has yet to make his mark in the senior league. Has made only a handful of appearances in his five years with Farense.

MAREGGINI, Gian Matteo (Fiorentina, Ita)

• 08.01.67 • Goalkeeper

Began his career with Fiorentina, but had to learn his trade in the Third Division with Rondinella, Lucchese and Carrarese originally. Returned to Florence in 1990 and stepped straight into the Fiorentina side as first choice keeper.

MARIO BARRETO (Beira-Mar, Por)

• 20.06.59 • Defender

Angolan born player who first played his football with the Imortal club. Joined Beira-Mar prior to the start of the 1990/91 season.

MARLON Romel Brandao (Boavista, Por)

• 01.09.63 • Striker

Brazilian born forward who began his career in Portugal with Sporting Lisbon in 1986. Spent the 1988/89 season with Amadora, before rejoining Sporting and then eventually moving to Boavista in 1990.

MAROCCHI, Giancarlo (Juventus, Ita)

• 04.07.65 • Midfield
• Italy 11 full caps

Experienced player who began his career with Bologna and made over 170 appearances for the club before moving on to Juventus.

MARQUEZ Lopez, Bartolome
(Figueres, Spa)
• 07.01.62 • Midfield

Joined Figueres from Espanol in 1988.

MARRAUD, David
(Nantes, Fra)
• 03.08.64 • Goalkeeper

Former INF Vichy number one who has been at La Beaujoire since 1985. Now approaching 200 senior games since his First Division debut, v Bastia, in November 1985.

MARTIN, Eric
(Nancy, Fra)
• 29.08.59 • Midfield
• France U21

Experienced left sided midfielder who re-joined the club from Paris St Germain in June 1989. He had begun his career with Nancy, making his debut against Metz, in August 1979.

MARTINI, Bruno
(Auxerre, Fra)
• 25.1.62 • Goalkeeper
• France 15 full caps

Joined Auxerre straight from school in 1981. Made his League debut while on loan at Nancy (v Laval, 21.9.83) - the only other club he has represented. France's first choice goalkeeper he missed a chunk of 1991/92 with a leg injury.

MARTINKENAS, Valdemaras
(Dynamo Kiev, UKR)
• Goalkeeper
• Lithuania full caps

Signed from Zhalgiris Vilnius during the 1991 season.

MARTIN VAZQUEZ, Rafael
(Torino, Ita)
• 25.09.65 • Midfield
• Spain 29 full caps

Promoted to the Real Madrid first team squad from nursery side Castilla in 1983 and became a very importanmt member of the side. Spent seven seasons with the Spanish giants before leaving his homeland for Torino in 1990.

MASNOV Margarit, Jordi
(Espanol, Spa)
• 20.02.71 • Midfield

Youngster who broke into the Espanol first team during the 1991/92 season.

MASSA, Claude
(Metz, Fra)

• 06.03.62 • Midfield

Born in Nice, he joined his home town club straight from school and made his First Divsion debut against Laval on 16th July 1985. Joined Metz in July 1991.

MASSAGIE, Carl
(Beveren, Bel)

• 06.03.65 • Defender

Beveren discovered him playing local football, and signed him straight from school in 1981. Had spells with Sint-Niklaas and Mechelen before returning to his first club.

MASSARO, Daniele
(Milan, Ita)

• 23.05.61 • Striker

Began career with Monza and then spent 5 years with Fiorentina before joining Milan in 1986. Loaned to Roma in 1988.

MASSON, Guillaume
(Lyon, Fra)

• 16.02.69 • Midfield

Reserve central midfielder who was previously with Montceau and Annecy. Joined the club in 1989 and made his senior bow v Cannet on 28th July 1990.

MATEUT, Dorin
(Zaragoza, Spa)

• 03.01.65 • Midfield
• Romania 53 full caps, 9 goals

Played for his country in the 1990 World Cup finals and signed by Zaragoza from Dinamo Bucharest after the tournament.

MATHIESON, Andy
(Glentoran, N.Ir)

• Midfield

Tireless performer who's never-say-die attitude makes him a great favourite at The Oval. Another player to find his shooting boots for the club during the glorious 1991/92 season. His goals and non-stop running in midfield were a major factor in Glentoran's comfortable Championship win.

MATHIJSSEN, Jacky
(Genk, Bel)

20.07.63 • Goalkeeper

First choice 'keeper who signed from Charleroi. Previously with Winterslag. Has played nearly 200 senior games.

MATIAS Manuel Amadeu Matos
(Vitoria Guimaraes, Por)

• 18.03.64 • Defender

Started his career with Porto but never made the first team and was transferred to Salgueiros in 1983. Spent five seasons there before moving to Uniao. Joined Vitoria for the 1901/92 season.

MATRISCIANO, Sylvian (Nancy, Fra)

• 06.07.63 • Goalkeeper

Formerly with Besancon and Lille. Short for a 'keeper (1.76m) he made his debut (v Auxerre) shortly after joining the club in August 1986.

MATTEOLI, Gianfranco (Cagliari, Ita)

• 21.04.59 • Defender

Very experienced player who joined Como from Cantu in 1976. After a couple of seasosn with Osimana and Reggiana he joined Sampdoria in 1986. A year later he moved on to Internazionale and stayed in Milan for four years before being signed by Cagliari in 1990.

MATTHAUS, Lothar (Internazionale, Ita)

• 21.03.61 • Midfield
• Germany 85 full caps, 23 goals

Started his career with Borussia Moenchengladbach. Finalist in German Cup 1984, later signing for winners

Bayern Munich for German record fee of £650,000. Signed by Inter for £2.4m in 1988. Won Italian League 1989, World Cup 1990 and UEFA Cup 1991. Ruptured knee ligaments while playing for Internazionale against Parma in April 1992, and is expected to be out of action until 1993. His driving force was sorely missed during the 1992 European Championship in Sweden. Was voted European and World Player of the Year after guiding West Germany to the 1990 World Cup with his inspirational leadership.

MATYSIK, Waldemar (SV Hamburg, Ger)

• 27.09.61 • Midfield
• Poland full caps

Signed from Auxerre in 1990. Previously with Gornik Zabrze.

MAUFROY, Marc (Lens, Fra)

• 16.02.70 • Striker

Signed from junior club JB Gauchy in 1985. Made his First Division debut in August 1988, against Sochaux.

di MAURO, Fabrizio (Roma, Ita)

• 18.06.65 • Midfield

First joined Roma in 1983 but failed to break into the first team. Spent three seasons with Arezzo in Serie B and one with Avellino in Serie A before rejoining Roma in 1988.

MAURO, Massimo
(Napoli, Ita)
• 24.05.62 • Midfield

Given his chance in Serie A by his home-town club Catanzaro during the 1979/80 season. Moved onto Udinese in 1982 and then Juventus in 1985. A big money transfer saw him move south to Napoli in 1989.

MAUROO, Bart
(Waregem, Bel)
• 08.04.68 • Defender

Fierce tackling defender who likes to get forward down the flanks and help out his attack. Signed from KVC Deerlijk Sport.

MAVRIDIS, Kostas
(Panathinaikos, Gre)
• Defender
• Greece 29 full caps

Left back who loves to get forward. His raiding displays helped the club to the 1990/91 League and Cup double. Former national captain.

MAX, Martin
(Borussia M'gladbach, Ger)
• 07.08.68 • Striker

Joined Gladbach from FC Recklinghausen in 1989.

MAYER, Andreas
(Bayern Munich, Ger)
• 13.09.72 • Midfield

Amateur signed from FC Augsburg in summer 1991.

MAZHEIKIS, Romas
(FC Krems, Aus)
• 28.04.64 • Defender
• USSR U21/Lithuania Full caps

Made his debut for Zhalgiris Vilnius in 1982 and made over 150 appearances in the Soviet Premier League before Lithuanian independence. Also played three games for the USSR U21 side. Signed by Krems during the 1991/92 season winter break.

MAZINHO II
(Bayern Munich, Ger)
• 26.12.65 • Midfield
• Brazil full

His real name is Waidemar Aureliano de Oliveira. Signed from Braganpino for £1.2m in August 1991, following the South American Championship in Chile.

MAZZOLINI, Stephane
(Auxerre, Fra)
• 28.11.86 • Defender

Another quality player to emerge off the production line at Abbe-Deschamps. Right back who made his debut v Matra in 1987.

McBREARTY, Joe
(Omagh Town, N.Ir)
• Goalkeeper

Proving that reaching 40 doesn't mean the end of your career, Joe's just finished his first season with Omagh. A salesman by profession. Formerly with Derry City and Sligo Rovers.

McBRIDE, Stephen
(Glenavon, N.Ir)
• Striker
• N.Ireland 2 full caps

Joined from Linfield in October 1985. Formerly with Motherwell. International debut v Denmark in October 1990. Scored a staggering 49 goals in 63 games in 1990/91. Regularly the Irish League's top scorer.

McCABE, Gerry
(Cork City, Eir)
• Striker

Scored on his debut for Cork (v Waterford, 18.08.91, League Cup). Formerly with Hibernian, Clyde, Clydebank and Hamilton Accies. Also spent several spells in Canada with Windsor Star, Toronto Italia and Victoria Vistas.

McCAFFREY, Conor
(Glentoran, N.Ir)
• Defender

Son of former Glentoran favourite Gerry McCaffrey. Attacking full back who's first team appearances have been limited in the last two seasons owing to the signing of Seamus Heath.

McCANN, Alan
(Glenavon, N.Ir)
• Defender

Committed Christian who combines playing for Glenavon with training, at Trinity College, to enter the Church of Ireland Ministry. A serious leg injury caused him to miss the whole 1989/90 season, after joining from Portadown in November. 1988. He recovered to play a huge part in the success of the next two seasons.

McCARROLL, Bryan (Ards, N.Ir)

• Striker

Civil Servant who will be celebrating his fourth season in senior soccer in 1992/93. Has been in and out of the side in that time, but three goals in five starts in 1990/91 certainly helped to press his claims for a regular first team spot. Previously with minor League sides Sirocco and Cromac.

McCARTAN, Paul (Distillery, N.Ir)

• Striker

Speedy front-man who is the 'Mr 100%' of the Distillery side. Formerly with Newry Town.

McCARTHY, Tony (Derry City, Eir)

• Defender

Signed for the club from UCD in July 1990. Solid and uncompromising defender.

McCARTNEY, Gary (Bangor, N.Ir)

• 15.08.60 • Midfield

Has been with the club since July 1989, but has only really made his presence felt in the last two seasons. Formerly with Liverpool, where he failed to make the breakthrough. He signed from Linfield.

McCAUL, Dermot (Omagh Town, N.Ir)

• Defender

Signed from Derry City, Dermot is one of a string of players to have signed for Omagh in the last two years. Strong in the air.

McCLOSKEY, Jim (Bangor, N.Ir)

• 14.12.71 • Midfield

Fine young player who began with Bangor's Colts team, before moving to England with Colchester United. A severe bout of homesickness saw him return to Bangor, though, and he's become a firm favourite at Clandeboye Park. Won the 1991/92 Lombard Ulster Cup with Bangor.

McCOLGAN, Declan (Omagh Town, N.Ir)

• Defender

Signed from Strabane, he has now completed four seasons with Omagh, scoring one goal in more than 70 games. A factory machinist by profession.

McCONKEY, Harry (Ballymena United, N.Ir)

• Midfield

A tireless worker in midfield whose strong takling and determination make him a firm favourite. He signed from Ballyclare Comrades in 1991.

McCONNELL, Graeme (Larne, N.Ir)

• Goalkeeper

Was ever-present during 1991/92, and his form between the sticks enabled Larne to complete their most successful season ever, by finishing fourth in the League.

McCONNELL, John (Linfield, N.Ir)

• Defender

Recruited by the Belfast blues from local junior soccer in 1990. Strongly built and reliable he broke into the first team during 1991/92.

McCONVILLE, Ffullan (Glenavon, N.Ir)

• Midfield

Counts N.Ireland manager Billy Bingham among his many admirers. Skilful and strong in the tackle he spent ten months with New Zealand club Napier City before returning to Glenavon in 1991. Has the unusual profession of warp-knitter.

McCORMICK, Gary (Linfield, N.Ir)

• Midfield

A long-throw expert who never stops running. A fringe player at Windsor Park, he was signed from Ballyclare Comrades.

McCOURT, Harry (Omagh Town, N.Ir)

• Striker

Trainee solicitor who has proved a thorn in the side of Irish League defender. Averaged a goal every other game with Omagh to the end of 1991/92. Formerly with Tobermore, Portadown and Limavady.

McCOURT, Thomas (Larne, N.Ir)

• Striker

Widely regarded as one of the quickest players in Ireland, he was Larne's leading scorer in 1991/92. Despite a lean spell through January and February he still recorded more than 20 strikes during the campaign, and his goals carried the club to an historic fourth spot in the League - their best ever finish to a season. Known as 'Tucker' to the Inver Court fans.

McCOY, Raymond
(Glenavon, N.Ir)

• Striker
• N.Ireland 1 full cap

Voted Ulster's 'Young Player of the Year' in 1987, he won his first cap v Yugoslavia in 1987. Joined from Coleraine in November 1990 for an Irish League record £32,000.

McCRACKEN, Tommy
(Distillery, N.Ir)

• Defender

Regarded as one of the Irish League's top defenders, Tommy was the subject of a £15,000 bid from Glenavon last season. Experienced player who's been with Distillery for several years.

McCREADIE, Barry
(Bangor, N.Ir)

• 20.10.61 • Striker
• Irish League Representative

Known as 'Big Mac', he has a very delicate touch for a target man. He holds the unique distinction of scoring Derry City's first ever goal on their return to senior football in the League of Ireland. Created a post-war record for Bangor when he scored in each of the first six games of 1990/91. Scored 10 goals in 24 League appearances during 1991/92, as well as helping the club to their Lombard Ulster Cup win.

McCREADIE, Chris
(Cliftonville,N.Ir)

• Defender

Widely regarded as the top player in Irish junior football until he signed pro with Cliftonville in May 1992. From Limavady United.

McCREADIE, Roy
(Omagh Town, N.Ir)

• Midfield

Born in Nottingham, this postman was appointed player/manager at Omagh at the beginning of 1991/92. Formerly with Portadown and Coleraine, he's a powerful midfielder who likes to get forward.

McCRYSTAL, Gavin
(Larne, N.Ir)

• Striker

Youngster who enjoyed his first season with the club in 1991/92, and chipped in with five goals as Larne went on to finish fourth in the Irish League - their best ever finish to a League campaign.

McCULLOUGH, Dean
(Glenavon, N.Ir)

• Defender

Returned to Glenavon in 1990 after three year absence with Coleraine and

Carrick Rangers. Experienced defender who's equally at home out wide or in the centre back slot.

McDERMOTT, Paul (Shelbourne, Eir)

• 07.07.71 • Midfield

Young midfielder who loves to score goals. Began with Shelbourne, where he broke into the senior set up in season 1990/91. Spent a period on loan at Limerick City later that same campaign.

McDONALD, Robert (Crusaders, N.Ir)

• Midfield

Slightly-built playmaker who is known as 'Jimmy Bean' to all at Seaview. Joined the club from local amateurs Grove United in June 1990, and scored the winner in the 1991/92 County Antrim Shield final.

McDONALD, Tom (Ards, N.Ir)

• Midfield

One of three ex-Larne players - the other two are Ian Bustard and Bryan McLoughlin - to have been re-united with ex-boss Paul Malone at Castlereagh Park. A postman by profession, he was also previously with Distillery.

McDONNELL, John (St Patrick's Athletic, Eir)

• 26.03.65 • Defender

Signed from Drogheda United.

McDONNELL, Martin (Sligo Rovers, Eir)

• 08.05.62 • Defender

Belfast-born player who moved down from the North with Galway United. Sligo Rovers snapped him up prior to the 1990/91 season. Strong defender who likes to come forward.

McEVOY, Ricky (Dundalk, Eir)

• 6.8.67 • Midfield

Born in Gibraltar, Ricky started his career with Luton Town (Eng) before moving to Shamrock Rovers in 1988. Ended Dundalk's long Euro-drought by scoring in 1-1 draw with Honved (Champions' Cup, September '91).

McEVOY, Ricky (Shamrock Rovers, Eir)

• 06.08.67 • Midfield

Born in Gibraltar, he began with Luton Town but failed to make the grade at Kenilworth Road and moved to Ireland with the Rovers in the summer of 1988. His League debut came v Dundalk on September 11, 1988 (lost 2-1). He spent part of the 1990/91 season on loan at Finn Harps.

McEWAN, James
(Distillery, N.Ir)

• Midfield

Tough tackling midfielder who returned to the first team after missing much of 1990/91 with a serious leg injury. The 'engine' in the Distillery machine.

McFADDEN, Jim
(Cliftonville, N.Ir)

• Midfield

Pacey wide man who is liable to chip in with important goals from the wing. Loves to take defenders on and use his speed to get into the area.

McGAUGHEY, Martin
(Linfield, N.Ir)

• Striker
• N.Ireland 1 full cap; Irish League Representative

One of the most prolific strikers in Irish League history, McGaughey has scored more than 300 goals in 450 plus games for the Blues. He represented his country v Israel in 1984 and in the same season was runner-up in the European Golden Boot competition. Has won every honour Irish football has to offer.

McGEE, Paul
(Sligo Rovers, Eir)

• 19.06.54 • Striker

Hugely experienced forward, who has been playing at the top level in Ireland for more than 20 years. Began with home town club Sligo Rovers, making his debut v Finn Harps way back in November 1970. He also had spells with Galway United and Derry City, before returning to his roots with Sligo in November 1990.

McGUINNESS, Ray
(Bangor, N.Ir)

• 26.04.64 • Defender

Much travelled central defender who's career has also taken in Finn Harps, Portadown and Derry City. He joined Bangor at the tail end of 1991/92, but had to sit out the remiander of the season as he was still serving a six match suspension.

McINALLY, Alan
(Bayern Munich, Ger)

• 10.02.63 • Striker
• Scotland 8 full; 3 goals

Nicknamed 'Rambo'. Began career with Ayr United and Celtic in Scotland, before moving to Aston Villa of England for £225,000 in July 1987. Signed by Bayern in 1989 for £1.1 million.

McINTYRE, Declan
(Galway United, Eir)

• 28.04.60 • Goalkeeper

Was first choice 'keeper ahead of Eire No 1 Packie Bonner (Celtic) while playing for Donegal Schools. Formerly with Sligo Rovers, Finn Harps and Derry City, before moving to Terryland Park in August 1989.

McKEEVER, Anthony
(Bray Wanderers, Eir)

• 13.02.63 • Defender

Known as Bo to the Carlisle Ground faithful. Made his League of Ireland debut against Longford Town on 21st October 1985 (lost 1-0), and played a big part in the club's promotion to the Premier League at the end of season 1990/91.

McKEEVER, Kevin
(Portadown, N.Ir)

• Defender

Versatile performer who has played right across the back four and in midfield for the club. Likes to get forward and help out his attackers.

McKEOWN, Kevin
(Crusaders, N.Ir)

• 12.10.67 • Goalkeeper
• Scotland Youth; U19

Began with Scottish Second Division side Stenhousemuir, where he played 17 games before transfering to Motherwell. Spent three years at Fir Park, and made just three first team appearances. First joined Crusaders in March 1989, on loan, and made the move permanent in December 1990. Is an inspiration in goal for the Crues.

McKEOWN, Michael
(Glenavon, N.Ir)

• Defender

Recently signed a new three-year contract with the club, keeping him at Glenavon until 1994. Usually a full back, but equally comfortable in central defence.

McLAUGHLIN, Paul
(Drogheda United, Eir)

• 08.08.65 • Defender

Birmingham-born player who has played all his senior football in Ireland. Hard working, he is equally happy playing in the centre of defence or midfield.

McLEOD, Duncan
(Cliftonville, N.Ir)

• Striker

Former Linfield player who signed for the club in the summer of 1990/91. Failed to live up to expectations in his first couple of seasons, with only a handful of goals.

McLOUGHLIN, Bryan (Ards, N.Ir)

• Midfield

A technical foreman with Northern Telecom by profession, he joined the club prior to the 1990/91 campaign. Previously with Bangor, Crusaders, Larne and Glenavon.

McNAMEE, Damien (Larne, N.Ir)

• Midfield

Attacking midfielder who can fill in up front if necessary. Signed from Limavady United at the beginning of the 1990/91 season his hard work and strong tackling in the midfield proved vital in the club's historic 1991/92 campaign.

McNEILL, Willie (Ballymena United, N.Ir)

• Striker

Formerly with B Division club Ballymoney United, he joined Ballymena in the summer of 1992.

McNULTY, Tom (Dundalk, Eir)

• 23.3.62 • Midfield

Scottish-born attacking midfielder in his second spell with the club after re-signing from Finn Harps in September 1989. Scored on his League of Ireland debut, v Cork City (16th September 1984). Knack of scoring important goals, including the one that clinched 1990/91 League title. Injured for much of 1991/92.

di MECO, Eric (Marseille, Fra)

• 07.09.63 • Defender
• France 6 full caps

Currently in his second spell at Olympique Marseille, having begun his career at the Velodrome back in 1980. His First Divsion debut came in August 1984, v Sochaux. Had spells with Nancy and Martigues before returning to his first club.

MEDVED, Dirk (Gent, Bel)

• 15.09.68 • Defender

Tough tackling defender who signed from Genk in 1990. Previously with Zwartberg. Solid and reliable he is a great favourite with the fans at Ottenstadion.

MEEUWS, Jimmy (Genk, Bel)

• 28.04.71 • Defender

Fine prospect of a full back who was snapped up from local side Overpelt in

June 1990. Came into the side during the 1990/91 season and has remianed a regular choice.

MEGE, Fabrice (St Etienne, Fra)

• 06.06.85 • Midfield
• France U21

The playmaker and lynch-pin of the side. Two-footed player who made his debut, for Nice v Bordeaux, back in July 1985. Has enjoyed two spells at both first club Nice, and Monaco, and also a brief period at Strasbourg. Joined St Etienne in June 1991 and his midfield prompting helped the club consolidate their mid-table position. Joint top scorer, with five goals, in the 1991/92 League campaign.

MEHMET, Ozdilek (Besiktas, Tur)

• 01.04.66 • Midfield
• Turkey 11 full caps

Can operate either as a winger, central midfielder or out-and-out striker. Especially dangerous at dead-ball situations, where his accurate crossing can create problems. The majority of his international appearances have been as substitute. He was Turkey's Player of the Year for 1990/91, and his playmaking ability makes him a fine prospect.

MEIER, Norbert (Borussia M'gladbach, Ger)

• 20.09.58 • Midfield
• West Germany 16 full caps

Formerly with St Pauli, Norbert was signed by Gladbach from Werder Bremen in 1989.

MEIER, Urs (Grasshoppers, Swi)

• 07.07.61 • Defender

Full back who joined Grasshoppers from SC Zug in 1983.

MELLI, Alessandro (Parma, Ita)

• 11.12.69 • Striker

First played for Parma when they were a Third Division side during the 1985/86 season. Had a brief spell with Modena in 1988, before returning to Parma and eventually helping them to reach Serie A in 1990.

MEL Perez, Jose (Betis, Spa)

• 28.02.63 • Striker

Formerley with Osasuna and Castellon, he joined Betis in 1990.

MELENDEZ Latorre, Carlos
(Espanol, Spa)

• 26.01.57 • Goalkeeper

Like Espanol's first choice keeper Biurrun, he joined the club from Atletico Bilbao.Now in his seventh season with the side although most of it has been spent in the reserves.

MELZIG, Jens
(Dynamo Dresden, Ger)

• 28.09.65 • Defender

When Dresden joined the newly united German League in season 1991/92 they needed to boost their squad quickly and cheaply. Jens, signed from Energie Cottbus, was one such acquisition.

MENDIONDO, Cesar Gonzalez Lopez
(Espanol, Spa)

• 25.06.66 • Defender
• Spain U21

Full back signed from Rayo Vallecano. Established himself as a regular in the Espanol side during the 1991/92 season.

MENDY, Roger
(Monaco, Fra)

• 08.02.60 • Defender
• Senegal full caps

One of the real characters of French football, this French-Senegalese stopper was one of the mainstays of the side that were League runners-up to Marseille in both 1990/91 and 1991/92. Dangerous in the air at free kicks and corners, he likes to get forward and chips in with some important goals. Formerly with Jeanne d'Arc Dakar and Toulon. Joined the club in 1989.

MENTXAKA Lorente, Juan Antonio
(Real Sociedad, Spa)

• 03.01.63 • Midfield

Superb passer of the ball who joined Sociedad from Espanol in 1990. Missed most of the 1991/92 season after falling out with manager John Toshack.

MENZO, Stanley
(Ajax, Hol)

• 15.10.63 • Goalkeeper
• Holland 3 full caps

Made just nine League appearances for Haarlem before being signed by Ajax. Has since made over 250 appearances for the Amsterdam club. Unpredictable 'keeper who is currently training to be a commercial pilot.Helped Ajax to win the 1991/92 UEFA Cup.

MERGAN, Hans
(Kortrijk, Bel)

• 29.01.66 • Midfield

Never-say-die midfielder who's fierce tackling made him a great favourite at previous club Molenbeek. Signed in June 1991. Began with SV Asse.

MERNAGH, Noel
(Galway United, Eir)
• 11.12.63 • Midfield

Slightly built local-boy who signed from West United in 1983.

MERTENS, Marc
(Lierse, Bel)
• 27.09.60 • Midfield

Great favourite with the fans at Het Lisp Stadion. He returned to the club for 1991/92 after a season spent on loan with Waregem. Tough-tackling midfielder who has now played more than 300 senior games. Lierse is his only full time club.

MESZAROS, Ferenc
(Lokeren, Bel)
• 01.08.63 • Striker
• Hungary 21 full caps

Prolific forward who signed from top Hungarian club Pecsi Muncas in 1987. The 1990/91 season was his best to date, when he grabbed 11 goals in 27 starts. Excellent close- control and a ferocious shot make him a real menace for defenders.

METGOD, Johnny
(Feyenoord, Hol)
• 27.02.58 • Midfield
• Holland 21 full caps

Began with Haarlem and later joined AZ Alkmaar. As libero helped club to Dutch title and UEFA Cup final in 1981. Moved on to Real Madrid in 1982. Joined Nottingham Forest in 1984 and sold to Tottenham for £250,000 in July 1987. Returned to Holland with Feyenoord. Captained the club to 1991 Dutch Cup victory.

METIN, Tekin
(Besiktas, Tur)
• 08.05.65 • Midfield
• Turkey 33 full caps, 2 goals

Equally happy playing as a wide midfielder or out-and-out forward. He began with Kocaelispor, before moving to Besiktas in December 1982. Has played a vital part as the club have made the League title their personal property over the past three seasons. Inspired them to a record 10-0 League victory over Adanaspor in 1989, scoring a hat-trick himself, as well as tearing the Adanaspor defence apart at will. He made his national debut in January 1983, while still only 19-years-old.

METZ, Gunther
(Karlsruher, Ger)
• 08.08.67 • Defender

Moved to Karlsruher from Kaiserslautern in 1987 and has now made well over 100 First Division appearances.

MICCICHE, Carmelo (Nancy, Fra)

• 16.08.63 • Striker
• France 2 full caps

Much-travelled striker, who played for Metz (twice), Quimper, Sarreguesmines, Marseille and Cannes. Played under current coach Marcel Husson at Metz, before following him to Nancy in 1991. Husson describes him as "fantastic - like Cantona without the problems". Made his debut, for Metz v Strasbourg, on 21st August 1984. Scored one goal during the 1991/92 League campaign.

MICHEL (Real Madrid, Spa)

• 23.03.63 • Midfield
• Spain youth, U18, U21, 61 full caps, 19 goals

Real name is Jose Miguel Gonzalez Martin del Campo. Superb passer of the ball who has spent all his career with Real and helped them to win the 1985 UEFA Cup. European U21 Champs finalist with Spain in 1984. Made senior debut v Austria November 1985. Played in 1986 and 1990 World Cup finals.

MIHAJLOVIC, Radmilo (Schalke, Ger)

• 19.11.64 • Striker
• Yugoslavia 6 full caps

Played for Sarajevo and Zagreb before being bought to Germany by Bayern Munich. Signed by Schalke in 1990.

MIHTARSKY, Petre (Porto, Por)

• 15.07.66 • Striker
• Bulgaria full caps

Followed fellow Bulgarian international striker Kostadinov to Porto when he joined the club from Levski Sofia prior to the start of the 1991/92 season.

MILD, Hakan (Gothenburg, Swe)

• 14.06.71 • Midfield
• Sweden 4 full caps, 1 goal; Olympic; U21; Youth

Originally joined Gothenburg Trollhatans youth club in 1990. Won youth, U21 and Olympic caps before making full debut v Denmark, June 1990. Very talented midfielder who was watched by scouts from all over Europe in 1991/92.

MILDE, Rocco
(Bochum, Ger)

• 08.06.69 • Striker

After playing for TSG Meissen and then Dynamo Dresden in Eastern Germany, Rocco was lured to the West by Bochum in 1989.

MILLA, Luis
(Real Madrid, Spa)

• 12.03.66 • Midfield
• Spain 3 full caps

Signed from Barcelona in July 1990.

MILL, Frank
(Borussia Dortmund, Ger)

• 23.07.58 • Striker
• Germany 17 full caps

Started his career with Rot-Weiss Essen before moving onto Borussia Moenchengladbach. Signed by Dortmund in 1986 and has now scored more than 100 First Division goals during his career.

MILLS, David
(Portadown, N.Ir)

• Midfield

Former Glentoran player who is the engine-room of the club's midfield. His all-action style resulted in him missing much of the early part of 1991/92 with an ankle injury.

MILOSEVIC, Cvijan
(RC Liege, Bel)

• 27.10.63 • Midfield
• Yugoslavia 2 full caps; U21

Signed from home country club Sloboda Tulsa in 1989 he has proved very adept as playmaker of the side, and helped them to the 1990 Belgian Cup. More than 50 senior games under his belt.

MILOVAC, Stevan
(Salgueiros, Por)

• 25.02.62 • Defender

Belgrade born defender who was bought to Salgueiros, along with fellow Slavs Djoincevic and Nikoloic, by the club Yugoslavian coach Zoran Filipovic.

MINO
(Espanol, Spa)

• 29.01.63 • Defender
• Spain U21

Real name is Bernardino Serrano Mori. A commanding central defender who was formerly with Seville.

MINOTTI, Lorenzo
(Parma, Ita)

• 08.02.67 • Defender

Libero who joined his local club Cesena as a teenager and made his League debut during the 1986/87 season. Moved to Parma in 1987 and helped the club into Serie A three years later. Skippered the side to their 1992 Italian cup victory over Juventus.

MIRANDA, Antonio Isaias Carvalho (Beira-Mar, Por)

• 20.08.64 • Midfield

Began his career with Varzim, his home town team, and made 80 First Division appearances for the club before joining Benfica in 1988. Moved on to Chaves after just one year and then joined Amadora in 1990. Joined Beira-Mar the following season.

MITCHELL, Noel (Ards, N.Ir)

• Defender

Manager Paul Malone has described him as the Irish League "find of the season". Signed from local parks side Coagh United, he celebrated his first month in senior soccer by being named "Guinness Player of the Month" in 1990/91. At 6ft 2in he is a commanding figure in the centre of the Ards defence.

MITO (Beira-Mar, Por)

• 26.09.65 • Midfield

Manuel Anselmo Simoes was born in Angola and began his career with Besteiros. Made his First Division debut with Porto during the 1984/85 season, but moved on to Academica the following term. Joined Beira-Mar in 1990.

MOISES Rodriguez Carrion (Zaragoza, Spa)

• 27.04.61 • Striker
• Spain U21

Tall and experienced striker originally from Seville. Joined Zaragoza from Castellon when they were relegated in 1991.

van MOL, Tom (PSV Eindhoven, Hol)

• 12.10.72 • Midfield

Belgian-born midfielder who spent eight years with Anderlecht in his home country before signing for PSV in 1990.

MöLLER, Andreas (Eintracht Frankfurt, Ger)

• 02.09.67 • Midfield
• Germany 24 caps, 4 goals

Exceptionally talented midfielder who has now become an established part of the German national side. Began his career with Frankfurt but was then sold to

Borussia Dortmund. Returned to Frankfurt in 1990, but is almost certain to start the 1992/93 season in Italy with Juventus.

MÖLLER, Andreas
(Schalke, Ger)

• 13.12.62 • Defender

Signed from Hannover 96 in 1988. Previously with VfB Stuttgart.

MOLLER, Frank
(Eintracht Frankfurt, Ger)

• 11.07.67 • Midfield

Began his career with Alemannia Laubenheim and then moved on to FSV Mainz in 1989. Signed by Eintracht during the 1992 mid-season winter break.

MOMMENS, Raymond
(Charleroi, Bel)

• 27.12.58 • Midfield
• Belgium 18 full caps

Solid force in the centre of midfield for Charleroi, who is approaching his 500th game in Belgian First Divsion football. Signed from Lokeren he was previously with SK Lebbeke.

MÖNCH, Marcus
(Bayern Munich, Ger)

• 07.09.72 • Midfield
• Germany Youth

Joined Bayern from top Bavarian youth club, SV Sandhausen in 1989. Capped 22 times at youth level.

MONCHU
(Sporting Gijon, Spa)

• 28.11.68 • Striker

Locally born target man who has forged a useful striking partnership at Gijon with the Czechoslovakian, Luhovy.

MONOS, Tamas
(RC Liege, Bel)

• 03.01.68 • Defender
• Hungary 14 full caps

Began his career with Hungarian First Division side Veszpremi, before moving to Belgium with Germinal Ekeren at the beginning of 1990/91. After 21 games (7 as sub) with Ekeren he signed for Liege at the beginning of season 1991/92.

MONTANIER, Philippe
(Caen, Fra)

• 15.11.64 • Goalkeeper

So highly do Caen rate their new 'keeper that they immediately gave him a five year contract on signing in 1991. Began with minor League club Evreux, and made his Division One debut, for Caen, at Toulon in February 1989. After a brief spell at Nantes, he returned to Caen in July 1991.

MOODY, Mick (St Patrick's Athletic, Eir)

• 24.02.66 • Midfield

Forceful, hard-running midfield man who was snapped up from Drogheda United.

MOORE, Terry (Glentoran, N.Ir)

• Defender
• Canada full caps

Club captain who lead the side to their runaway League success in 1991/92, when they won the title by 12 clear points. Currently in his third spell with the club, he has recently signed a new, long-term contract at The Oval.

MORAN, Joseph (Bray Wanderers, Eir)

• 08.09.60 • Goalkeeper

Known as Josh to the Carlisle Ground faithful, he was signed from Limerick City. His form between the sticks was a major reason behind Wanderers' tremendous defensive record when they won promotion to the Premier Division in 1990/91.

MORAVCIK, Lubomir (St Etienne, Fra)

• 22.06.65 • Midfield

Signed from little known Czechoslovakian club Plastika Nitra in the summer of 1990, his debut in the French First Division came against Rennes on 21st July 1990. Proved himself a good find, scoring seven times in 37 games in his first season.

MORDT, Per Edmund (Gothenburg, Swe)

• 25.03.65 • Midfield
• Norway 23 full caps, U21, Youth

Began his career as a left-back with Norweigan club Valerengen, but then bought to Sweden by Gothenburg in 1985 and converted into midfielder. Missed the decisive penalty in the 1985 Champions' Cup Semi-final shoot-out against Barcelona.

MOREAU, Thierry (Le Havre, Fra)

• 17.01.67 • Midfield

Home-grown, right-sided player who joined the club as a schoolboy, signing pro on his 18th birthday in 1985. Scored four League goals during the 1991/92 campaign.

MOREIRA DE SA Manuel Arnaldo (Vitoria Guimaraes, Por)

• 03.02.66 • Striker

Was on Porto's books for a while but couldn't break into the team. Something of a nomad in the Portuguese League, spending a seasons each with Rio Ave, Leixoes, Maritimo and Penafiel, since 1986/87. Joined Vitoria for the 1991/92 season.

MORGADO, Maria Jorge Castro (Porto, Por)

• 31.12.69 • Defender

MORLEY, Pat (Cork City, Eir)

• 18.05.65 • Striker

Signed from Sunshine George Cross (Australia). Voted PFA Player of the Year in 1990/91, when he also set new club record, scoring 15 League goals in a season. Previously with Waterford United (twice) and Limerick City.

MORONI, Paulo Ricardo (Sporting Braga, Por)

• 29.08.61 • Defender

Brazilian born defender who moved to Portugal and joined Sporting Braga in 1987. Has spent all of his time in Portugal with the club.

MURRAY, Robert (Bray Wanderers, Eir)

• 02.04.66 • Goalkeeper

Signed from local boys' club St Joseph's Boys as cover for Josh Moran. He played six games during the 1990/91 promotion season.

MORRIS-BURKE, Johnny (Galway United, Eir)

• 06.12.66 • Defender

Versatile player equally at home in defence or midfield. Born in Newport Pagnell in England. Joined club from Athlone Town in August 1990 and previously with Longford Town and Temple Villa. Likes to get forward, particularly down the right flank.

MORRISON, Allen (Ards, N.Ir)

• Defender

Utility man, who is equally happy performing in central midfield or defence. A shipping manager by profession, he is a ferocious tackler.

Signed from Coleraine, he was also previously on the books at Ballyclare Comrades and Bangor.

MORRISON, Martin (Athlone Town, Eir)

• 27.11.61 • Midfield

Joined in June 1988 from St Pat's Athletic - a valuable breeding ground for Athlone. Strong tackler who likes to get forward, particularly at dead-ball situations.

MORRISON, Raymond (Glentoran, N.Ir)

• Midfield

Hard tackling midfielder who enjoyed his testimonial year with the club in 1991/92 and celebrated by scoring 12 goals as the club raced to the League title. Known as 'Nuts' to the Oval faithful he missed a chunk of the season through injury, and then suspension, before returning in the drive for the Championship. Was voted the Irish League's Player of the Year for 1991/92.

MOSER, Hans-Werner (Wattenscheid, Ger)

• 24.09.65 • Defender

Signed from Hamburger SV in 1990.

MOSTOVOI, Alexander (Benfica, Por)

• 22.08.68 • Midfield
• CIS/USSR Olympic, 13 full caps, 3 goals

Moscow-born midfielder who joined Benfica from Spartak during the 1991/92 season. His transfer also involved him getting married to a Portuguese girl at the same time to get around imigration laws! Has had terrible luck with injuries which have caused him to sit out both the 1990 World Cup and the 1992 European Championships.

MOZER, Jose Carlos (Marseille, Fra)

• 19.09.60 • Defender
• Brazil full caps

Known as Carlos, he is one of the most effective sweepers in France. His calmness on the ball and excellent reading of the game make him a shining light in Marseille's multi-million pound side.

MUHAMMED, Altinas (Galatasaray, Tur)

• 30.03.64 • Midfield
• Turkey 11 full caps

Spent a year in the international wilderness before being recalled for the game against Poland in September 1991. He enjoyed a fine game that evening, and has been a regular in Sepp Piontek's line-ups ever since.

MULDOON, John (Bangor, N.Ir)

• 12.01.62 • Defender
• N.Ireland Youth

Joined the club from Cliftonville in March 1991 as cover for George Gibson, who had broken his arm. Was a great favourite at Cliftonville, where he made 359 senior appearances, and even had a branch of the supporters' club named after him. Had a brief spell with Swansea City, but failed to break through at the Vetch. A member of the club's 1991/92 Lombard Ulster Cup winning side.

MULLAN, John (Distillery, N.Ir)

• Defender

Born and still lives in Dublin. Joined Distillery from Ards during 91/92. Very comfortable on the ball for a central defender he's become a vital part of the side.

MULLER, Peter (Cologne, Ger)

• 15.12.69 • Striker

Began his career with Cologne, but left Germany for Belgium before even making his League debut. Rejoined his original club from Mechelen in 1991.

MULLER, Rene (Dynamo Dresden, Ger)

• 11.02.59 • Goalkeeper
• East Germany 46 full caps

Highly experienced keeper who joined Dresden from Sachsen Leipzig in 1991. Before that he had been with the better known Leipzig club, Lokomotiv.

MUNARON, Jacques (RC Liege, Bel)

• 08.09.56 • Goalkeeper
• Belgium 8 full caps

Former Dinant player who signed for Liege from Anderlecht. Has more than 370 senior games to his credit.

MURPHY, Albert (Athlone Town, Eir)

• 06.11.63 • Midfield

Prolific central midfielder or winger who is a great favourite at St Mel's Park. Signed from Drogheda United in October 1987. Always likely to cause problems with his tremendous shooting ability.

MURPHY, Barry (Shamrock Rovers, Eir)

• 01.04.59 • Defender

He signed for the club from Bohemians in summer 1988.

MURPHY, Jack
(Bangor, N.Ir)

• 16.07.63 • Midfield
• Irish League Representative

Previously with Portadown, he was signed from Queen's University - where he is studying law - in the summer of 1990. Deadly from free-kicks, he made his Representative debut against the English League in 1990/91.

MURPHY, Liam
(Cork City, Eir)

• 20.12.61 • Defender
• Eire Youth

Skipper of the side. Previously with Cork United and Limerick City.

MURPHY, Ronnie
(Dundalk, Eir)

• 3.9.62 • Defender

Bit of a hard-man in defence for Dundalk. He played a significant role in the 1991 double-winning side. Signed from Bohemians in 1990.

MURRAY, Derek
(Bohemians, Eir)

• Midfield

Attacking midfielder who was signed from Home Farm.

MURRAY, Martin
(Crusaders, N.Ir)

• Midfield

Vastly experienced player who's know-how has proved invaluable at Seaview. Won the FAI Cup with Home Farm when he was 16, and then transferred to Everton, then managed by Billy Bingham. Failed to settle at Goodison, though, and returned to Ireland with Drogheda. In 1982 he was a double-winner with Dundalk, and also played for St Pat's Athletic before joining Crues in September 1991.

MURRAY, Martin
(St Patrick's Athletic, Eir)

• Midfield

Came to Harold's Cross from Ashtown Villa prior to the 1990/91 season but has struggled to hold down a regular first team spot.

MUSONDA, Charles
(Anderlecht, Bel)

• 22.08.69 • Midfield
• Zambia 13 full caps

Hard-working midfield ball-winner who began with Mufulira Wanderers, before moving to Belgium with Brugge as a 17-year-old. Has dual Belgian-Zambian nationality. Anderlecht signed him in August 1987.

MUSSI, Roberto
(Torino, Ita)

• 25.08.63 • Defender

Joined Parma from Third Division
Massese in 1984 before being signed by
Milan three years later. After two seasons
with Milan he was sold to Torino.

MUSZNAY, Zsolt
(Antwerp, Bel)

• 20.06.65 • Midfield

Creative playmaker who likes to get
forward and among the goals. Romanian-
born, he began with Steaua Bucharest
before moving to Hungarian side
Videoton. Antwerp snapped him up in the
summer of 1991, as countless former
Eastern bloc players fled to the West.

MUZZI, Roberto
(Roma, Ita)

• 21.09.71 • Striker

Locally born player who has spent all his
career with Roma. Made his debut for the
club at the end of the 1989/90 season.

MYYRY, Marko
(Lokeren, Bel)

• 15.11.67 • Midfield
• Finland 36 full caps, 2 goals

Attacking midfielder who joined the club
midway through the 1988/89 season.
Began with home town club Haka
Valkeakoski before moving to Meppen,
from where Lokeren snapped him up.
Creative player who likes to get forward.

NACHTWEIH, Norbert (Eintracht Frankfurt, Ger)

• 04.06.57 • Midfield

Rejoined Frankfurt from Cannes in 1991. Has also had spells with Bayern Munich and Chemie Halle.

NADAL, Miguel (Barcelona, Spa)

• 28.07.66 • Midfield
• Spain 2 full caps

After an impressive 1990/91 season with Mallorca, Migeul was snapped up by Barcelona during the 1991 close season. His move to the Nou Camp coincided with his promotion to the Spanish national side.

NADON, Jean-Claude (Lille, Fra)

• 21.11.64 • Goalkeeper
• France U21

Such a favourite at the club that, when his last contract expired in July 1990, they signed him on for a further six years. Formerly with Guingamp he moved to Lille in 1989, making his senior debut in July of that year at home to Caen. Has missed only a handful of games over the past two seasons.

NAKHID, David (Waregem, Bel)

• 15.05.64 • Midfield

Made his name with FC Zurich, before moving to Baden. Waregem snapped him up at the beginning of season 1990/91 and his dangerous raids down the wing have created havoc in opposing defences.

NANDO (SV Hamburg, Ger)

• 03.07.66 • Striker

Real name is Fernando Pereira Pinho. Signed from Flamengo of Brazil in 1989.

NANDO (Barcelona, Spa)

• 30.10.67 • Defender
• Spain 7 full caps

Fernando Munoz Garcia is a full back who began his career with Seville, his home town club. Signed by Barcelona in 1990 and played in the 1991 European Cup-Winners' Cup defeat by Manchester United, although he was sent off during the game.

NAPIER, Stephen (Cork City, Eir)

• Defender
• Eire Schools, Youth

Spent two years with Middlesbrough, but failed to make the grade at Ayresome Park and moved to Cork City in 1991.

de NAPOLI, Fernando (Napoli, Ita)

• 15.03.64 • Midfield
• Italy 52 full caps, 1 goal

Picked up by Avellino in 1981, but had to move on to Rimini a year later to make his League debut. Returned to Avellino in 1983/84 and finally signed by Napoli three years later.

NARBEKOVAS, Arminas (FK Austria, Aus)

• Midfield
• Lithuania full caps

Made first team debut for Zhagiris Vilnius in 1983, aged 18, and joined FK Austria from Zhagiris Vilnius along with fellow Lithuanian Valdas Ivanauskas in 1990. Won Austrian League Championship medal in first season. Won gold medal with the USSR team at the 1988 Olympics. His penalty against Georgia in May 1990 was Lithuania's first international goal for fifty years.

NARCISO Rodriguez de Armas (Burgos, Spa)

• 05.10.62 • Striker

Originally with Las Palmas, he joined Burgos from Sporting Gijon in 1991.

NARDINI, Mauro (Cagliari, Ita)

• 19.02.64 • Defender

Joined Cagliari from Barletta in 1990 after they had won promotion to the Serie A. Had previously spent all his career in the lower leagues with Romagnano, Sarzanese, Pontedera and Spal.

NASSEN, Daniel (RWD Molenbeek, Bel)

• 24.11.66 • Defender

Raiding full back who joined the club from Standard Liege in July 1991. Previously with Vlijtingen.

NAUDTS, Patrick (Lokeren, Bel)

• 29.07.65 • Defender

Solid and reliable defender who has come up through the ranks at the club and has now played more than 100 senior games.

N'DINGA Mbote (Vitoria Guimaraes, Por)

• 11.09.66 • Midfield
• Zaire full caps

One of two Kinshasa-born Zairean internationals in the Vitoria line-up, he is a pacey, attack-minded midfielder who has made over 150 appearances for the club since joining them in 1986/87.

N'DORAM, Japhet (Nantes, Fra)

• 27.02.66 • Striker
• Chad full caps

Lightning fast striker who signed for Nantes from Tonnerre de Yaounde in 1990, scoring twice in 17 starts in his first season.

NEHL, Josef (Bayer Leverkusen, Ger)

• 13.06.61 • Midfield

Arrived at Leverkusen from Bochum during the 1991/92 season to help boost their push for Europe. Had previously joined Bochum from Viktoria Kîln in 1986.

NEILL, George (Glentoran, N.Ir)

• Defender

Right full back who is one of the quickest players in the Irish League. Loves to get forward down the flanks to support his attacking players. The 1991/92 season was his 11th at The Oval. Also plays rugby union and American football.

NELA, Sebastiano (Roma, Ita)

• 13.03.61 • Defender

Made his League debut with Genoa in Serie B during the 1978/79 season. Was given his chance in the top flight by Roma who signed him in 1981. Has now made over 200 appearances in Serie A for the club.

NELINHO Nelio Frutuoso Marques (Uniao, Por)

• 16.04.58 • Defender

Steady full-back who has been ever-present in the side since joining them in 1989/90

NELO (Boavista, Por)

• 25.08.67 • Midfield
• Portugal 3 full caps

Manuel Antonio Guimaraes ia a locally born player who began his career with Boavista but had to move to Farense to get his break in First Division football. Returned to Boavista in 1988.

NELSON, Dean (Bangor, N.Ir)

• 28.03.73 • Midfield
• N.Ireland Youth

Played for Watford and Aberdeen as a youngster, but failed to make the grade on the other side of the Irish Sea and returned to Northern Ireland. Captained the Bangor Colts side to the 1989/90 Irish Youth Cup. Very strong in the tackle.

NELSON, Fernando (Sporting Lisbon, Por)
• 05.11.71 • Defender

Began his career with his home-town club Porto, but did not manage to break into the first team. had to move onto Salgueiros to make his First division debut. Joined Sporting in 1991.

NEMTSOUDIS, Georgious (Grasshoppers, Swi)
• 01.01.73 • Defender

Greek-born full back who made his Grasshoppers first team debut in October 1989.

NENO (Benfica, Por)
• 27.01.62 • Goalkeeper
• Portugal youth, 2 full caps

Made his League debut with Vitoria Guimaraes in 1984 after first choice 'keeper Silvano had been sold to Benfica. Followed Silvano to the Portuguese giants a year later, but struggled to make the first team. Had a season with Setubal, followed with two more back at Guimaraes, before returning to Benfica in 1990 and claiming the number one shirt from rival Silvano. Made his international debut against Brazil in June 1989.

NERI, Maurizio (Lazio, Ita)
• 21.03.65 • Midfield

Despite one season with Fiorentina, Maurizio spent most of his early career in the lower Leagues with Bellaria, Fano, Reggiana and Ancona. Returned to Serie A in November 1988 with Napoli, but moved on to Pisa two years later. Signed by Lazio in 1991.

NERLINGER, Christian (Bayern Munich, Ger)
• 21.03.73 • Midfield
• Germany Youth

Joined Bayern from TSV Forstenried in 1987. Turned pro summer 1991.

NEUBARTH, Frank (Werder Bremen, Ger)
• 29.07.62 • Striker
• Germany 1 full cap

Tall, powerful striker who joined Werder from Concordia Hamburg. Scored over 90 Bundesliga goals for Bremen.

NEUHAUS, Uwe (Wattenscheid, Ger)

• 26.11.59 • Defender

Signed from BVL Remscheid in the summer of 1989.

NEUN, Jorg (Borussia Moenchengladbach, Ger)

• 07.05.66 • Midfield

Signed from SV Waldhof Mannheim in 1987.

NEVILLE, Mick (Shelbourne, Eir)

• Midfield

Ball-winning midfielder who is very strong in the air. Signed from Derry City in June 1990.

NEWE, Paul (Shelbourne, Eir)

• 20.04.64 • Striker

Devastating front-man who signed from Dundalk in the summer of 1990. Fourteen goals in 20 starts quickly endeared him to the Tolka Park faithful.

NGOTTY, Bruno (Lyon, Fra)

• 10.06.71 • Defender
• France U21

Home-grown youngster who is approaching 100 senior games since making his bow in a baptism of fire at home to Marseille in July 1989. Was one of three defenders making their debut that day - the others were Fugier and Garde - and the trio have gone on to become the bedrock of Lyon's First Division squad.

NICOLINI, Eligio (Atalanta. Ita)

• 19.01.61 • Midfield

Started his career in the lower divisions with Omegna before moving to Vicenza in 1980. Spent his first season on loan to Ternan, before returning to Vicenza and winning a regular first team place. Signed by Atalanta in 1987.

NIEDERBACHER, Richard (Waregem, Bel)

• 07.12.61 • Striker
• Austria 4 full caps

Hugely experienced and widely travelled goalscorer now returned for his second spell at the Regenboogstadion. Previous clubs include Gleisdorf, Sturm Graz, Paris St Germain, Stade de Reims, Vienna SK and Rapid Vienna. Not the most delicate of players, he can always be relied upon to stir up defences and create and take chances.

NIELSEN, Allan
(Sion, Swi)
• 13.03.71 • Midfield

Joined Bayern Munich from Esbjerg of Denmark in 1988. Moved on to Sion in 1991.

NIELSEN, Henrik
(Lille, Fra)
• 29.03.65 • Striker

Another of Lille's Danish contingent. Very strong in the air, he was previously with Greve before moving to Fenerbahce (Tur). Averages a goal every 2.5 games for Lille since making his debut at Metz in July 1990.

mio NIELSEN, Mickael
(Lille, Fra)
• 12.02.65 • Midfield
• Denmark full caps

One of Lille's Danish midfield trio. Signed from Fram Copenhagen in July 1990. Made his debut away to Metz later that same month. Prefers to play down the left-flank, but can operate in centre.

NIJSKENS, Angelo
(Charleroi, Bel)
• 01.06.63 • Midfield

Equally comfortable in attack or midfield, he is happiest playing wide as a conventional winger. Dutch-born, with Belgian national status, he was previously with Hulst, Lokeren and Bayer Uerdingen, before signing from RC Liege in the middle of 1991/92.

NIKOLIC, Doucq
(Salgueiros, Por)
• 11.07.59 • Midfield

Belgrade born defender who was bought to Salgueiros along with fellow countrymen Milovac and Djoincevic by Yugolavian coach Zoran Filipovic.

de NIL, Alain
(Cercle Brugge, Bel)
• 17.08.66 • Striker

Equally happy as a wide midfielder or up front, he signed from Mechelen. Previously with SCUP Jette and Molenbeek.

NILIS, Luc
(Anderlecht, Bel)
• 25.06.67 • Striker
• Belgium 18 full caps

Former Halvenweg Zonhoven and Winterslag player who signed for Anderlecht in October 1986. Has won two League titles and two Belgian Cups with the club. Was leading scorer (19 goals) during the 1991 Championship season.

NILSSON, Joakim (Sporting Gijon, Spa)

• 31.03.66 • Midfield
• Sweden 27 full caps, 1 goal

Talented player who has yet to really fulfill his obvious potential. Played in the 1990 World Cup finals for Sweden and earned himself a move to Real Zaragoza that summer on the back of his performances there. Remained in Spain but later moved onto Sporting Gijon.

NILSSON, Mikael (Gothenburg, Swe)

• 28.09.69 • Midfield
• Sweden 8 full caps; U21; Youth

Sweeper who joined the Gothenburg youth section from IFK Falkoping in 1987. Promoted to first team squad during the following season.

NOGUEIRA, Antonio Jose (Boavista, Por)

• 21.09.63 • Midfield

Born in Lisbon and originally from the Boa Hora club. Viseu gave him the chance to play First Division football in 1988 and he resumed his career there with Penafiel in 1990. Signed by Boavista prior to the 1991/92 season.

NOGUEIRA, Manuel (Cannes, Fra)

• 01.09.68 • Midfield

Progressed through the junior ranks at the club, but has struggled to make a real impact at first team level. His Division One debut came against Auxerre on 21st October 1989.

NOLAN, Jimmy (Galway United, Eir)

• 06.01.64 • Defender

One of the club's longest serving players, signed from Mervue United in 1982. Happy anywhere in defence or midfield, he even spent part of 1991/92 in goal after a 'keeper crisis at Terryland. Played in Galway's last Cup final appearance, v Shamrock Rovers, 1985.

NOLAN, John (Sligo Rovers, Eir)

• 16.04.64 • Defender

Began with Shamrock Rovers, with whom he made his League of Ireland debut, against Home Farm, in April 1987 (won 3-1). Joined the Rovers from Drogheda United in the summer of 1990.

NORTAN, Paul
(Feyenoord, Hol)
• 01.12.63 • Defender

Signed from AZ Alkmaar in 1988. Can also play in midfield.

NOUMA, Pascal
(Paris St Germain, Fra)
• 06.01.72 • Striker
• France U21

Exceptionally tall youngster (6ft 4in) who has come up through the ranks at the club to which he's been affiliated since age 14. Has made only a handful of senior appearances since his debut, at Lille, in February 1990.

N'SUMBU, Ngoy
(Germinal Ekeren, Bel)
• 30.10.72 • Midfield
• Zaire 2 full caps

Very much a flair player, he can tear teams apart when he's on his game - but can be equally frustrating. Signed from Ban Limpopo midway through the 1990/91 season.

NUCIARI, Giulio
(Sampdoria, Ita)
• 26.04.60 • Goalkeeper

Joined Sampdoria from Monza in 1989. Also with Montecatini, Ternana and Milan.

NUGENT, Martin
(Bray Wanderers, Eir)
• 05.08.65 • Midfield

Contributed four goals in 26 games from central midfield as Bray Wanderers won promotion to the Premier Division.

NUTT, Colin
(Cliftonville, N.Ir)
• Defender

Attacking full back who made a big impression during his first season at Solitude Stadium. Signed from local junior club Limavady United, he was ever present until four weeks from the end of the season, when a knee injury forced him out of action.

N'WANU, Chidi
(Beveren, Bel)
• 01.01.67 • Defender

Nigerian-born full back who signed from Diest in the summer of 1991, as the club sought to strengthen an already sound defence for life back in the First Division. Previously with home-town club Lagos and also VC Westerlo.

O'BRIEN, Dave
(Sligo Rovers, Eir)
• 06.05.63 • Midfield

Known to everyone in the League of Ireland as Rocky. Hard-working midfield general, who, like several of his Sligo team-mates, began with Bohemians. Ironically, his League of Ireland debut, which came in September 1981, was against his present club.

O'CALLAGHAN, Brendan
(Drogheda United, Eir)
• 07.01.66 • Defender

Can play in central defence, midfield or up front, and scored some vital goals in the run up to promotion from the First Division to the Premier in 1990/91.

OCEANO Andrade da Cruz
(Real Sociedad, Spa)
• 29.07.62 • Midfield

Goalscoring midfielder who arrived at the club from Sporting Lisbon along with Carlos Xavier in 1991.

O'CONNOR, Barry
(Shamrock Rovers, Eir)
• 17.06.72 • Striker

A bright future has been predicted for this talented young forward, with several envious glances being cast from across the Irish Sea. Signed from local League side Cherry Orchard, he made his League of Ireland debut, v Dundalk, in September 1989. Gave notice of his goalscoring ability with a fabulous burst of seven goals in 11 games during the 1990/91 campaign.

O'CONNOR, John
(Bangor, N.Ir)
• 28.01.60 • Midfield

Known as 'Jock' to all at Clandeboye Park. Signed from Ards in 1987, and quickly became a firm favourite with his tireless running and non-stop hard work. Won the club's "Player of the Year" award in 1989/90. He has also played for Portadown and Clifton, where he won an Irish Cup winners' medal in 1979. A member of Bangor's 1991/92 Lombard Ulster Cup winning side.

O'CONNOR, Michael
(Athlone Town, Eir)
• 08.10.60 • Striker

Born in Athlone, but it was with Dundalk that he got his first chance. Failed to make the grade at Oriel Park, and moved to Athlone in 1979. Made his League of Ireland debut, v Drogheda, in March of that year. Currently one of the longest serving players at the club.

O'CONNOR, Tony
(St Patrick's Athletic, Eir)

• 15.11 66 • Midfield

Central midfielder who likes to get
forward and score goals.

O'DRISCOLL, Maurice
(St Patrick's Athletic, Eir)

• 02.08.66 • Midfield

Strong-tackling, hard-running 'engine' of
the St Pat's midfield.

OECHLER, Marc
(Nuremburg, Ger)

• 11.02.68 • Midfield

Locally discovered midfielder who has
managed to force his way into the first
team set up.

OGUN, Temizkanoglu
(Trabzonspor, Tur)

• 14.04.68 • Defender
• Turkey 3 full caps

Something of an oddity in the Turkish
national team in that he does not play for
one of the Istanbul giants Besiktas,
Fenerbahce or Galatasaray. Solid and
reliable defender who prefers to sit back
and let his team mates do the attacking.

OGUZ, Cetin
(Fenerbahce, Tur)

• 15.02.63 • Midfield
• Turkey 19 full caps, 2 goals

His international bow came in a rare, and
famous, Turkish victory - v Greece in
September 1988 (3-1).

O'KANE, CIARAN
(Glenavon, N.Ir)

• Midfield
• N.Ireland Youth

A fine prospect who made a sparkling
debut v Omagh Town in April 1991.
Began season in third team and quickly
progressed to firsts.

O'KANE, Sean
(Cliftonville, N.Ir)

• Striker

Hit a rich seam in 1991/92 when he
chipped in with 20 goals for the club. Like
fellow front-runner Billy Drake he suffered
a lean period in 1991/92 (9 goals), but his
pace and touch always cause problems.

OKPARA, Godwin
(Eendracht Aalst, Bel)

• 20.09.72 • Defender

One of seven new players to join the club
in the wake of promotion in 1990/91.

Nigerian-born, but with Belgian nationality, he previously had a season in the top flight with Beerschot, playing 21 senior games.

OLIVEIRA, Antonio Henrique Jesus (Beira-Mar, Por)

• 08.06.58 • Defender
• Portugal full caps

Very experienced player who was signed by Benfica from Maritimo in 1983. Made 98 League appearances for the club before returning to Maritimo in 1987. Signed by Beira-Mar three years later.

de OLIVEIRA RUBEN, Vinicius (Caen, Fra)

• 11.10.71 • Midfield

Brazilian-born left sided midfielder who was signed as a trainee from Fluminense in his home country.

OLMETA, Pascal (Marseille, Fra)

• 07.04.61 • Goalkeeper
• France U21

Experienced 'keeper who began with home-town club Bastia and has now made more than 300 First Division appearances. Faces intense challenge for first team spot from Alain Casanova, but won out towards the

end of 1991/92 when his rival broke his leg.

OLSEN, Jesper (Caen, Fra)

• 20.03.61 • Midfield
• Denmark 43 full caps, 5 goals

Winger turned central midfielder who has played top level football in four countries. Began in his native Denmark with Naestved before moving on to Dutch giants Ajax, where he was a huge hit. From 1984 to 1988 he was at Manchester United, where he scored 21 goals in 139 League games. Then moved on to Bordeaux before joining Caen in the summer of 1990. Creative hub of the side.

OLSEN, Lars (Trabzonspor, Tur)

• 02.02.61 • Defender
• Denmark 62 full caps, 3 goals

Libero who captained Brondby to Danish League title in 1991. Joined Trabzonspor that summer. Played for his country in the 1988 and 1992 European Championships, where his assured performances at the back helped his country to their first ever trophy when they beat Germany 2-0 in the final.

OMAM-BIYIK, Francois (Cannes, Fra)

• 21.05.66 • Striker
• Cameroon full caps

Main claim to fame is scoring THAT goal v Argentina at World Cup Italia '90. Signed for Cannes in 1991, from Rennes. Tall, strong and excellent in the air, he was also formerly with Laval. Averages a goal every three games and was linked with Marseille during the 1991/92 close season.

O'NEILL, Alan (Dundalk, Eir)

• 2.7.57 • Goalkeeper
• League of Ireland Representative

Veteran 'keeper and club captain at Oriel Park. Began with Shamrock Rovers, moved to UCD in 1983 and then on to Dundalk in summer 1985. Was an essential part of the club's double-winning side in 1987/88 and also the 1990/91 title win. Brother of Derry City 'keeper Dermot O'Neill. Kept 23 clean sheets in 33 games during 1990/91.

O'NEILL, Derek (Athlone Town, Eir)

• 19.07.63 • Defender

Dublin-born stopper who migrated to Australia to try his luck with Wollongong City, south of Sydney. Returned to his home country with Athlone in July 1990.

O'NEILL, Dermot (Bohemians, Eir)

• 27.11.60 • Goalkeeper

Veteran stopper who has been with the club since signing from Dundalk back in 1981. A firm favourite at Dalymount Park, he is the club's longest serving player.

O'NEILL, Kevin (Omagh Town, N.Ir)

• Midfield

Signed from Ballymena in October 1991, and quickly established himself in the side thanks to his accurate crossing ability.

ONORATI, Robert (Genoa, Ita)

• 05.02.66 • Midfield

Left-sided midfield player previously with Pistoiese, Fiorentina and Avellino.

van OOSTEN, Albert (Den Haag, Hol)

• 04.10.66 • Defender

After spells with VVM and ADO, Albert signed for Den Haag in July 1985. Had to wait 14 months for his first team debut and has now played over 180 times.

OOSTERVEER, Arnold (Rennes, Fra)

• 01.03.63 • Defender

Towering central defender (6ft 4in) who, not surprisingly, wins just about everything in the air. Born in Groningen, Holland, he began his pro career with

Niort, moving to Rennes in the wake of promotion from Division Two. His debut came in October 1990 v Caen.

ORDENEWITZ, Frank (Cologne, Ger)

- 25.03.65 • Striker
- Germany 2 full caps

Joined Cologne from Werder Bremen in 1989 after previously playing for junior side TSV Dorfmark.

O'REILLY, Charlie (Drogheda United, Eir)

- 06.11.62 • Defender

Stong tackling right back who's drive and determination helped Drogheda to the First Division Championship in 1990/91.

OREJUELA Rivero, Antonio Jose (Atletico Madrid, Spa)

- 02.12.60 • Midfield
- Spain U21

Joined Atletico Madrid in 1988 from Mallorca.

ORHAN, Cikrikei (Trabzonspor, Tur)

- 16.04.67 • Striker
- Turkey 2 full caps

Made his senior international debut away to Bulgaria in August 1991.

ORLANDO, Allessandro (Sampdoria, Ita)

- 01.06.70 • Defender

Signed by Sampdoria from Udinese during summer 1991. Spent the 1989/90 season with Parma.

ORLANDO Lins Mancini (Farense, Por)

- 14.12.59 • Defender

Has spent three years out of the Farense side after an impressive start, but still a valued member of the squad.

ORLANDO, Manuel Vieira Silva (Sporting Braga, Por)

- 07.07.69 • Goalkeeper

Locally born keeper who has been with Sporting Braga all of his career. Promoted to the first team squad at the start of the 1991/92 season.

ORLANDO, Massimo (Fiorentina, Ita)

- 26.05.71 • Defender

Began his career with Conegliano before moving to Second Division Reggina in 1988. Signed by Juventus in 1990, but later allowed to join Fiorentina.

OSAM, Paul
(St Patrick's Athletic, Eir)

• 20.12.67 • Midfield

Began with minor League side Mount Merrion, before joining St Pat's in the summer of 1988. His League of Ireland debut came a year later, in September 1989, away to Limerick City (lost 0-1). Still struggling to hold down a regular first team spot at Harold's Cross.

OSIO, Marco
(Parma, Ita)

• 13.01.66 • Midfield

Made just six League appearances in three years at Torino before joining Empoli in 1986. Was on his travels a year later, joining Parma and immediately becoming a first team regular.

OSONDU, Philip
(RWD Molenbeek, Bel)

• 28.11.71 • Striker

Nigerian-born forward who was granted Belgian citizenship in 1990. Began with El Kaname in his home country before being snapped up by Belgian giants Anderlecht. Failed to make the breakthrough there, and transferred to Molenbeek in July 1990.

O'TOOLE, Alan
(Drogheda United, Eir)

• 16.04.66 • Midfield

Has had trouble establishing himself over the past couple of seasons at Drogheda. Equally happy playing as a wide midfielder or an out-and-out striker.

OTT, Thorsten
(Bayern Munich, Ger)

• 18.06.73 • Striker

Amatuer signed from Kickers Offenbach in summer 1991.

OTTEN, Johnny
(Werder Bremen, Ger)

• 31.01.61 • Defender
• Germany 6 full caps

Joined Bremen from SV Hagen in 1979. Over 275 Bundesliga games for the club.

OTTO, Heine
(Den Haag, Hol)

• 24.08.54 • Striker
• Holland U21

Began his career with FC Amsterdam and FC Twente before leaving Holland and moving to England. Spent four seasons with Middlesbrough as a first team regular before returning home and signing for Den Haag in July 1985.

OUDEC, Nicolas (Nantes, Fra)

• 28.10.71 • Striker
• France Schools; Youth

Made a terrific impact on his introduction to the first team in August 1990, when he grabbed 2 goals in his first four games. Home-grown player with a very bright future predicted. Joined the club from school in 1987.

OUDJANI, Cherif (Sochaux, Fra)

• 09.12.64 • Striker
• Algeria full caps

At 6ft 1in tall, and almost 14st Oudjani's a handful for any defence, and he averages a goal every 2.5 games at Sochaux. Signed from Lens in 1989. Ironically, his League debut came for Lens, v Sochaux, in February 1984.

van OVERTVELDT, Herve (Beveren, Bel)

• 22.10.71 • Midfield

Home grown player who helped the club to promotion in 1990/91. Signed straight from school in 1987, making his first team debut during the relegation season of 1989/90.

OYEKANNI, Taju (Kortrijk, Bel)

• 23.02.73 • Striker

Speedy and exceptionally skilful on the ball, if a little lightweight. Coach Boudewijn Braem has predicted a bright future for this young Nigerian signed from Lagos City in May 1991.

OZCAN, Gokhan (Genk, Bel)

• 27.07.69 • Midfield

Turkish-born midfield ball-winner who was recently granted Belgian citizenship. Joined the club in the wake of their promotion from the Second Divsion in 1989/90.

PACHECO, Antonio Manuel
(Benfica, Por)

• 01.12.66 • Midfield

• Portugal U21, 5 full caps

Began his career with little Torralta and made his League debut with Portimonense in 1986. Moved to Benfica a year later and proved a great success in his first term. Has made over 100 League appearances .

PACIONE, Marco
(Genoa, Ita)

• 27.07.63 • Striker

Formerly with Atalanta, Torino, Juventus and Verona.

PADRAO, Carlos Manuel Costa
(Porto, Por)

• 01.09.58 • Goalkeeper

Born in Angola and began his League career with Belenenses in 1981. Moved onto to Vitoria Setubal a year later and spent three seasons with the club before joining Chaves in 1985. Had one season at Boavista before signing for Porto in 1990.

PAGE, Oliver
(Dynamo Dresden, Ger)

• 10.04.71 • Defender

Had very few first team chances at Bayer Leverkusen so decided to move on to Dresden in 1991.

PAGLIUCA, Gianluca
(Sampdoria, Ita)

• 18.12.66 • Goalkeeper

• Italy 4 full caps

Failed to make grade with home-town club Bologna and joined Sampdoria in 1986. In Italy squad for 1990 World Cup, but did not make international debut until 1991, coming on as substitute in the final of the Scania 100 Tournament and making the vital save in the penalty shoot-out to beat USSR.

PAILLE, Stephane
(Caen, Fra)

• 27.06.65 • Striker

• France 9 full caps

Returned to the club in 1991/92, having spent much of the previous season on loan at Portuguese giants Porto, where he scored four times in 11 starts. Previously with Sochaux and Bordeaux he has proved himself an accomplished goalscorer everywhere he's played.

PAIVA Marco Paulo
(Maritimo, Por)

• 07.02.73 • Midfield

A much fancied youngster, he burst onto the League scene in 1990 when he played

20 games for Maritimo, his home-town club. Since then has been a regular member of the team.

PALATSI, Jerome (Montpellier, Fra)

- 10.12.69 • Goalkeeper
- France Schools, U21

Home-grown reserve 'keeper who spent the 1990/91 season on loan at Ales.

PALMERS, Erwin (Lokeren, Bel)

- 28.03.68 • Midfield

Re-joined the club prior to the 1991/92 season after a season on loan at Second Division side Eeklo. Began with Berchem Sport.

PANCEV, Darko (Internazionale, Ita)

- 07.09.65 • Striker
- Yugoslavia 24 full caps, 17 goals

Began with Vardar Skopje and was League's top scorer in 1984, his first full season. Signed by Red Star Belgrade in 1990. 34 goals in 1991 made him Europe's top scorer. His full international debut came as an 18-year-old v Hungary in March 1984. Signed a pre-contract agreement to move to Internzaionale when the club's foreign complement will allow him to play.

PAPIN, Jean-Pierre (Milan, Ita)

- 05.11.63 • Striker
- France 37 full caps, 21 goals

Despite Marseille president Bernard Tapie going on record as saying that "Papin will not leave Marseille at any cost", a multi-million pound offer from Milan tempted him to Italy in the summer of 1992. Top scorer in the French League for five successive, and success filled, seasons with Marseille. He is France's greatest international asset. Began with Valenciennes before moving to Belgian club Brugge, where he won rave reviews. Bernard Tapie snapped him up in August 1986. His goals have been rewarded with four League title wins, a French Cup victory and a place in France's 1986 World Cup squad. Romped away with the French League's top scorer title once again in 1991/92, with 27 strikes. Was voted "European Footballer of the Year" in 1991.

PARDEZA Richardo, Miguel (Zaragoza, Spa)

- 08.02.65 • Striker
- Spain 5 full caps

A popular player who has been the mainstay of the Zaragoza frontline since his return to the club in 1987 following a brief spell with Real Madrid.

PARENTE, Carlos Alberto (Salgueiros, Por)
• 08.04.61 • Midfield

Experienced midfielder who began his career with Sintrense and then made his name at Boavista. Moved on to Salgueiros prior to the start of the 1991/92 season.

PARI, Fausto (Sampdoria, Ita)
• 15.09.62 • Midfield
• Italy Youth

Made just 1 League appearance for Inter before joining Parma on free transfer. Moved to Sampdoria in 1983.

PASSI, Franck (Toulon, Fra)
• 28.03.66 • Midfield
• France U21

Like elder brother Gerald (Monaco) he began with Montpellier. But it wasn't until he moved to Marseille that he got his chance in the First Division, making his debut v Toulouse in August 1986. He later followed his brother to Toulouse before signing for Toulon in June 1990. Scored just one League goal during the 1991/92 campaign.

PASSI, Gerald (Monaco, Fra)
• 21.01.64 • Midfield
• France 9 full caps

Scored the goal that won the Cup against Marseille in 1991 and is the creative force around which Monaco's recent success has been built. Formerly with Montpellier and Toulouse he joined the club in 1990, and has made more than 200 senior appearances in French Division One.

PATTERSON, Alan (Linfield, N.Ir)
• Goalkeeper

Formerly with Glentoran and English League club Queens Park Rangers, this tall, commanding 'keeper has settled well at Linfield. Was called up to the Irish League Representative XI in 1991/92.

PATTERSON, Eddie (Cliftonville, Eir)
• Midfield

Happy to play anywhere across the midfield, Eddie is a good squad player who can be relied upon to always give 100%.

PATTINAMA, Ton (Den Haag, Hol)
• 30.07.56 • Defender

Highly experienced performer who has made over 500 League appearances for his five League sides. Made his debut during the 1975/76 season while with Excelsior. Moved on to Den Bosch in 1984 and then spent the two years with Utrecht. Signed by Heracles in 1988 and finally by Den Haag in March 1992.

PATXI FERREIRA
(Atletico Madrid, Spa)
• 22.05.67 • Defender
• Spain U21

Signed from Atletico Bilbao in the summer of 1989.

PATXI SALINAS
(Atletico Bilbao, Spa)
• 17.11.63 • Defender

Francisco Salinas Fernandez is a long serving defender who is now in his tenth season with the Basque side.

PAUK, Thierry
(Metz, Fra)
• 25.07.64 • Defender
• France U21

Joined the club straight from school in 1980, making his debut v Monaco four years later. Solid and uncompromising central defender.

PAULINO Roque da Silva
(Beira-Mar, Por)
• 13.09.57 • Goalkeeper

Angolan born keeper who returned to his first club, Beira-Mar from Estoril in 1984.

PAULO JORGE Gomes Bento
(Vitoria Guimaraes)
• 20.06.69 • Midfield

Not renowned as a great playmaker, he tends to do the legwork in midfield while his Brazilian born team-mate Joao Batista provides the flair. Moved to Vitoria in 1991/92 after three seasons at Est Amadora.

PAULO MADEIRA
(Benfica, Por)
• 06.09.70 • Defender
• Portugal youth, U21, 1 full cap

Born in Angola and played his football in the African country with St Antonio. Joined Benfica as a 16-year-old and made his League debut for the side during the 1989/90 season. Won a call-up to the Portuguese national squad during the 1991/92 season and made his international debut in Februiary 1992 against Malta.

PAULO PEREIRA
(Porto, Por)

• 27.08.65 • Defender

One of a number of Brazillian players in the Porto squad, Paulo Pereira is currently the longest serving having originally joined the club in 1988.

PAULO TORRES
(Sporting Lisbon, Por)

• 25.11.71 • Defender

Began his career with little Evora in his home town and made his League debut with Sporting in 1989. Has struggled to gain a regular first team place.

PAUWELS, Raf
(Lierse, Bel)

• 14.06.68 • Midfield

Began with minor League club Hooikt before joining Lierse in the wake of promotion from Division Two in 1988.

PEAN, Eric
(Toulon, Fra)

• 10.09.63 • Defender
• France U21

Experienced centre back who has been playing top class football for more than 10 years since taking his bow for Lille v Nice in March 1981. Moved on to Bordeaux, and then Caen before joining Toulon at the beginning of 1990/91.

PEDEMAS, Olivier
(Toulouse, Fra)

• 31.08.68 • Goalkeeper

Understudy to first choice 'keeper Robin Huc. Came through the ranks at the club and has made a handful of Division One appearances.

PEDERSON, Tore
(Gothenburg, Swe)

• 29.09.69 • Defender
• Norway 16 full caps; Olympic; U21; Youth

Reliable Norweigan who joined Gothenburg from Fredrikstad in 1990. His international debut came against the USSR in September 1990 (lost 2-0).

PEDRAZA Lamilla, Angel
(Mallorca, Spa)

• 04.10.64 • Midfield

Joined Mallorca from Barcelona in 1988.

PEDRO, Eduardo
(Salgueiros, Por)

• 30.06.67 • Defender

Like team mate Madureira he was formerly

with the Leixoes club. First team regular who helped Salgueiros win the Portuguese Second Division title in 1990.

PEERSMAN, Luc
(Beveren, Bel)

• 28.01.69 • Defender

Came up through the ranks at Beveren to make his debut during season 1989/90. Sadly, the club were relegated that same year, but Luc showed his loyalty by signing a new contract and then helping Beveren bounce back into the top flight in 1990/91.

PEETERS, Rene
(Eendracht Aalst, Bel)

• 10.10.61 • Defender

Experienced lower-divisions player who is currently enjoying his second spell at the club. Began with Anderlecht, but never made the break through and transferred to Eendracht. Had a spell at Eeklo before returning in time to help Aalst to their dramtic Second Divsion play-off win in 1990/91.

PELE, Abedi
(Marseille, Fra)

• 05.01.62 • Midfield
• Ghana full caps

Attacking midfielder who kept Eric Cantona out of the first team at Marseille. African Footballer of the Year for 1991.

First came to notice helping Niort to promotion from Division Two in 1987, and with a name like Pele was always going to be remembered. Was the inspiration behind Marseille's historic run to the 1991 Champions' Cup final.

PELLEGRINI, Luca
(Verona, Ita)

• 24.03.63 • Defender

Sweeper who joined Sampdoria from his home-town club, Varese, in 1980. Moved to Verona in October 1991.

PERCY, Keith
(Glenavon, N.Ir)

• Midfield

Goal-grabbing midfielder who rejoined Glenavon in January 1992 after three years with Armagh City. A plumber, he was Armagh's second highest scorer (15 goals) in 1990/91. From Bleary.

PEREIRINHA, Joaquim
Miguel Pedreirinho
(Farense, Por)

• 26.11.58 • Midfield

Now one of the old men of the Portugeuse game, he has found it hard to stay with the pace in recent years. Started at Amora in 1980 then had a brief spell with Belenenses before slotting into the Farense side in 1986/87.

PEREZ, Christian
(Paris St Germain, Fra)

• 13.05.63 • Midfield
• France 21 caps, 2 goals

Approaching his 200th senior appearance, this cultured playmaker is an inspiration to those around him for club and country. Equally happy causing trouble up front or prompting from the midfield. He is a favourite of French coach Michel Platini. Joined the club in 1988, from Montpellier, and began his career with Nimes in March 1980.

PEREZ, Lionel
(Nimes, Fra)

• 24.04.67 • Goalkeeper

Consolidation in Divison One was the aim of newly-promoted Nimes, and they achieved it, thanks in no small part to the vital saves of the giant Perez. Discovered by the club playing local junior football, he signed pro in 1987.

PERILLEUX, Philippe
(Monpellier, Fra)

• 16.09.63 • Midfield
• France U21

Talented playmaker, who likes to get forward and score goals, and is the source of many of the club's attacking moves. Began with Valenciennes before moving to Lille in 1984.

PERRONE, Carlo
(Atalanta, Ita)

• 08.07.60 • Midfield

Began his career with Vicenza, but actually made his League debut while at Empoli during the 1979/80 season. Left Vicenza in 1983 and arrived at Atalanta in 1990 following spells with Triestina, Campobasso and Bari.

PERUZZI, Angelo
(Juventus, Ita)

• 16.02.70 • Goalkeeper
• Italy U21

Made his League debut for Roma during the 1987/88 season, but did not get a regular first team place until joining Verona for the 1989/90 campaign. Returned to Roma the following season, but was suspended for a year - along with ex-Roma team-mate Andrea Carnevale - after failing a dope test. Signed by Juventus in 1991.

PESCHEL, Peter
(Bochum, Ger)

• 26.01.72 • Striker

Joined Borussia Dortmund while still a schoolboy, but failed to make the grade. Moved on to Bochum in 1988.

van PETEGHEM, Roald (Eendracht Aalst, Bel)

• 08.02.64 • Midfield

Now in his second spell at the club, having also enjoyed two stays with Gent, his first club. Signed from Second Division Eeklo after Aalst won promotion in 1990/91.

PETEREYNS, Frederic (Caen, Fra)

• 08.12.69 • Goalkeeper

Began with his home town club Maubeuge, before being signed as cover for first choice 'keeper Philippe Montanier in 1990. His first - and only - appearance to date was against Nantes on 24th May 1991.

PETERSEN, Dan (Ajax, Hol)

• 06.05.72 • Striker

Danish born, scored on Ajax debut v Willem II Tilburg October 1991.

PETIT, Emmanuel (Monaco, Fra)

• 22.09.70 • Defender
• France 2 full caps

Towering centre back who joined Monaco from ES Arques in 1985, but had to wait four years to make his senior debut, against Sochaux in March 1989. Has progressed in leaps and bounds since then and has become an important member of Platini's French squad. French Cup winner in 1991.

PETROV, Petar (Beira-Mar, Por)

• 20.02.61 • Defender
• Bulgaria full caps

Left his native Bulgaria to join Beira-Mar in the Portuguese prior to the start of the 1989/90 season.

PETRY, Zsolt (Gent, Bel)

• 23.09.66 • Goalkeeper
• Hungary 11 full caps

Has become Hungary's first choice 'keeper under coach Kalman Meszoly. Fine shot-stopper who began with Videoton. Joined Gent from Honved in June 1991.

PETTERSEN, Stefan (Ajax, Hol)

• 22.03.63 • Striker
• Sweden 24 full caps, 1 goal

Began his career in Sweden with IFK Vasteras in 1980. Joined IFK Norrkoping two years later and in his first season helped the club into the Swedish First Division. Moved on to Gothenburg in 1984, before signing for Ajax in 1988.

PFANNKUCH, Thomas (Borussia Moenchengladbach, Ger)

• 21.02.70 • Defender

Joined Gladbach from KSV Baunatal in 1990.

PFLÖGLER, Hans (Bayern Munich, Ger)

• 27.03.60 • Defender
• Germany 11 full caps

Left-sided defensive player who joined Bayern as junior in 1975 from minor League side SV Vötting-Weihenstephan. Has played over 350 first team games and won more than 10 caps. Member of German 1988 European Championships and 1990 World Cup squads.

PHILLIPS, Colm (Shamrock Rovers, Eir)

• 05.03.57 • Defender

One of several 'old heads' to have been introduced to the Shamrock Rovers line-up by player/manager Noel King. Signed from Bray Wanderers in January 1991.

PIACENTINI, Giovanni (Roma, Ita)

• 09.04.68 • Midfield

Born in Modena and made his debut for his home club in the Third Division in 1985. Helped the club to win promotion in 1986 and then joined Padova in 1987. Signed by Roma two years later.

PICASSO, Mauro (Foggia, Ita)

• 16.07.65 • Striker

Made his League debut in Serie B with Genoa during the 1984/85 season. Later played for Pavia, Campania and Messina before joining Foggia in 1990.

PICCIONI, Enrico (Cremonese, Ita)

• 23.11.61 • Midfield

Made his League debut with Sambenedettese and joined Forli after just one appearance. Later moved on to Empoli, Perugia and Catanzaro, before signing for Cremonese in 1987.

PICKEU, Olivier (Caen, Fra)

• 24.02.70 • Striker
• France U21

Along with strike-partner Stephane Paille he was loaned out during 1990/91 - to Tours - to gain some valuable experience while Graham Rix carried on scoring goals at Caen. Returned in the summer of 1991, signed a new contract and pledged his future to the club. Previously with INF

Clairefontaine and Lille, the Caen management have high hopes for this U21 international.

PIERLEONI, Angelo (Ascoli, Ita)

• 15.12.62 • Midfield

Began his career with Third Division Teramo in 1979 and had spells with Benevento, Fermana and Massina before joining Brescia ten years later. Soon moved onto Cesena and then arrived at Ascoli in 1990. Was involved in the on field argument with Ascoli team mate Antonio Aloisi against Internazionale in April 1992 that led to both players being banned by the club for the remainder of the 1991/92 campaign.

PILZ, Uwe-Hans (Dynamo Dresden, Ger)

• 10.11.58 • Midfield
• East Germany 35 full caps

Played for Sachsenring Zwickau and Dresden before moving to the Bundesliga with Fortuna Koln. Returned to Dresden for the start of the 1991/92 season

PIN, Gabriele (Lazio, Ita)

• 21.01.62 • Midfield

Lazio captain who began his career with Juventus. After spells with Sanremese, Forli and Parma, Gabriele left Juve for Lazio in 1986.

PINEDA, Michel (Toulon, Fra)

• 09.06.64 • Striker

Big, bustling goal scorer of French-Spanish descent. Began with Auxerre, where he played his first pro game, v Nantes, in July 1983. Moved on to Spanish giants Barcelona before returning to France with Toulon in 1990. Didn't have to wait long for his first goal, scoring in the fourth match of the season v Brest.

PIOLI, Stefano (Fiorentina, Ita)

• 19.10.65 • Defender

Born in Parma and began his career with his local club in the Third Division in 1982. Two years later he was snapped up by Juventus who then sold him to verona in 1987. Transferred to Fiorentina in 1989.

PISTER, Thierry (Standard Liege, Bel)

• 02.09.65 • Midfield

Franco-Belgian who signed from Toulon in June 1990. Missed much of the 1990/91 season through injury. Began with Gent before moving, via Antwerp, to France and Toulon.

PITICO Manuel Inacio Filho
(Farense, Por)

• 01.07.63 • Striker

Burst onto the scene in 1988/89 with six goals in 33 games. Has remained consistent to that and always commands a spot in the Farense line-up.

PIVETEAU, Fabien
(Le Havre, Fra)

• 28.10.63 • Goalkeeper

Giant 'keeper (6ft 4in) who began with Angers in 1984. Kicked off his pro career with Nice, making his debut at Racing Club Paris in May 1987. Moved to Le Havre in 1990.

PIZZI, Juan Antonio
(Tenerife, Spa)

• 07.06.68 • Striker

Formidable Argentinian forward who joined Tenerife in 1991 from Mexican club Toluca.

van der PLAS, Arjan
(Feyenoord, Hol)

• 06.09.71 • Defender

Full back who has spent 1990/91 season on loan with Excelsior.

PLATT, David
(Juventus, Ita)

• 10.06.65 • Midfield
• England 31 full caps, 11 goals

After serving his apprenticeship at Old Trafford, David was released by Manchester United and finally turned pro with little Crewe. Signed by Aston Villa for £200,000 in February 1988 and went on to establish himself as a regular in the England side. His performance at the 1990 World Cup finals in Italy persuaded Bari to pay £5.5m in the summer of 1991, a record fee for a British player at the time. Despite Bari's poor form in 91/92, Platt was a huge success during his first term in Italian football. Juventus swooped for his signature in June 1992 for a staggering £8 million, and he is expected to forge a lucrative partnership with another new-boy Gianluca Vialli.

PLESSERS, Gerard
(Kortrijk, Bel)

• 30.03.59 • Defender
• Belgium 13 full caps, 1 goal

Vastly experienced centre back who is approaching 300 senior games. Previously with Overpelt Fabriek and Standard Liege before spending a successful spell with Hamburg in Germany. Returned to Belgium with Genk and signed from Kortrijk in 1990. International debut came v Scotland (lost 3-1) in December 1979.

PLOVIE, Pascal
(Club Brugge, Bel)

• 07.05.65 • Defender
• Belgium 5 full caps

A favourite of Belgian manager Guy Thys, he made his international debut v Mexico (June 1990), coming on as sub for Eric Gerets. Also played at Italia '90. Versatile full back or wide midfielder who has tremendous ball skills. In his second spell with Club Brugge, having started at the club before moving to Antwerp, he has enjoyed ten seasons at the Olympiastadion.

POINT, Christophe
(Caen, Fra)

• 26.05.65 • Defender

Home-grown central defender who joined the club as an 11-year-old schoolboy in 1976. Made his debut as one half of a new defensive partnership alongside Franck Dumas, at Cannes in July 1988. Has now made more than 100 first team appearances.

POLICANO, Roberto
(Torino, Ita)

• 19.02.64 • Midfield

Began with Third Division Latina in 1981 and spent two seasons in the Third Division before joining Genoa in Serie A. His stay in the top flight lasted just one season as Genoa were relegated in his first season. Returned to Serie A in 1987 when signed by his home-town club Roma. Joined Torino two years later.

POLLEY, Prince
(Germinal Ekeren, Bel)

• 05.04.69 • Striker

Scored seven goals in 26 games for Beerschot in 1990/91, which tempted Ekeren to swoop for his signature during the close season and take him to Veltwijckpark. Ghana-born goalscorer who was previously with Ashanti Kotoko and Sparta Rotterdam.

POLSTER, Anton
(Logrones, Spain)

• 10.03.64 • Striker
• Austria 44 full caps, 15 goals

One of Austria's best known stars. Played for Austria Vienna, Torino and Seville before joining Logrones in 1991.

PONS, Frederic
(Toulouse, Fra)

• 14.05.62 • Defender

Algerian-born full back who began with Metz, taking his League bow v Strasbourg in December 1985. Moved on to Toulon before joining Toulouse in 1990. Made his 200th senior appearance during season 1991/92.

POPESCU, Gheorge
(PSV Eindhoven, Hol)

• 09.10.67 • Defender
• Romania 29 full caps, 1 goal

Began with Universitatea Craiova in Romania. Had a short spell with Steaua Bucharest, but returned to Craiova. Joined PSV after 1990 World Cup finals.

PORRINI, Sergio
(Atalanta, Ita)

• 08.11.68 • Defender

Libero who spent the first three years of his career at Milan without ever making a League appearance. Finally got his chance in Serie A when he joined Atalanta in 1989 and has now become a first team regular.

PORRO, Alessandro
(Foggia, Ita)

• 29.06.67 • Defender

Joined Maceratese in 1984 and spent three seasons with the club before moving on to Fano. Spent the 1988/89 season with Lanciano and joined Foggia in 1990.

PORTE, Krist
(Gent, Bel)

• 07.09.68 • Striker

Home grown player who's first team outings have been restricted since the arrival of Marc van der Linden and Erwin Vandenburgh at the club.

PORTELA Jorge Manuel Duarte
(Farense, Por)

• 12.03.65 • Defender

Began his career with his home-town club of Sporting Lisbon but made just eleven appearances in two seasons from 1988. Moved to Farense in 1990/91 and has developed as an attacking full-back.

POSCHNER, Gerhard
(Borussia Dortmund, Ger)

• 23.09.69 • Midfield

Began his career with Stuttgart, but moved on to Borussia Dortmund at the age of 21. Has played over 80 First Division games.

POST, Edwin
(Den Haag, Hol)

• 11.01.66 • Striker

Was given his chance in League football by PEC Zwolle, but after just one season he was signed by Den Haag in August 1988.

POUTCH, Neil
(Shamrock Rovers, Eir)

• 27.11.69 • Midfield

Dublin-born central midfielder who began with Luton Town, but failed to make the grade at Kenilworth Road and transferred to the Rovers in June 1990. He made his League of Ireland debut in September of that year, v Athlone Town.

Played for both Moscow Dynamo and Moscow Torpedo as a youth. Joined Spartak Moscow in 1980 making debut in 1982. Member of USSR European U21 Championship winning side in 1990. Joined Stahl in 1991.

POVLSEN, Flemming (Borussia Dortmund, Ger)

• 03.12.66 • Striker
• Denmark 49 full caps, 14 goals

Highly experienced forward who played for Aarhus and Viby in his native Denmark before joining Castilla in Spain. Had his first spell in Germany with Cologne before moving country yet again to join PSV Eindhoven in Holland. Sold by Bobby Robson to Dortmund in 1990.

POWER, Philip (Sligo Rovers, Eir)

• 22.08.67 • Striker

Joined first club Shelbourne straight from school, going on to take his bow in the League of Ireland against Waterford United in December 1987. Sligo snapped him up prior to the 1990/91 season.

POZDNYAKOV, Boris (Stahl Linz, Aus)

• 31.05.62 • Defender
• USSR U21 full caps

PREUD'HOMME, Michel (Mechelen, Bel)

• 24.01.59 • Goalkeeper
• Belgium 33 full caps

His international appearances have been limited due to the presence of Jean-Marie Pfaff in the Belgian goal, but he has remained the first choice for his country since 1987. His international debut came in May 1979, v Austria (0-0). Approaching 500 senior games he previously donned his gloves for Standard Liege and Malinois.

PRINZEN, Roger (Wattenscheid, Ger)

• 04.03.69 • Midfield

Previously with Kaiserslautern and Eintracht Frankfurt, but failed to make the grade. Moved on to Darmstadt and signed for Wattenscheid in 1991.

PRIOU, Franck (Cannes, Fra)

• 17.10.63 • Striker

Began with Mulhouse, where he made his League debut, v Toulouse, in July

1989. Moved to Sochaux and then on to Cannes in 1991.

PROGNA, Domenico (Bari, Italy)

• 07.08.63 • Defender

A midfielder turned sweeper, Domenico began his career with Lecce before joining Campobasso in 1982. Three years later he joined Pisa, but he could not prevent their relegation from the Serie A during his first season. Joined Atalanta in October 1986, but again suffered relegation in his first term. However, the club bounced back to the top flight the follow season and Progna was part of the Atalanta side that reached the European Cup-Winners' Cup Semi-Finals in 1988. Signed by Bari for £1m in 1991.

PROSINECKI, Robert (Real Madrid, Spa)

• 12.01.69 • Midfield
• Yugoslavia 16 full caps, 4 goals

Born in Germany of Croatian parents. A precocious midfielder who had a serious knee injury that kept him out of action for the whole of 1991/92. Had moved to Real from Red Star Belgrade, where he had won the European Cup in June 1991. Played in the 1990 World Cup and the 1987 World Youth Championships, in Chile, which was won by Yugoslavia. He missed the final of that competition, but was still voted "Player of the Tournament" in his absence.

PROTASOV, Oleg (Olympiakos Piraeus, Gre)

• 14.02.64 • Striker
• USSR 66 full caps, 28 goals

Made his international debut for the USSR against West Germany in 1984, but hit the headlines a year later when he set a Soviet League record by scoring 35 goals in 34 games with Dnepr. Made a fleeting appearance in the 1986 World Cup finals and later moved from Dnepr to Dynamo Kiev. Moved to Olympiakos in 1990.

PRUNIER, William (Auxerre, Fra)

• 14.8.67 • Defender

Young defender who has close to 200 senior games to his credit. On the fringes of the international set-up, his height is a great asset at the back for Auxerre.

PUDAR, Ivan (Boavista, Por)

• 16.08.61 • Goalkeeper
• Yugoslavia full caps

Born in Split, Yugoslavia and joined Boavista from another Portuguese side, Sporting Espinho, during the summer of 1991.

PUEL, Claude
(Monaco, Fra)

• 02.09.61 • Midfield
• France U21

Home grown player who joined the club as 15-year-old in 1976. Took his senior bow on 25th May 1979 against Paris St Germain. A hard-running midfielder who has played more than 330 senior games for the club.

PUGLISI, Carmelo
(Torino, Ita)

• 03.02.72 • Midfield

Played just one season with Messina in Serie B before being snapped up by Torino prior to the 1991/92 season.

PURVIS, Edwin
(Den Haag, Hol)

• 24.10.61 • Defender

Has now been with Den Haag for 12 years, making over 380 appearances in the process.

PUSZAMSZIES, Toni
(MSV Duisburg, Ger)

• 14.08.58 • Defender

Made around a dozen first team appearances for Bayer Uerdingen before joining Duisburg in 1985.

QUAIN, Didier
(RC Liege, Bel)

• 15.12.60 • Midfield

Formerly with Tournaisienne and Kortrijk, he celebrated his 300th First Division appearance during 1990/91.

QUARANTA, Raphael
(Antwerp, Bel)

• 29.12.57 • Defender

Experienced central defender and club captain who is approaching 400 senior games. Previously with CS Visetois and Cercle Liege.

QUERTER, Alex
(Club Brugge, Bel)

• 18.12.57 • Defender

One of several hugely experienced players in the Brugge side, he signed from Cercle Brugge. Injury has restricted his appearances to a handful over the past two seasons. Previously with Lokeren.

QUEVEDO, Jose Maria
(Cadiz, Spa)

• 01.06.69 • Midfield

Tall midfielder who is now in his third season with Cadiz.

QUIGLEY, Nigel (Glenavon, N.Ir)

• Defender

Signed from home-town club Coleraine in January 1992 for an undisclosed fee. A joiner by occupation, he was Coleraine's Player of the Year in 1989/90.

QUIM Joaquim Carvalho Azevedo (Farense, Por)

• 23.08.59 • Midfield
• Portugal full caps

Has been in the top flight for over a decade and had three seasons with Porto from 1985/86 when he also represented the national side. Started his career with three years at Rio Ave from 1981 then went to Porto and Tirense before being signed by Farense in 1990/91.

QUIM Joaquim Gomes Carneiro (Gil Vicente, Por)

• 19.06.54 • Goalkeeper

Much travelled keeper whose previous clubs include Maritimo, Fafe, Beira-Mar and Penafiel.

QUIM MACHADO Joaquim M Goncalves (Vitoria Guimaraes, Por)

• 10.10.66 • Midfield

A hard-working player who has made his name thorough his fitness and tackling. Played over fifty times in two seasons for Brage before switching to Vitoria in 1991/92.

QUIQUE (Valencia, Spa)

• 02.02.65 • Defender

Left back whose real name is Enrique Sanchez Flores. Joined Valencia in 1984 from Madrid junior club, Peqaso.

RABESANDRATANA, Eric
(Nancy, Fra)

- 18.09.72 • Defender
- France Schools; Youth

A commentator's nightmare (the name is Madagascan in origin), he's nicknamed Rabe. Flexible player who likes to quickly turn defence into attack, he has been compared to Milan's Frank Rijkaard. Came through the ranks at Nancy, signing on, aged 14, in 1986.

RADANOVIC, Ljubomir
(Standard Liege, Bel)

- 21.07.60 • Defender
- Yugoslavia 33 full caps

One of the Belgian League's leading players he is equally comfortable playing sweeper or central defence. 1991/92 is his fourth season with the club, which he left for Nice in 1990/91, and then returned to when the French club was declared bankrupt. Formerly with Lovcen and Partizan Belgrade in his home country.

RAMBAUDI, Roberto
(Foggia, Ita)

- 12.01.66 • Striker

Joined Torino in 1984, but failed to make the first team. Made his League debut in 1985 while with Omegna and joined Foggia after periods with Pavia and Perugia.

RAMON Calvo Val
(Celta, Spa)

- 07.08.62 • Midfield

Tall midfield player who had spells with Valladolid and Deportivo before joining Celta.

RAMON Vazquez Garcia
(Seville, Spa)

- 14.02.64 • Striker
- Spain 3 full caps, 1 goal

Bought by Seville from Recreativo de Huelva in 1986 and is a consistant goalscorer for the club.

RAMOS, Tab
(Figueros, Spa)

- 21.09.66 • Midfield
- USA full caps

Born in Uruguay, but opted to play for the United States. A member of the States World Youth Cup squad in 1983 aged just 16 and made his full international debut against Guatemala in January 1988. His performance in the 1990 World Cup finals earned him a contract with Figueros in Spain.

RAMPULLA, Michelangelo (Cremonese, Ita)

• 10.08.62 • Goalkeeper

Began his career with Fourth Division Pattese, but failed to make a League appearance before moving on to Varese in Serie B. After three seasons with the club he spent a further two at Cesena before joining Cremonese in 1985. Twice helped the club to gain promotion to Serie A and created history in 1992 by becoming the first goalkeeper to score in a Serie A game when he equalised with a header following a corner in injury time of the game against Atalanta.

RAUDNEI Anversa Freire (Gil Vicente, Por)

• 18.07.65 • Striker

Frontman from Sao Paulo, Brazil who began his Portugese league career with Porto. Signed from Belenenses at start of 1991/92 season.

RAVELLI, Thomas (Gothenburg, Swe)

• 13.08.59 • Goalkeeper
• Sweden 91 full caps; U21; Youth

His brother Andreas was also a Swedish international. Thomas became Sweden's most capped keeper with his 78th appearance v West Germany in 1990. Signed by Gothenburg from Osters Vaxjo in 1989 as a replacement for Erik Thorstvedt who was sold to Tottenham Hotspur. Rumoured to be a target for First Division Luton Town.

RAVERA, Alain (Cannes, Fra)

• 25.02.65 • Defender

Home grown player who has come up through the ranks at the club he first came to the notice of as a nine-year-old in 1974. Made his senior debut against Lens in August 1987 and has now played more than fifty times in the First Division.

RAVNIC (Valladolid, Spa)

• Goalkeeper

Experienced Yugoslavian 'keeper who re-signed for Valladolid in 1992 following the departure of Columbian international Rene Higuita. Had previously been with Valladolid in the mid 1980s.

RECEP, Cetin (Besiktas, Tur)

• 01.10.65 • Defender
• Turkey 13 full caps

An integral member of the Besiktas back line that conceded just 17 goals, and didn't lose a single game, on the way to their third successive League title in 1991/92.

Made his international debut v Hungary in March 1988, but then spent 18 months out in the cold before being recalled for the game against England in October 1991. Can play at right full back or central defence.

RECHA
(Betis, Spa)
• 07.06.67 • Midfield

Jose Maria Alvarez de la Rosa moved into the Betis first team squad from the reserves in 1988 and has stayed theer ever since.

RECK, Oliver
(Werder Reck, Ger)
• 27.02.65 • Goalkeeper

Bremen's first choice number one, signed from Kickers Offenbach in 1985. Has made over 150 League appearances for the club.

REDONDO, Joao
Antonio Cunha
(Beira-Mar, Por)
• 08.01.62 • Defender

Began his career with Os Limianos and got his chance in the Portuguese First Division with Beira-Mar during the 1988/89 season. Has now made over 100 appearances for the club in the top flight.

REEKERS, Rob
(Bochum, Ger)
• 07.05.66 • Defender
• Holland 3 full caps

Former Dutch international who used to play for FC Twente in his native country. Joined Bochum from ASC Schîppingen in 1986.

REHN, Stefan
(Gothenburg, Swe)
• 22.09.66 • Midfield
• Sweden 25 full caps, 5 goals; Olympic; U21; Youth

Won promotion from Swedish Second Division with Djurgardens in 1987 and, after making international debut v East Germany in January 1988, joined Everton in England. Could not settle and quickly brought back to Sweden by Gothenburg in 1990. Won League and Cup double in 1991.

REICH, Burkhard
(Karlsruher, Ger)
• 01.12.64 • Defender
• East Germany 6 full caps

Began his career with Dynamo Furstenwalde, before joing FC Berlin. Wsa given his chance in the Bundesliga when signed by Karlsruher in 1991.

REICHERT, Peter
(Karlsruher, Ger)

• 04.08.61 • Striker

Former VfB Stuttgart forward who quit Germany to try his luck in France. After spells with Racing Strasburg and Toulouse he returned home with Karlsruher in 1990.

REID, Noel
(Athlone Town, Eir)

• 14.03.67 • Striker

Former St Pat's and Bohemians forward who joined the club in the summer of 1990. Scored on his League of Ireland debut, for Bohemians v Galway United, on 26th October 1986.

REINHARDT, Alois
(Bayern Munich, Ger)

• 18.11.61 • Defender
• Germany 4 full caps

Joined Bayer Leverkusen from 1.FC Nuremburg in 1984. Signed by Bayern for £300,000 in November 1991.

REKDAL, Kjettil
(Lierse, Bel)

• 06.11.68 • Midfield
• Norway 11 full caps

Prolific midfielder who's done much to boost Lierse's 'goals for' tally over the past two seasons. Began with home town club Molde FK before joining Borussia Moenchengladbach in Germany.

van RETHY, Ronny
(Antwerp, Bel)

• 21.11.61 • Defender

Experienced lower division player with Zwaluwen Olmen and KFC Beringen. Has made more than 230 senior appearances since joining Antwerp.

REUTER, Stefan
(Borussia Dortmund, Ger)

• 16.10.66 • Defender
• Germany 36 full caps, 2 goals

Like Juve team-mate Jurgen Kohler, he was a member of West Germany's 1990 World Cup winnning side. Followed Kohler from Bayern Munich to Juventus in 1991 for £3m. Returned to his native Germany with Dortmund in June 1992. Nicknamed Turbo for his lightning raids down the flanks.

REUZEAU, Bertrand
(Montpellier, Fra)

• 01.04.66 • Defender
• France U21

Short for a right-back (5ft 7in), he signed from Marseille in 1991, having spent the 1990/91 season on loan at Lille. Began with Laval, for whom he made his League debut, v Auxerre, in August 1984.

REVAULT, Christophe (Le Havre, Fra)

• 22.03.72 • Goalkeeper

Home grown player who has progressed the ranks at the club. Understudy to first choice 'keeper Fabien Piveteau.

REVELLES, Patrick (Toulon, Fra)

• 20.09.68 • Striker

Local discovery who joined the club from school in 1985. Was signed as a midfielder, but has revealed such an eye for goal that he was pushed up front in 1992/93. Earned his debut, v Nancy, in August 1990 and went on to score ten goals in 28 games during his first senior season. The 1991/92 season saw him grab eight goals.

REYNDERS, Eric (Genk, Bel)

• 28.01.65 • Midfield

Creative midfielder who signed from Antwerp in the wake of Genk's promotion from Division Two in 1989/90. Previously with Beringen.

REYNOLDS, Joe (Shelbourne, Eir)

• 16.03.64 • Defender

Former Shamrock Rovers stopper who's fierce tackling makes him a firm favourite at Tolka Park.

REYNOLDS, Kevin (Bray Wanderers, Eir)

• 14.07.65 • Midfield

Made his League of Ireland debut against Newcastlewest on 11th September 1988 (won 2-1). Was a member of the club's 1990/91 promotion winning side.

RHODE, Frank (SV Hamburg, Ger)

• 02.03.60 • Defender
• East Germany 42 full caps

Former Dynamo Rostock defender who joined Hamburg from FC Berlin in 1990.

RIBAR, Jean-Luc (Rennes, Fra)

• 26.02.65 • Midfield
• France U21

One of only a handful of players at the club with extensive experience in the top flight. Spent four seasons with St Etienne and Lille before dropping down to Division Two with Quimper in 1988.

Rennes snapped him up in 1989 and his prompting from the wings helped the club to promotion in 1990.

RIBEIRO, Jose Manuel Vidal

(Beira-Mar, Por)
• 14.04.64 • Defender

Began his career with Vista Alegre and joined Beira-Mar in the Portuguese First Division prior to the start of the 1990/91 season.

RICARDO AGUIAR Miguel Teieira (Maritimo, Por)

• 27.05.63 • Defender

Signed for Maritimo in 1987 but has failed to find a regular first team spot, playing only a handful of games since joining.

RICARDO (Gomes), Remondo (Paris St Germain, Fra)

• 13.12.64 • Defender
• Brazil full caps

Nine goals in 36 games during the 1990/91 season with Benfica prompted Paris-SG to sign this outstanding sweeper from Rio. His goals tally speaks volumes about the way he likes to bring the ball out from the back and get involved in attacking moves. Began with Fluminese in his native Brazil before travelling to the

Stadium of Light in 1987. Paris-SG signed him in the summer of 1991.

RICARDO LADEIRA Alexandre Gomes (Maritimo, Por)

• 31.05.65 • Midfield

Can score goals but prefers a steady role, marshalling the midfield. For three years from 1988 was a regular member in the Nacional line-up before Maritimo signed him up.

RICARDO Narusevicius (Farense, Por)

• 27.09.61 • Striker

Holds dual Portuguese and Brazilian nationality and has been a regular member of the first team for four years.

RICARDO JORGE Andrade Fernandes (Uniao, Por)

• 30.10.64 • Defender

A consistent defender who started with the club in 1989, left for a season with Gil Vincente, but was re-signed a year later.

RICE, Paul (Cliftonville, N.Ir)

• Goalkeeper

Signed professional with the club in 1990 and has attracted interest from English and Scottish League clubs.

RICKY
(Boavista, Por)

• 16.07.61 • Striker
• Nigeria full caps

Began his career in Portuguese football with Benfica in 1988, but after failing to score in four League outings he was off loaded to Amadora. Spent two seasons with the club and scored 28 League goals to earn himself a move to Boavista prior to the 1991/92 season.

RIDVAN, Dilmen
(Fenerbahce, Tur)

• 15.08.62 • Striker
• Turkey 23 full caps, 5 goals

Widely regarded, along with countryman Colak Tanju, as one of the most dangerous forwards in the European game. When fit he is a real menace - and truly earns his 'Little Devil' nickname. The match against England in October 1991 was his first international for some time, and it was welcome return. He had spent the previous year struggling with a serious knee injury that threatened to end his career, and, just as that appeared to be clearing up, he dislocated a shoulder. Fenerbahce signed him from local League club Sariyer.

RIEDLE, Karl-Hienz
(Lazio, Ita)

• 16.09.65 • Striker
• Germany 24 full caps, 9 goals

Played lower League football in Germany with Augsburg and Blau-Weiss Berlin, before joining Werder Bremen. Cost Lazio £4m to bring him to Italy. He is also a fully qualified butcher. His partnership with Lazio team-mate Thomas Doll has earned the pair the nickname "Romulus and Remus" after the fabled founders of Rome. He has been described by Germany captain Rudi Voller as "the best header of the ball in Europe."

RIJKAARD, Frank
(Milan, Ita)

• 30.09.62 • Midfield
• Holland 54 full caps, 5 goals

Began career with Ajax, but fell out with manager Johan Cruyff. Arrived at Milan in summer 1988. Sent off in 1990 finals v Germany for spitting at Rudi Voller and afterwards announced his retirement from international football, although he later changed his mind and played in Holland's ultimately disappointing 1992 European Championship side.

RIO, Michel
(Caen, Fra)

• 07.03.63 • Midfield

Left-sided midfielder, who loves to get behind the defence. Previously with Guingcamp, Nantes and Metz, he joined Caen in 1989. His senior debut came for Nantes in November 1986, when he came on as sub in their game v Brest. More than 20 goals in over 150 first team games so far for the club.

RIPODAS, Patxi
(Atletico Bilbao, Spa)

• 13.09.60 • Midfield

Big money signing who joined Bilbao in the summer of 1989 from fellow Basque side Osasuna.

RITTER, Thomas
(Stuttgarter Kickers, Ger)

• 10.10.67 • Defender

Signed from Fortschritt Bischofswerda in 1990. Previously with Dynamo Dreseden in the old East Germany.

RIX, Dennis
(Linfield, N.Ir)

• Midfield

Something of a squad player, he was signed from Ballyclare Comrades in the summer of 1991. Hard-working and useful in front of goal, Rix formerly played with Ards.

RIX, Graham
(Le Havre, Fra)

• 23.10.57 • Midfield
• England 17 full caps; U21

Joined Arsenal from school, and spent 13 productive seasons at Highbury, appearing in three FA Cup finals (one win) and one Littlewoods (League) Cup final. After six games on loan at Third Division Brentford he transferred to Caen. moving to Le Havre in July 1991. Injury has severely restricted his appearances over the past two years. Missed the vital penalty in Arsenal's 1980 Cup-Winners' Cup final shoot-out v Valencia. Considered retirement at the end of the 1991/92 season

RIZA, Calimbay
(Besiktas, Tur)

• 02.02.63 • Defender
• Turkey 25 full caps

Another fine player to come off the quality youth production line at Besiktas. He made his international debut v Austria back in November 1982 (lost 4-0) and has not missed a national game since October 1989. Attacking full back who likes nothing more than to get forward and take people on, his prompting from the wings has helped his club to their utter domination of the League Championship in Turkey, which they have won for the last three years running.

RIZZITELLI, Ruggiero (Roma, Ita)

• 02.09.67 • Striker
• Italy 9 full caps, 3 goals

Began his career in the Italian Second Division with Cesena and helped the club gain promotion in 1987. After one year in the top flight he was snapped up by Roma.

ROBERT, Christophe (Monaco, Fra)

• 30.03.64 • Striker
• France U21

Quick, tricky striker who joined from Nantes in summer 1991. Had spent nine years at La Beaujoire, where he made his debut against Nancy in April 1982. Previously with Saint-Seurin.

ROBERTO Santamaria Calavia (Osasuna, Spa)

• 12.03.62 • Goalkeeper

Has been first choice between the posts for Osasuna for the past six years.

di ROCCO, Giovanni (Ascoli, Ita)

• 27.12.70 • Defender

Born in Naples and made his debut for Napoli while still a teenager. After spending a season in the Third Division with Torres, he joined Ascoli in the summer of 1990.

ROCHA, Ricardo (Real Madrid, Spa)

• 11.09.62 • Defender
• Brazil 53 full caps

Formerly with Sporting Lisbon in Portugal and Sao Paulo in his native South America.

ROCHE, Alain (Auxerre, Fra)

• 14.10.67 • Defender

Former Bordeaux and Marseille player who many have tipped to be a future international star. Calm on the ball and comfortable going forward he forms a sound partnership with William Prunier for the whites.

ROCHE, Stephane (Lyon, Fra)

• 25.09.70 • Midfield

Joined the club as a 15-year-old straight from school in 1985. Progressed through the Lyon's junior sides to make his senior debut on 30th August 1989, against Racing Paris. Has now played more than 50 Division One games. Scored two goals during the 1991/92 League campaign.

RODGERS, Derek
(Galway United, Eir)

• 06.10.67 • Defender

Most versatile player who has performed in
defence and midfield for Galway. Began
with Home Farm, then Shamrock Rovers,
before joining United in 1986.

RODLUND, Johnny
(IFK Norkopping, Swe)

• Striker
• Sweden full caps

Scored 16 goals in 30 games as a youth
international and made his U21 debut aged
18. Four goals in his first 10 games at that
level earned him a full international debut.

RODRIGUEZ, Bernard
(Toulon, Fra)

• 16.02.64 • Midfield

Had spent his entire career with minor
League club Sete before moving to Toulon
in 1990, making his debut at Monaco in
July of that year.

ROGERIO LEITE
(Sporting Braga, Por)

• 09.12.65 • Midfield

Began his career with Vitoria Guimaraes
and joined Sporting Braga via Fafe in
1990.

ROGERIO PIMENTA
(Sporting Braga, Por)

• 16.12.62 • Defender

Began his career with Gil Vicente but had
to move on to Chaves to make his debut in
the First Division. Made 93 appaearances
for the club at that level before moving to
Sporting Braga in 1991.

ROLLAIN, Herve
(Lille, Fra)

• 24.02.68 • Defender

Speedy young full back who joined from
minor-League club Angers in July 1991.
Likes to get forward down the flanks and
support the midfield and attack.

ROLLMAN, Jurgen
(Werder Bremen, Ger)

• 17.10.66 • Goalkeeper

Ex-Kickers Offenbach, 1860 Munich and
FSV Frankfurt. Joined Bremen in 1988 as
cover for Oliver Reck.

ROMANO, Serge
(Metz, Fra)

• 25.07.64 • Defender

Home grown player who first came to the
club as a 20-year-old, and has been with
them ever since. Made his Division One
debut against Toulon in July 1987 and

was a member of the victorious 1988 French Cup winning squad. Predominately a right back, but can play in central defence or wide midfield.

ROMARIO, Faria de Souza
(PSV Eindhoven, Hol)

• 29.01.66 • Striker
• Brazil full caps

Signed by PSV from Vasco Da Gama in Brazil, October 1988. Scored remarkable 67 goals in 69 League games during first three seasons in Holland. Top scorer in 1988 Olympic Games.

ROMMEL Fernandez Gutierrez
(Valencia, Spa)

• 15.01.66 • Striker

Panamanian attacker who originally began with Alianza de Panama. Arrived at Valencia via Tenerife in 1991. Regular scorer for the club.

RONDAGS, Patrick
(Lierse, Bel)

• 12.12.64 • Goalkeeper

Has made the number one spot his own since the departure of Kris de Fre to Beerschot at the beginning of 1991/92. Formerly with Rapid Spouwen and SK Tongeren.

ROONEY, Ray
(Sligo Rovers, Eir)

• 22.08.67 • Striker

One of three brothers currently on the books at the Showgrounds. Kieran and Philip have yet to establish themselves in the first team. Ray made his debut at Cobh Ramblers in September 1989, and scored the only goal of the game as Sligo won 1-0.

ROOS, Axel
(Kaiserslautern, Ger)

• 19.08.64 • Midfield

Came to Kaiserslautern as a 15-year-old in 1979 and has now made over 150 appearances for the club.

van ROOSBROECK, Kurt
(Lierse, Bel)

• 10.10.66 • Defender

Commanding centre back who was spotted playing for minor League club KFC Begijnendijk and signed for Lierse in 1987.

de ROOVER, Bart
(Gent, Bel)

• 21.08.67 • Defender

Began with minor League club Zwarte Leeuw before joining Lokeren. Signed for Gent in July 1991.

van ROOY, Frans (Standard Liege, Bel)

• 03.07.63 • Midfield

Astonishingly overlooked by Holland, he took Belgian citizenship in November 1991 in an attempt to gain international recognition. Magical player who can turn a match with one flash of brilliance. Forms a tremendous midfield axis with Guy Hellers. Joined the club from Antwerp for an undisclosed fee described as "huge" by coach Arie Haan. Previously with minor League club Woensel, and Eindhoven.

ROSEZ, Dirk (Standard Liege, Bel)

• 05.01.61 • Goalkeeper

Understudy to Gilbert Bodart. The 1992/93 season will be his third with the club, and he's still played less than 10 senior games. More than 120 First Division appearances to his credit with previous clubs Eendracht Denermonde, Eendracht Aalst and Beveren (twice).

ROSLER, Uwe (Dynamo Dresden, Ger)

• 15.11.68 • Striker
• East Germany 5 full caps

Had spells with the Leipzig clubs Lokomotiv and Chemie as a youth before moving on to Magdeburg. Signed by Dresden in 1990.

ROSSI, Sebastiano (Milan, Ita)

• 20.07.64 • Goalkeeper

Joined Cesena in 1981, but had to have loan spells with Forli, Empoli and RM Firenze, before breaking into Cesena side. Helped club to promotion from Second Division in 1987. Signed by Milan during summer 1990.

ROTH, Dietmar (Eintracht Frankfurt, Ger)

• 16.09.63 • Defender

After playing junior football with Liedolsheim, Dietmar was signed up by Karlsruher. Moved on to Schalke before arriving at Eintracht in the summer of 1987.

ROUSSEAU, Pascal (Rennes, Fra)

• 04.03.62 • Goalkeeper
• France Youth

Widely travelled 'keeper who is vying with Pierrick Hiard for the number one shirt at the club. Brought in as replacement for Franck Mantaux, who moved to Chateauroux in 1991. Was previously with Paris FC, Racing Paris, Laval and Marseille. Rennes signed him from Reims in July 1991.

ROUSSET, Gilles
(Lyon, Fra)

• 22.08.63 • Goalkeeper
• France 2 full caps

Made only his second international
appearance when he played against
England in February 1992, but earned a
place in France's squad for Sweden '92 as
understudy to Auxerre's Bruno Martini.
Giant 'keeper (6ft 6in) who joined Lyon in
June 1990, after spells with Boulougne-
Billancourt and Sochaux.

ROUX, Bruno
(Le Havre, Fra)

• 11.07.63 • Striker

Signed from Paris St Germain in 1988.
Made his senior debut, for Paris-SG,
against his present club, in July 1987.

ROUYR, Thierry
(RWD Molenbeek, Bel)

• 11.09.66 • Midfield

Former Jupille and Seraing player who
signed from Standard Liege. Approaching
200 senior appearances.

ROY, Bryan
(Ajax, Hol)

• 12.02.70 • Striker
• Holland 12 full caps, 2 goals

Has spent all his career with Ajax and
made his first team debut in 7-1 thrashing
of FC Twente in September 1987. Has
now made more than 100 appearances for
the club.

le ROY, Paul
(Lens, Fra)

• 12.02.70 • Defender

Home grown player who has progressed
through the ranks after being snapped up
from boys' club Bethune as a 14-year-old.
Made his senior debut against Bordeaux
on 25th March 1989.

RUFER, Wynton
(Werder Bremen, Ger)

• 29.12.62 • Striker
• New Zealand 9 full caps

Born in New Zealand of a Kiwi mother
and a Swiss father. Began his career with
local club Wellington Diamond and
represented his country in the 1982 World
Cup finals. Moved to Europe and played
for Norwich City, Zurich, FC Aarau and
Grasshoppers before joining Bremen in
1989. His brother, Shane Rufer, was with
Gillingham in the 1991/92 season.

RUDY, Andrzej
(Cologne, Ger)

• 15.10.65 • Midfield
• Poland 12 full caps

Signed from Polish side GKS Katowitz in

1989. Also played for Slask Breslau and Odra Scinawa in his home country.

RUI AGUAS
(Benfica, Por)

• 28.04.60 • Striker
• Portugal 22 full caps. 7 goals

The son of Jose Aguas, captain of Benfica's 1961 and 1962 European Cup winning sides. Began his career with his father's club, but moved away to Portimonense in 1983. Made his international debut while there, and was re-signed by Benfica in 1985. Helped the club to the League title in 1987 and the European Cup in 1988. Signed by Benfica's big rivals Porto prior to the start of the 1988/89 season, but returned home to Benfica for the third time in 1990.

RUI ALBERTO
(Salgueiros, Por)

• 21.03.67 • Striker

Began his career with Tirsense, but established himself at Rio Aves. Left the club during the summer of 1991 to join Salgueiros.

RUI BENTO
(Benfica, Por)

• 14.10.72 • Defender
• Portugal youth, 1 full cap

Joined Benfica from his home-town club Silves in 1987 and was promoted to the first team squad prior to the 1991/92 season. Member of Portugal's World Youth Cup winning squad in 1991.

RUI COSTA
(Benfica, Por)

• 29.03.72 • Defender
• Portugal youth

Talented full back who was a member of the Portuguese side that won the 1991 World Youth Cup. Picked up by Benfica as a youngster and loaned out to Fafe for experience. Returned to Benfica prior to the 1991/92 season.

RUI FRANCA
(Salgueiros, Por)

• 11.08.62 • Midfield

Another long serving Salgueiros player who made his First Division debut for the club back in the 1982/83 season. Began his career with Porto but failed to break into the first team set-up. Won Second Division championship medal with Salgueiros in 1990.

RUI JORGE Costa
Rodrigues
(Uniao, Por)

• 23.09.64 • Midfield

An unspectacular journeyman of the Portuguese league who spent several seasons in the lower divisions before joining Leixoes in 1988 and then moving on to Amadora. He had difficulty making the grade at both sides and is not a regular in the Uniao line-up.

RUI VIEIRA Manuel Pereira (Maritimo, Por)

• 21.05.62 • Defender

Started his career with Vitoria Guimaraes in 1984 but switched to Maritimo after four seasons. A sturdy defender who has scored just twice in over 150 League appearances.

RUMMENIGGE, Michael (Borussia Dortmund, Ger)

• 03.02.64 • Midfield
• Germany 2 full caps

The younger brother of former West German international striker Karl-Heinz Rummenigge. Struggled to match his brother's achievements at Bayern Munich, but after his move to Dortmund in 1988 Michael managed to prove himself.

RUOTOLO, Gennaro (Genoa, Ita)

• 20.03.67 • Midfield

Signed in 1988 after spells at Sorrento and Arezzo.

RUSSELL, Andy (Glenavon, N.Ir)

• Defender

In his second spell with the club after a 15-month sports scholarship in Alabama, USA. Was outstanding in the 1988 Cup final v Glentoran, and is the target of several clubs across the Irish Sea in England.

RUTJES, Graeme (Anderlecht, Bel)

• 26.03.60 • Defender
• Holland 13 full caps, 1 goal

Signed to help strengthen the defence in August 1990, he quickly established himself at Anderlecht and helped lead the club to their 21st League Championship in 1991. He scored three goals in 33 matches in that campaign. An experienced campaigner, with more than 35 European games under his belt with Anderlecht and previous club Mechelen. Also played for Nieuwkerk, Portland and Excelsior.

RYAN, John (St Patrick's Athletic, Eir)

• 27.02.68 • Striker

Now back at Harold's Cross having been transferred to Bray Wanderers at the beginning of the 1990/91 campaign. St Pat's quickly realised their mistake, and re-

signed him in February 1991. Made his
League of Ireland debut, v Cork City, in
September 1988.

RYDLEWICZ, Rene (Bayer Leverkusen, Ger)

• 18.07.73 • Striker

Began his career with East German side
Energie Cottbus, before moving to
Dynamo Berlin. Followed the example of
Andreas Thom and quit Berlin for
Leverkusen in 1990.

RZEHACZEK, Michael (Bochum, Ger)

• 17.01.67 • Midfield

Has played over 100 First Division games
since joining Bochum from FC
Recklinghausen in 1987.

SABAS, Juan
(Atletico Madrid, Spa)

• 13.04.467 • Striker

Made his name with Rayo Vallecano before moving on to Atletico Madrid in 1989.

SABAU, Ioan
(Feyenoord, Hol)

• 12.02.68 • Midfield

• Romania 32 full caps, 7 goals

Starred for Romania in 1990 World Cup finals while still playing club football for Dinamo Bucharest in his home country. Attempts to secure his signature after the finals were blocked by Romanian FA and Feyenoord only completed deal after UEFA and FIFA stepped in.

SABAU, Ion
(Mallorca, Spa)

• Goalkeeper

• Romania full caps

Played for his country in the 1990 World Cup finals in Italy and moved to Spain a year later, replacing the Morrocan Ezaki in the Mallorca goal.

SABBADINI, Marino
(Germinal Ekeren, Bel)

• 10.12.69 • Defender

Signed from minor League side Smeermaas in 1989/90, he has established himself as a firm favourite at Veltwijckpark. Likes to get forward and score goals from defence.

SALILLAS, Francesco
Garcia
(Celta, Spa)

• 07.01.66 • Striker

Formerly with Zaragoza, he joined Celta in 1991.

SALINAS, Julio
(Barcelona, Spa)

• 11.09.62 • Striker

• Spain 29 full caps, 8 goals

Member of the Spanish U21 side that reached the final of the 1984 European Championship. After starting out at Atletico Bilbao and then moving on to Atletico Madrid in 1986, Julio arrived at Barcelona in 1988. His first international goal came against the USSR during Spain's World Cup warm up in 1986.

SALVA, Salvador
Garcia
(Logrones, Spa)

• 04.03.61 • Defender

• Spain 6 full caps

Central defender who was capped by his country while with Barcelona, prior to moving to Logrones.

SALVI, Daniel
(Grasshoppers, Swi)

• 29.01.72 • Striker

Made his Grasshoppers debut v Lugano in March 1991.

SAMARAS, Yannis
(Panathinaikos, Gre)

• Striker
• Greece 16 full caps

Joined the club from OFI Crete in December 1988.

SAMMER, Matthias
(VfB Stuttgart, Ger)

• 05.09.67 • Midfield
• East Germany 23 full caps, 4 goals/Germany 10 full caps, 1 goal

Talented playmaker who is one of the few East German players to have forced their way into the united German national side on a regular basis. Played for Dynamo Dresden in the East, before moving West to VfB in 1990. Likely to be with Internazionale, of Milan, for the 1992/93 season.

SAMSON, Siasia
(Lokeren, Bel)

• 14.08.67 • Striker
• Nigeria 18 full caps

Lightning fast forward who has been a huge hit at the club since joining in 1986. Began at the Flash Flamingoes stable, a source of so many top Nigerian players, and also played with El Kalimi (twice) and Julius Berger FC.

SAMUEL Antonio
Silva Quina
(Boavista, Por)

• 03.08.66 • Defender

Spent seven seasons with Benfica, making 113 League appearances for the club before joining Boavista prior to the 1991/92 season.

SANCHEZ, Hugo
(Real Madrid, Spa)

• 11.07.58 • Striker
• Mexico 98 full caps

Previously with Universidad in Mexico. Joined Real in July 1985. His contract at Real Madrid was terminated towards the end of the 1991/92 campaign, following a "difference of opinion" with coach Leo Beenhakker. Well known for his spectacular goals, and lavish celebrations of them.

SANCHIS, Manuel
(Real Madrid, Spa)

• 23.05.65 • Defender
• Spain U18, Olympic, U21, 47 full caps, 1 goal

Madrid-born stopper who progressed to the Real first team squad via nursery side Castilla.

SANDERS, Koenraad (Mechelen, Bel)

• 17.12.62 • Defender
• Belgium 4 full caps

Former Brugge full back who has become a firm favourite at Mechelen. More than 300 senior games to his credit. International debut came v Yugoslavia in May 1989. More of a conventional, defensive, player
than many European full-backs.

SANE, Souleyman (Wattenscheid, Ger)

• 26.02.61 • Striker
• Senegal International

Signed from 1.FC Nuremburg in 1990. Previously with SC Freiburg. Member of Senegal squad at 1992 African Nations Cup.

SARAVAKOS, Dimitris (Panathinaikos, Gre)

• Striker
• Greece 65 full caps, 19 goals

A free-kick specialist, with a tremendous right foot shot, he is probably Greece's greatest asset. Began as a winger with Panionios, where his father Thanassis was a great favourite. Joined Panathinaikos in 1984, and has gone on to become one of the most feared forwards in Europe. Scored 33 goals in League and Cup competitions as the club raced to the Greek League and Cup double in 1990/91. He is well on course to beat Nikos Anastopolous' Greek record appearances (73) and goals (29) at international level. He first appeared for the national side against Switzerland in 1982, and scored five goals in a 6-1 trouncing of Egypt in October 1990.

van der SAR, Edwin (Ajax, Hol)

• 29.10.70 • Goalkeeper

Understudy to the experienced Stanley Menzo, he made his first team debut v Sparta Rotterdam in April 1991.

SARRIUGARTE Montoya, Felix (Oviedo, Spa)

• 06.11.64 • Striker

Signed by Oviedo from Atletico Bilbao prior to the 1989/90 season.

de SART, Jean-Francois (Anderlecht, Bel)

• 18.12.61 • Defender
• Belgium 3 full caps

He played 264 games for Liege, his first and only club, before moving to

Anderlecht in the summer of 1991. Solid central defender. Made his international debut against Yugoslavia in May 1989 (won 1-0).

SASSUS, Jean-Luc (Cannes, Fra)

• 04.10.62 • Defender
• France U21; B

Attacking full back who has played more than 200 First Division games since his debut, for Toulouse, against Nantes in October 1982. Joined Cannes in 1986 and has established himself as a firm favourite with the fans.

SAUVAGET, Patrice (Lille, Fra)

• 24.06.66 • Striker

Slightly built, but with deceptive speed and a cannonball shot. Signed from minor-League club Angers in 1989. He took his First Division bow at home to Caen in July that year.

SAUZEE, Franck (Marseille, Fra)

• 28.10.65 • Midfield
• France U21; 26 full caps, 7 goals

Lethal from a dead ball situation, he began with Sochaux in 1989. Joined Marseille, but surprised many by leaving soon after for Monaco. Proved to be a good decision

as he lead the club to runners-up spot in the League, and a French Cup win over Marseille. The whites promptly re-signed him in summer 1991.

SAVICEVIC, Dejan (Milan, Ita)

• 15.09.66 • Striker
• Yugoslavia 26 full caps, 7 goals

Joined OFK Titograd as a boy and moved to Buducnost in 1983. Scored on his international debut three years later against Turkey. Joined Red Star Belgrade in 1988 and helped the club to the final of the 1990/9 European Cup, but was dropped for the vital Marseille match. Milan paid almost £12 million for his services in the summer of 1992.

SCAPPATICCI, Mario (Portadown, N.Ir)

• Defender

Has two older brothers playing in N.Ireland - Tony with Glentoran and Freddie. Came up through the ranks at Shamrock Park.

SCAPPATICCI, Tony (Glenavon, N.Ir)

• Defender

Signed from Banbridge Town in March 1989. Strong in the air, and comfortable on the ball he's been a vital part of Glenavon's recent success story.

SCHACHT, Dietmar (Schalke, Ger)

• 28.09.62 • Defender

Joined Schalke in 1989 after spells with Alemannia Aachen, Arminia Bielefeld and Tennis Borussia Berlin.

SCHAFER, Gunter (VfB Stuttgart, Ger)

• 09.06.62 • Defender

Joined Stuttgart as a 13-year-old and is currently the longest serving player at the club. Has witnessed two Bundesliga Championship titles and has made almost 300 appearances for the club.

SCHAFER, Oliver (Kaiserslautern, Ger)

• 27.02.69 • Midfield

Played all his football outside of the First Division before joining Kaiserslautern from Freiburg in 1991.

SCHEEPERS, Twan (PSV Eindhoven, Hol)

• 08.11.71 • Striker
• Holland Olympic

Product of PSV youth policy. Signed pro in 1989 and made League debut that season.

SCHELLEVIS, Leo (Den Haag, Hol)

• 07.01.67 • Defender

Like so many of Den Haag's squad, Leo was discovered by his home-town club playing in local football. Made his debut for the side at the end of the 1985/86 season

de SCHEPPER, Ludo (Waregem, Bel)

• 24.09.64 • Goalkeeper

Understudy to Marc Huysmans at the club, which he joined from Oostkamp, his only previous side.

SCHERR, Uwe (Kaierslautern, Ger)

• 16.01.66 • Midfield

After playing junior football with Amberg, Uwe was signed by Nuremburg. Joined Kaiserslautern via Augsburg.

SCHEUER, Sven (Bayern Munich, Ger)

• 19.01.71 • Goalkeeper
• Germany U21

Joined Bayern from Stuttgart amateur club, SV Böblingen in 1988.

SCHILLACI, Salvatore
(Internazionale, Ita)

• 01.12.64 • Striker
• Italy 16 full caps, 7 goals

'Toto' shot to fame in Italia '90 when he was the tournament's leading scorer with 6 goals in the finals. Born in Palermo and spent seven seasons with little Messina before moving to Juventus in 1989. Signed a three year contract with Internazionale in June 1992.

van't SCHIP, Johnny
(Genoa, Ita)

• 30.12.63 • Striker
• Holland 35 full caps, 2 goals

Experienced forward who has spent all of his career with Ajax. Made his debut for the club v Haarlem in December 1981 and has now played over 300 games for the side. Moved to Italy with Genoa in June 1992.

SCHIPPERS, Nick
(Eendracht Aalst, Bel)

• 16.12.61 • Goalkeeper

Experienced 'keeper who signed from Antwerp. Previously with Beershot. Played a big part in the club winning the Second Division play-offs in 1990/91 to achieve Division One football for the first time since 1962.

SCHLIPPER, Gunter
(Schalke, Ger)

• 13.08.62 • Midfield

Began his career with Cologne, but failed to establish a regular first team place. Moved to Schalke in 1988.

SCHLOTTERBECK, Nils
(MSV Duisburg, Ger)

• 12.03.67 • Midfield

Signed from SC Freiburg in 1991. Previously had spells with VfB Stuttgart, Stuttgarter Kickers and Offenburg.

SCHMALER, Nils
(VfB Stuttgart, Ger)

• 10.11.69 • Defender

Twin brother of Stuttgart striker Olaf Schmaler. Has found it somewhat easier than his brother to make the first team since arriving at VfB from Eintracht Braunschweig in 1988.

SCHMALER, Olaf
(VfB Stuttgart, Ger)

• 10.11.69 • Striker

Has followed the same career path as his twin Nils, both beginning to play their football with Victoria Braunschweig. The twins later moved on to Eintracht Braunschweig before both joining

Stuttgart in 1988. Has yet to win a regular first team place.

SCHMIDT, Bodo (Borussia Dortmund, Ger)

• 03.09.67 • Defender

Failed to make the grade at Bayern Munich as a youngster and moved on to SpVgg Unterhaching. Given his chance back in the First Division by Dortmund in 1991.

SCHMIDT, Ferenc (MSV Duisburg, Ger)

• 28.07.63 • Striker

Began his career with Cologne and moved on to Luttringhausen and Bocholt before joining Duisburg for the first team. Later moved on to Wuppertaler before returning to MSV in 1989.

SCHMIDT, Lars (Karlsruher, Ger)

• 13.09.65 • Midfield

Joined club from SpVgg Bad Homburg in 1985. Previously with Kickers Offenbach.

SCHMOLLER, Frank (Germinal Ekeren, Bel)

• 21.08.66 • Striker

German-born goalscorer who began with home-town club TSV Niendorf before moving, via SV Hamburg and SVW Mannheim, to Belgium with Lierse. In 1990/91, his first season at Ekeren, he scored 10 goals in 27 games.

SCHNEIDER, Martin (Borussia Moenchengladbach, Ger)

• 24.11.68 • Midfield

Signed by Borussia from Nuremburg in the summer of 1990. Previously with Bayern Munich.

SCHOLL, Mehmet (Bayern Munich, Ger)

• 16.10.70 • Midfield

The son of a migrant Turkish work, Mehmet was signed by Bayern from Karlsruher in May 1992 for a then German record fee of £3.7m. He had begun his football life with Karlsruher at the age of 13.

SCHOLTEN, Arnold (Feyenoord, Hol)

• 05.12.62 • Midfield

Signed by Ajax from Den Bosch, but could not establish a regular place in Amsterdam and moved to Feyenoord in 1989.

SCHOLZ, Heiko
(Dynamo Dresden, Ger)

• 07.01.66 • Midfield
• East Germany 7 caps

Involved with Dresden as a youngster, but developed at Lokomotiv Leipzig. Returned to Dynamo in 1990.

SCHON, Alfred
(Nancy, Fra)

• 13.01.62 • Defender
• Germany B; Olympic

Speedy defender who signed in 1991, after making 180 appearances in Bundesliga II, with Mannheim. Fine athlete who fills the sweeper's role at Marcel-Picot and has become a firm favourite with the fans.

SCHOOFS, Johan
(Lokeren, Bel)

• 14.02.64 • Defender

The club's longest serving player, he is approaching 300 senior appearances at the Daknamstadion. Began with Eendracht Genenbos and then moved to Beringen, before hitting the big time with Lokeren.

SCHOSSLER, Detlef
(Dynamo Dresden, Ger)

• 03.10.63 • Defender
• East Germany 18 full caps

Spent all his junior and early career with Magdeburg before being signed by Dresden in 1989.

SCHREIER, Christian
(Fortuna Dusseldorf, Ger)

• 04.02.59 • Midfield
• Germany 1 full cap

Signed from Bayer Leverkusen in 1991. Previously with VfL Bochum.

SCHREUDER, Alfred
(Feyenoord, Hol)

• 02.11.72 • Midfield

Came up through the junior ranks with brother Dick at PSV Eindhoven before being snapped up by Feyenoord in 1991.

SCHREUDER, Dick
(PSV Eindhoven, Hol)

• 02.08.71 • Striker

Joined PSV from Feyenoord as a junior.

de SCHRIJVER, Hans
(Eendracht Aalst, Bel)

• 16.11.65 • Goalkeeper

Former Anderlecht number one who never made the breakthrough at Constant Vanden Stock Stadium. Understudy to Nick Schippers.

SCHRODER, Marco (Bayer Leverkusen, Ger)

• 18.05.66 • Striker

Joined Bayer from junior side VfL Leverkusen in 1987, but has struggled to make an impression in the First Division.

SCHRODER, Michael (SV Hamburg, Ger)

• 10.11.59 • Midfield

Returned to Hamburg from VfB Stuttgart in 1989.

SCHULTZ, Frank (Borussia Moenchengladbach, Ger)

• 18.02.61 • Midfield

Ex-VfL Bochum and Eintracht Frankfurt. Signed from VfL Osnabruck in 1990.

SCHULZ, Axel (Hansa Rostock, Ger)

• 20.05.59 • Midfield
• East Germany 3 full caps

Long-serving midfielder who has spent all his career with Rostock. Originally joined the club as a schoolboy.

SCHULZ, Michael (Borussia Dortmund, Ger)

• 03.09.61 • Defender

After playing junior football with TuS Syke and Nettlingen, Michael joined Oldenburg and earned himself a move to Kaiserslautern. Signed by Dortmund in 1989.

SCHUMACHER, Harald (Bayern Munich, Ger)

• 06.03.54 • Goalkeeper
• Germany 76 full caps

Nicknamed Toni. Former West German captain, twice German Footballer of the Year. World Cup runner-up 1982, 1986. Spent most of career with Cologne, but was sacked in 1987 following publication of his controversial autobiography. Resumed career in Turkey with Fenerbahce until injury forced him to quit at end of 1990/91 season. Came out of retirement October 1991 to help out during Bayern's injury crisis.

SCHUPP, Markus (Wattenscheid, Ger)

• 07.01.66 • Midfield

Midfield playmaker signed from 1.FC Kaiserslautern in 1991. Tipped as possible international last season.

SCHUSTER, Bernd
(Atletico Madrid, Spa)

• 22.11.59 • Midfield
• West Germany 21 full caps, 4 goals

Gifted and highly experienced midfielder who has, quite incredibly, played for Barcelona, Real madrid and Atletico Madrid. Has not played for the national side since 1984, but has said that he now wishes to return to Berti Vogts' team.

SCHUTH, Philippe
(Metz, Fra)

• 15.12.66 • Goalkeeper

Stand-in goalkeeper behind Michel Ettorre at the club. Began with Strasbourg, for whom he made his First Division debut, against Rouen, in March 1985. Also played for Angers and Dunkerque before joining Metz in July 1989.

SCHUTTERLE, Rainer
(Karlsruher, Ger)

• 21.03.66 • Midfield

Originally arriced at Karlsruher from junior side Kehler KV. Left to play for VfB Stuttgart, but returned in 1989.

SCHWABE, Dieter
(Eendracht Aalst, Bel)

• 12.09.56 • Defender

Solid and reliable central defender who has played more than 350 Belgian First Division games, mainly with his previous club Kortrijk. His experience was brought in to help the club consolidate after winning promotion in 1991/92. Played with Cologne, Bonn and Bayer Uerdingen in his native Germany.

SCHWABL, Manfred
(Bayern Munich, Ger)

• 18.04.66 • Midfield
• Germany full caps

Spent 8 years with Bayern as a junior before leaving for 1.FC Nuremburg in 1986. Re-signed in 1989 for £800,000.

SCHWANKE, Jorg
(Bochum, Ger)

• 12.01.69 • Defender
• East Germany 1 full cap

Came to Bochum in 1991 from East German club Energie Cottbus. Was previously with Dynamo Berlin.

SCHWARZ, Stefan
(Benfica, Por)

• 13.04.69 • Midfield
• Sweden 16 full caps, 2 goals

Plays on the left side of midfield and is always likely to cause problems at set pieces with his blistering left foot shot. Born in Sweden of a German father, he began his career with his home-town club, Malmo. Bayern Munich attempted to sign Stefan, but the deal fell through because he refused to take up the German citizenship which would have allowed Bayern to field an extra 'foreigner'. His decision to play for Sweden instead earned him appearances in the 1990 World Cup, the 1992 European Championships and a move to Benfica in Portugal.

SCIFO, Enzo
(Torino, Ita)
• 19.02.66 • Midfield
• Belgium 53 full caps, 11 goals

Born in Belgium of Italian parents he began his career with La Louviere before being given a chance with Anderlecht. Proved his ability and earned himself a move to Internazionale in 1984. Struggled to make his mark on the Italian game and was loaned out to French clubs Bordeaux and Auxerre to gain experience. Bought back to Italy by Torino in 1991. His international debut came against Hungary in June 1984 (drew 2-2).

SCLOSA, Claudio
(Lazio, Ita)
• 28.02.61 • Midfield

Much travelled player who had spells with Turin, Bologna, Como and Bari before joining Lazio from Pisa in 1988.

SCULLY, Gerry
(Drogheda United, Eir)
• 29.11.62 • Midfield

Signed from Emfa. Equally happy playing in midfield or as an out-and-out striker. Helped the club to promtion to the Premier League in season 1990/91.

SECHET, Jean-Phillipe
(Nancy, Fra)
• 16.07.65 • Defender

Multi-purpose defender, who's one of the best man-markers in the French game. Formerly with Grenoble and Gueugnon. Very quick to get forward and support his midfield. Nine goals in 1991/92.

SECKLER, Erich
(Bayer Leverkusen, Ger)
• 26.09.63 • Defender

Joined Bayer as an 18-year-old from Baumberg, but has had limited first team opportunities since.

SEDLACEK, Roman
(Hansa Rostock, Ger)
• 12.01.63 • Striker
• Czechoslovakia 3 full caps

Signed from Sigma Olomouc in 1991. Previously with Banik Ostrava.

SEGERS, Didier
(Lierse, Bel)
• 21.02.65 • Defender

Strong in the air he is very dangerous from dead-ball situations. Formerly with Molenbeek and Stade Leuven.

SEMEDO, Jose Orlando Rocha
(Porto, Por)
• 05.03.65 • Midfield
• Portugal 9 full caps, 1 goal

Formerly with the Sporting Esmoriz club, he made his League debut for Porto during the 1983/84 season and scored on his one and only appearance. Took a further four years until he gained a regular first team spot with the side.

SEMPERE Macia, Jose Maria
(Valencia, Spa)
• 15.02.59 • Goalkeeper

Has been with Valencia since 1981, but has been forced to wait as understudy to Otxoterena. Finally took over as the club's first choice 'keeper during 1991/92

SENOUSSI, Al Habo
(Rennes, Fra)
• 15.10.66 • Midfield

Former Nice, Le Touquet and Quimper player who joined the club in 1989 and helped them to promotion in 1990. Got his first taste of top flight football v St Etienne, 21st July 1990.

SERGIO DUARTE dos Santos
(Farense, Por)
• 20.01.65 • Midfield

One of seven Brazilians in the Farense squad, this six feet two inch front man has made a habit of finding the target in crucial matches but doesn't seem to reproduce that touch game in, game out. Has been with the club for four seasons.

SERGIO, Joao
(Sporting Lisbon, Por)
• 03.01.66 • Goalkeeper

Began his career as a youngster with Barreirense and got his chance in the top flight with Portimonense. Made his League debut during the 1986/87 season and moved to Sporting three years later.

SERGIO, Manuel Freitas Abreu
(Sporting Braga, Por)
• 16.05.67 • Defender

French defender who's first Portuguese club was Fafe. Moved on to Tirsense in 1989 and spent two seasons with the club before signing for Sporting Braga before the start of the 1991/92 campaign.

SERGIO, Raffaele
(Lazio, Ita)

• 27.08.66 • Defender

Left-back who loves to get forward. Played for Cavese, Benevento and Mantova in the Third Division before joining Lazio in 1989. Now a first team regular.

SERNA, Ricardo
(Barcelona, Spa)

• 21.01.64 • Defender
• Spain 6 full caps

Impressive full back who was signed by Barcelona from Seville in 1988. Made his Spanish international debut v Northern Ireland in December of that same year.

SERRA Jose Carvalha
Goncalves
(Pacos De Ferreira, Por)

• 09.12.61 • Midfield

Spent seven years at Sporting Braga where he gained a reputation as a skilful and attacking midfielder. In 1987 moved to Desportivo Chaves for two seasons and then on to Vitoria Setubal, before joining his present club.

SERR, Michael
(Kaiserslautern, Ger)

• 14.07.62 • Goalkeeper

Joined Kaiserslautern in 1985. Previously with Phonix Bellheim and ASV Landau.

SERREDSZUM, Cyril
(Metz, Fra)

• 02.10.71 • Midfield
• France Youth

Attacking wide midfielder with a sweet right foot. Has made only a handful of first team appearances since his debut against Lyon, in December 1989, but a bright future is predicted by coach Joel Muller.

SERRINHA
(Beira-Mar, Por)

• 28.06.65 • Midfield

Joao Mario Goncalves made his Portuguese First Division debut with Sporting Braga during the 1986/87 season. Joined Beira-Mar prior to the start of the 1991/92 season.

SEVEREYNS, Francis
(Mechelen, Bel)

• 08.01.68 • Striker
• Belgium 5 full caps, 1 goal

Like current team-mate Marc Emmers he made his international debut v Israel, in

January 1988. Formerly with Westmalle, Antwerp and Pisa he enjoyed a particularly successful season in 1990/91, when he grabbed 13 goals in 21 starts.

SFORZA, Ciriaco (Grasshoppers, Swi)

• 02.03.70 • Defender
• Switzerland full caps

Converted into central defender from midfield. Joined Grasshoppers from Wohlen and made debut in August 1986. Watched by Bayern Munich for much of the 1992/93 season.

SHAKHOV, Evgueni (Dnepr, CIS)

• Striker

Won the USSR title with Dnepr in 1988 and was the League's leading scorer with 16 goals. Prior to that he had breif spell in Germany with Kaiserslautern.

SHALIMOV, Igor (Internazionale, Ita)

• 02.02.69 • Midfield
• USSR youth, U21, 24 full caps, 1 goal

Member of the Soviet U21 team that won the 1990 European Championships and later progressed to the full international side, making two appearances in the 1990 World Cup finals. Signed by Foggia in 1991 and then sold to Inter in May 1992

for £9.2m, making him the second most expensive player in the world at the time.

SHELLEY, Mick (Dundalk, Eir)

• 21.1.60 • Defender

Has played every position except goalkeeper for his club. Made the left-back spot his own when ex-captain Martin Lawlor moved to Shamrock Rovers. Won the 'double' with Dundalk in 1988 and, previously, a League Cup medal with Bohemians.

SIGNORI, Giuseppe (Lazio, Ita)

• 17.02.68 • Midfield

Given his break in League football while at Leffe and then joined Piacenza in 1986. Joined Foggia, after a spell at Trento, in 1989. Transferred to Lazio in June 1992.

SIGNORINI, Gianluca (Genoa, Ita)

• 17.03.60 • Defender

Started career with Parma and signed by Roma in 1987. Unable to settle and moved to Genoa in 1988.

SIKORA, Eric (Lens, Fra)

• 04.02.68 • Defender

Home grown player who was first affiliated to the club as a 12-year-old in 1980. Made his First Division debut at Sochaux in October 1985, and has gone on to play more than 100 senior games.

SILAS
(Sampdoria, Ita)
• 27.08.65 • Midfield
• Brazil 26 full caps, 1 goal

Won World Youth Cup with Brazil in 1985 and made full debut year later v Hungary. Left Brazil and Sao Paulo club to join Sporting in Portugal. Bought to Italy by Cesena and joined Sampdoria in summer 1991. Member of Brazilian World Cup squads in 1986 and 1990.

SILENZI, Andrea
(Napoli, Ita)
• 10.02.66 • Striker

Born in Rome and joined Third Division Lodigiani in 1984. Had a season with Arezzo before moving onto Reggiana in 1987. Helped the club gain promtion in his first season and then hit 23 goals in 36 games the following year. That goalscoring feat earned him a move to Napoli prior to the 1990/91 season.

SILOOY, Sonny
(Ajax, Hol)
• 31.08.63 • Defender
• Holland 21 full caps

Began his career at Ajax and made his first team debut v Sparta Rotterdam in May 1981. Seven seasons later he moved to Racing Club Matra of Paris. Returned to Ajax in 1989.

da SILVA, Victor
(Lille, Fra)
• 21.04.62 • Midfield

Born in Portugal, he has spent all his professional career in France. Began with INF Vichy, and also played for Monaco and Ales before signing for Lille in June 1988. Made his First Division debut, for Monaco, against Nancy on 24th September 1983.

SILVESTRE, Franck
(Sochaux, Fra)
• 05.04.67 • Defender
• France 11 full caps

Paris-born central defender who arrived at Sochaux as a trainee from Le Bourget back in 1981. Made his League debut away to Paris St Germain in September 1985. Recently signed a new four-year contract at Sochaux.

SIMBA, Amara
(Paris St Germain, Fra)
• 23.12.61 • Striker
• France 3 games, 2 goals

Explosive goal-scorer who joined the club in the wake of their 1986 Championship win. He began with Versailles where he became something of a local hero before moving on loan to Cannes. Paris-SG snapped him up in the summer of 1986, but he had to wait ten months for his chance in the first team, coming on against Bordeaux in April 1987. Equally comfortable in midfield, where he plays at international level. Injured before the 1992 European Championships in Sweden, and was replaced by in the French national side by Fabrice Divert, of Montpellier.Six League goals in 1991/92

SIQUET, Thierry
(Cercle Brugge, Bel)
• 18.10.68 • Defender

Learned his trade with minor League club Union Hutoise before moving on to Standard Liege in 1988. Cercle signed him up in the summer of 1991.

SILVANO de Almeida
Louro
(Benfica, Por)
• 05.03.59 • Goalkeeper
• Portugal youth, U21, 19 full caps

Began his career with Vitoria Setubal in his home town and made his Portuguese League debut during the 1980/81 season. Moved onto Vitoria Guimaraes two years later and made his international debut against Hungary in 1983. Was signed by Benfica in 1984 and had a spell on loan to Aves in 1985. Recalled to the club to take over between the posts after first-choice

keeper Manuel Bento broke his leg while preparing for the 1986 World Cup.

SIVEBAEK, Johnny
(Monaco, Fra)
• 25.10.61 • Defender
• Denmark 83 full caps, 1 goal

Well known to British fans having spent a season at Manchester United. Attacking full back who is comfortable on the ball. Began with Danish club Vejle, before moving to United in 1985/86. Moved to France the following year, when he joined St Etienne. making his debut in August 1987 against Marseille. Joined Monaco in the summer of 1991. He is the second most capped player in Danish history. Was substituted during Denmark's historic 2-0 European Championship final win over Germany, having unfortunately carried an injury into the game.

SIX, Vincent
(Kortrijk, Bel)
• 24.12.72 • Striker

Highly regarded, lightning-fast front man who formed part of the club's new look front line for season 1991/92. Signed from minor League club Zonnebeke.

SKUHRAVY, Tomas
(Genoa, Ita)
• 07.09.65 • Striker
• Czechoslovakia 35 full caps, 11 goals

The Czechoslovakian Football Federation had to grant special dispensation to allow Tomas to play in the First Division before his eighteenth birthday. Made a big impact with his scoring ability for Czechoslovakia in the 1990 World Cup finals in Italy, scoring five goals to finish as the tournament's second highest scorer. Signed by Genoa from Sparta Prague immediately after the finals. He was an immediate success, scoring 15 goals in his first season in the ultra-defensive Italian League. Unusually for a Serie A goalscorer, none of that tally were penalties. His international debut came against Holland in September 1986, but it took him almost three years to score his first goal, v Luxembourg in 1989.

SLATER, Robby
(Lens, Fra)
• 22.11.64 • Midfield

British-born Australian citizen who has spent his entire pro career in Europe. Began with mighty Anderlecht, where he won the Beglian Cup in 1988 and 1989, and is one of only a handful of Aussies to have proved a big hit on the continent. Joined Lens in summer 1990, and helped guide the club to promotion the following season.

SLISKOVIC, Blaz
(Rennes, Fra)
• 30.05.59 • Midfield
• Yugoslavia full caps

Hugely experienced midfield ball-winner who has played at the very top level for club and country. Began with Yugoslav giant Hadjuk Split, before transferring to Marseille in 1986, making his debut in France against great rivals Monaco in August of that year. Next stop was Pescara, Italy, where he spent two seasons before returning to France with Lens and then dropping into Division Two with Mulhouse. Rennes swooped for his signature to help bolster their midfield in July 1991.

de SMET, Stefaan
(Lierse, Bel)
• 03.04.69 • Defender

Home grown star who likes to get forward and help out in attack. Broke into the side at the back end of the 1989/90 season and has become a firm favourite of coach Herman Helleputte.

SMIDTS, Rudy
(Antwerp, Bel)
• 12.08.63 • Defender

Home-grown star who has now made more than 220 first team appearances.

SMITH, Alan
(Bray Wanderers, Eir)
• 02.07.67 • Defender

Was a member of the club's 1990/91 promotion winning side.

SMITH, Francis
(Bangor, N.Ir)

• 29.04.58 • Striker

Scored five goals in the last four games of 1990/91, after joining the club in February 1991, to help clinch a UEFA Cup spot. Currently in his second spell at the club, having also spent time at Distillery, Sheffield Wednesday, Portadown, Glenavon and Larne. Scored 10 goals in 20 League games in 1991/92.

SMYTH, Dean
(Glentoran, N.Ir)

• Goalkeeper

Signed from Crusaders, he began season 1991/92 as first choice 'keeper at The Oval, playing 27 consecutive games, before a serious shin injury forced him out of action towards the end of the campaign.

SMYTH, Gary
(Glentoran, N.Ir)

• Defender

A target for several Football League clubs, he unfortuantely suffered a viral illness midway through 1991/92, which restricted his first team appearances. Calm on the ball, he likes to play his way out of trouble and is dangerous at dead-ball situations.

SMYTH, Michael
(Ballymena United, N.Ir)

• Defender
• Irish League Representative

Has been at the Showgrounds since he was a schoolboy. Captained the club to their 1988 Irish Cup triumph.He is regarded as one of the top left backs in Irish League football.

SNELDERS, Eddy
(Germinal Ekeren, Bel)

• 09.04.59 • Midfield
• Belgium 1 full cap

Widely travelled central midfielder, who has played more than 430 senior games. Has enjoyed spells with Antwerp, Lokeren, Lierse, Standard Liege and Kortrijk. His single international appearance came v Holland, in October 1981 (won 3-0).

SOBIECH, Jorg
(Wattenscheid, Ger)

• 15.01.69 • Defender

Signed from Schalke 04 in 1987.

SODA, Antonio
(Bari, Ita)

• 24.06.64 • Striker

Made his Serie A debut during the

1982/83 season with his local club Catanzaro, and played his football with Catanzaro, Carbonia, Empoli and Triestina in the lower Leagues for the next seven years. Returned to the big time with Bari in November 1990.

SOEIRO Jose Manual Guedes Silva (Vitoria Guimaraes, Por)

• 17,04.66 • Midfield

A product of the club's youth programme, he joined Vitoria when he was seventeen and has played over a hundred times for them since.

SOENENS, Kurt (Cercle Brugge, Bel)

• 09.01.67 • Midfield

Began with minor League club Ingelmunster, before signing pro with Cercle in 1986/87. Does the fetching and carrying in the midfield and provides countless openings for partner Karacic.

SOLA Elizalde, Miguel Angel (Osasuna, Spa)

• 29.09.57 • Midfield
• Spain youth

Arrived at Osasuna in 1984, having previously been with Atletico Bilbao.

SOLDA, Roberto (Lazio, Ita)

• 28.05.59 • Defender

Dominating sweeper who joined Lazio in 1989 from Verona. Previously had spells with Ravenna, Forli, Como, Atalanta and Juventus.

SOLER, Miguel (Atletico Madrid, Spa)

• 16.03.65 • Defender
• Spain 8 full caps

Tall stopper who joined Atletico from Barcelona in 1991.

SOLOZABAL, Roberto (Atletico Madrid, Spa)

• 15.09.69 • Defender
• Spain youth, Olympic

Locally born full back who graduated to the first team squad from the reserves.

SONGO'O, Jacques (Toulon, Fra)

• 17.03.64 • Goalkeeper

Signed from Canon de Yaounde, Cameroon, in 1989 as cover for first choice 'keeper Luc Borrelli. Has played more than 30 senior games, and is vying to become number one at Stade Bon-Rencontre.

SONOR, Luc
(Monaco, Fra)

• 15.09.62 • Defender
• France 9 full caps

Former Metz player who joined the club in 1986 and was an integral part of the success story of the mid-to-late 1980s, when Monaco won the League (1988) and French Cup (1991). Has played almost 300 senior games.

SORDO, Gianluca
(Torino, Ita)

• 02.12.69 • Midfield

Began his career with Torino in 1986, back failed to break into the League side. Spent the 1988/89 season at Third Division Trento before returning to Torino and helped them gain promotion back to Serie A in his first season back.

SORIN, Michel
(Rennes, Fra)

• 18.09.61 • Defender

Signed from Brest in 1989, this centre back was instrumental in driving the club to promotion from Division Two in 1990. Plenty of experience of top level football, having spent several seasons with Laval (227 games, 3 goals) before transferring to Brest in 1987. Ever-present during Rennes first season back in the top flight (1990/91).

SOSA, Ruben
(Lazio, Ita)

• 25.04.66 • Striker
• Uruguay full caps

Considered to be his country's number one player, Ruben was even selected as one of the six stars who made the draw for the 1990 World Cup. Helped his country to the final of the 1989 South American Cup where they were beaten by Brazil.

SOUDAN, Yves
(Beveren, Bel)

• 23.10.67 • Striker

Former SK Wondelgem and Gent striker who signed for the club in June 1991, after Beveren won the Division Two title.

da SOUZA, Elber
(Milan, Ita)

• 23.07.72 • Striker
• Brazil Youth

Signed from Brazillian club Londrina in 1991. Loaned to Grasshoppers for all of 1991/92. World Youth Cup finalist 1991.

SOUSA, Antonio
Augusto Gomes
(Beira-Mar, Por)

• 28.04.57 • Midfield
• Portugal full caps

Very experienced midfielder who began playing his football with Sanjoanense. Made his First Division debut with Porto dduring the 1980/81 season and spent four years as a first team regular with the club before moving on to Sporting Lisbon. Returned to Porto in 1986 and had a further three seasons with the club before signing for Beira-Mar in 1989.

SOUSA, Paulo Carvalho (Benfica, Por)

• 30.08.70 • Midfield
• Portugal youth, U21

Joined Benfica from his home town club Viseu in 1985 and made his League debut for the club at the end of the 1989/90 season.

SPASIC, Pedrag (Osasuna, Spa)

• 13.05.65 • Defender
• Yugoslavia 30 full caps, 1 goal

Tall,balding, Croatian-born defender who spent two seasons with Real Madrid before joining Osasuna.

SPASSOV Yulian Assenov (Pacos De Ferreira, Por)

• 29.05.63 • Striker

A strong and pacey frontman, he was picked up from the Bulgarian leagues by Farense in 1986. Scored five goals in 28 games there before moving to Beira-Mar and notching another six. A proven goal scorer signed by Pacos De Ferreira in 1991.

SPEAK, Jon (Ballymena United, N.Ir)

• Striker

Began with Dundalk, making his League of Ireland debut, v Cork City, in September 1984. Derry signed him from Ballymena United in the summer of 1990, and he celebrated his first season at The Brandywell by becoming joint top scorer, with Stuart Gauld, with eight goals. Moved North to Ballymena in June 1992.

SPIERS, Eddie (Larne, N.Ir)

• Defender

'Steady' Eddie was signed from Barn United after a chance meeting with former Larne boss Paul Malone, now in charge at Ards. Hugely experienced, his calm leadership helped the club to its most successful ever season in 1991/92, when it finished fourth in the Irish League.

SPIES, Michael (Hansa Rostock, Ger)

• 09.07.65 • Midfield

Signed from Moenchengladbach in 1991. Previously with Karlsruher and Stuttgart.

SPROULE, Keith
(Omagh Town, N.Ir)
• Midfield

Developed through the youth ranks at St Julian's Road, this teenager is currently enjoying his third senior season with the club. From Castlederg.

STADLER, Joachim
(Borussia Moenchengladbach, Ger)
• 15.01.70 • Defender

Signed from 1.FC Kaiserslautern in 1991.

STAELENS, Lorenzo
(Club Brugge, Bel)
• 30.04.64 • Defender
• Belgium 7 full caps

One of the club's two international full-backs (the other is Pascal Plovie), he was signed from Kortrijk. Equally happy playing in midfield - either wide or central. Previously with White Star Lauwe.

STALMANS, Patrick
(Genk, Bel)
• 31.10.59 • Defender

Hugely experienced centre-back who was brought in to help the club stabilise on their return to the top flight. Signed from Lokeren in July 1991, he was previously with Gerhees, Diest, Meerhout and Beveren.

STAM, Rene
(Den Haag, Hol)
• 27.01.65 • Goalkeeper

Began his career with AZ 67 but failed to make his League debut. Signed by Den Haag in July 1984 and has now made over 300 first team appearances for the club.

STAUCHE, Ghintaras
(Spartak Moscow, Rus)
• 24.12.69 • Goalkeeper
• USSR U21, Youth, Olympic

Lithuanian who joined Spartak in 1990

STEFFEN, Horst
(Borussia Moenchengladbach, Ger)
• 03.03.69 • Midfield

Signed from Bayer Uerdingen in 1991.

STEINER, Paul
(Cologne, Ger)
• 23.01.57 • Midfield
• Germany 1 full cap

Signed from MSV Dusiburg in 1981. Has made over 300 German First Division appearances.

STEININGER, Frank-Josef
(MSV Duisburg, Ger)

• 09.07.60 • Midfield

Originally joined Duisburg after playing for junior sides Hamborn and Buschhausen. Later moved on to Union Solingen and Sarrbrucken, before rejoining MSV in 1989.

STEINMANN, Rico
(Cologne, Ger)

• 26.12.67 • Midfield
• East Germany 23 full caps

Experienced former international from Chemnitz who was given his chance in the German First Division by Cologne in 1991.

STEIN, Uli
(Eintracht Frankfurt, Ger)

• 23.10.54 • Goalkeeper
• West Germany 6 full caps

Controversial keeper who was sent home from the 1986 World Cup finals for critising manager Franz Beckenbauer in the German press. Began his career with Arminia Bielefeld before moving on to Hamburg. Won the European Cup with the club in 1983 and then joined Frankfurt four years later.

STERNKOPF, Michael
(Bayern Munich, Ger)

• 21.04.70 • Midfield
• Germany U21

Signed by Bayern from Karlsruher SC in summer 1990 for £1.1m. Previously with SV Nordwest Karlsruher.

STEWART, Alfie
(Portadown, N.Ir)

• Defender

Brings the European-style to Portadown by filling the sweeper's role at Shamrock Park, and was a major reason behind the club winning its first League title in 1990 and then retaining it the following season. Signed from Glentoran for £15,000, he is described by manager Ronnie McFall as "the bargain of the decade".

STEWART, Stephen
(Crusaders, N.Ir)

• Defender

Previously with Linfield and Ballyclare Comrades, he has enjoyed six seasons at Seaview. Ever present in season 1991/92, he was voted Player of the Year at the club for the previous campaign. Possesses a tremendous shot and is dangerous from dead-ball situations around the box.

STITT, Lawrence (Cliftonville, N.Ir)

• Defender

Happy at full back or in central defence he is very much the club's elder statesman. Has missed just a handful of games in the past two seasons.

STOICHKOV, Hristo (Barcelona, Spa)

• 08.02.66 • Striker
• Bulgaria 36 full caps, 4 goals

Bulgarian Footballer of the Year in 1989, 1990 and 1991, Hristo became his country's most expensive footballer ever when signed for £2 million from CSKA Sredets by Barcelona in 1990. Played in the 1992 European Cup Final at Wembley Stadium.

STOJANOVIC, Stevan (Antwerp, Bel)

• 29.10.64 • Goalkeeper

One of two Yugoslav 'keepers at the club (the other is Ratko Svilar) he was snapped up from Red Star Belgrade in the summer of 1991. Made vital penalty saves to win the European Champions' Cup for Red Star, against Marseille, in 1991. Also made huge contribution to the 1990 and 1991 League title victories. Fine capture for Antwerp.

STOJIC, Ranko (Charleroi, Bel)

• 18.01.59 • Goalkeeper
• Yugoslavia 14 full caps

First choice 'keeper at the club since he joined from Anderlecht in 1989/90. Began in Belgium with Liege, having played in his home country with Iskra, Partizan Belgrade and Dinamo Zagreb.

STOJKOVIC, Dragan (Verona, Ita)

• 03.03.65 • Striker
• Yugoslavia 39 full caps, 9 goals

Scored twice on his League debut for local side Radnicki Nis at the age of 18. Made his international debut against France in November 1983 and thus created a record by representing his country at youth, U21, Olympic and full levels within less than 12 months. Moved from Radnicki to Red Star Belgrade in July 1986 for a reported fee of four floodlight pylons, which must go down as one of the football bargains of all time. Won the League Championship with Red Star in 1988 and 1990. Joined Mareseille and won a European Cup runners-up medal in 1991 after coming on as substitute against his former club-mates at Red Star. Also runner- up in 1991 French Cup final v Monaco, again as substitute. Joined Verona for £4.4 million in June 1991.

STOPYRA, Yannick (Metz, Fra)

• 09.01.61 • Striker
• France 33 full caps

One of the most experienced and dangerous strikers in France. Approaching 500 senior games and 150 League goals during a career which has taken in Sochaux, Rennes, Toulouse, Bordeaux and Cannes. Signed for Metz in July 1991 and is still terrorising top flight defences. Had a quiet season in 1991/92, scoring just two League goals.

STRAIN, Brian (Portadown, N.Ir)

• Defender

A physiotherapist by profession, this highly-rated central defender spent a period on trial at Manchester United during 1991/92, but decided to remain at Shamrock Park. Likes to get forward and pops up with some vital goals. Club captain. He was signed from Glentoran.

STRAKA, Frantisek (Hansa Rostock, Ger)

• 21.05.58 • Defender
• Czechoslovakia 35 full caps

Signed from Borussia Moenchengladbach in 1991. Previously with Sparta Prague.

STROMBERG, Glenn Peter (Atalanta, Ita)

• 05.01.60 • Midfield

Made his name in Sweden with Gothenburg and earned himself a move to Benfica in 1983. Spent two years in Portugal before moving to Atalanta prior to the 1984/85 season.

STRUDER, Stefan (Eintracht Frankfurt, Ger)

• 30.01.64 • Midfield

Started out at SV Hamburg before moving across town to St Pauli. Signed by Frankfurt in 1988.

STRUNZ, Thomas (Bayern Munich, Ger)

• 25.04.68 • Midfield
• Germany 2 full caps

Signed by Bayern from MSV Duisburg in 1989 before making his Bundesliga debut. Two dozen League games later, made international debut v Sweden, in 1990.

STUBNER, Jorg (Dynamo Dresden, Ger)

• 23.07.65 • Midfield
• East Germany 47 caps.

Highly experienced midfielder who also spent some time with Motor Halle as a junior.

STUMPF, Reinhard (Kaiserslautern, Ger)

• 26.11.61 • Defender

Signed from Kickers Offenbach in 1989. Previously with Karlsruher.

SURAY, Olivier (Charleroi, Bel)

• 16.10.71 • Defender

One of two brothers to come up through the ranks at the club and break into the first team. Brother Eric, a midfielder, was sold to Union at the end of season 1990/91, but Olivier was retained. Has played more than 60 senior games.

SUSS, Thomas (Karlsruher, Ger)

• 08.04.62 • Defender

Swiss defender who moved to Germany with Karlsruher from Basle in 1987.

SUTTER, Alain (Grasshoppers, Swi)

• 22.01.68 • Midfield
• Switzerland 21 full caps, 2 goals

Talented playmaker, formerly with Bumpliz 78 and Young Boys of Berne.

SUVRIJN, Wilbert (Montpellier, Fra)

• 26.10.62 • Midfield
• Holland U21; 8 full caps

Signed from Dutch club Roda Sport in July 1989, he made his debut, days after signing, against Cannes. He was the ball-winner for Carlos Valderrama, and now performs the same job alongside Philippe Perilleux. French Cup winner with Montpellier in 1990.

SVERRISSON, Eyjolfur (VfB Stuttgart, Ger)

• 03.08.68 • Striker
• Iceland 2 full caps

Joined Stuttgart from UMF Tindastoll in his native Iceland in 1990.

SVILAR, Ratko (Antwerp, Bel)

• 06.05.50 • Goalkeeper
• Yugoslavia 10 full caps

One of two Yugoslav 'keepers at the club, the other is Stevan Stojanovic, he joined from Vojvodina Novi Sad in 1984/85. Now a naturalised Belgian citizen.

SWAN, Derek (Shamrock Rovers, Eir)

• 24.10.66 • Striker

Joined the club from Port Vale in November 1990, and quickly made a big impression by grabbing 10 goals in 17 games during his first season.

SZENYREI, Jozsef (Cadiz, Spa)
• 25.04.54 • Goalkeeper
• Hungary full caps

Signed by Cadiz from Malaga in 1988.

TABB, Marty (Cliftonville, N.Ir)
• Defender

One of the country's leading centre backs who was signed from Coleraine midway through the 1991/92 season and has become an integral part of the Reds defence.

TACCONI, Stefano (Juventus, Ita)
• 13.05.57 • Goalkeeper
• Italy 3 full caps

Played for Spoleto, Inter, Pro Patria, Livorno and Sambenedettese before settling down with Avellino in 1980. Moved to Juventus in 1983 where he eventually replaced Dino Zoff in the Juve goal.

TAFFAREL, Claudio (Parma, Ita)
• 08.05.66 • Goalkeeper
• Brazil full caps

Highly-rated Brazilian keeper who left Internacional in his homeland for Parma after the 1990 World Cup finals.

TAHAMATA, Simon (Ekeren, Bel)
• 26.05.56 • Striker

Had already played for Piel, Ajax, Standard Liege, Feyenoord and Beerschot before moving to Ekeren and helping them win a UEFA Cup spot for the first time in 1990/91. Boasts three nationalities, Moluccan, Dutch and Belgian, and was joint-winner, with Franky van der Elst of the 1991 Footballer of the Year trophy.

TAIBI, Calogero (Lokeren, Bel)

• 16.11.66 • Midfield

Italian-born winger or central midfielder who holds Belgian citizenship. Began with CS Couillet and also played for Charleroi.

TALBUT, Mark (Germinal Ekeren, Bel)

• 23.07.62 • Defender

English-born stopper with Belgian nationality, who has notched up in excess of 220 First Division appearances with Ekeren and his previous clubs, Mechelen and Beerschot. In the finest tradition of Ekeren defenders he is adept at getting forward and making a nuisance of himself.

TAMAYO Tornadijo, Pedro Luis (Burgos, Spa)

• 03.11.62 • Defender

Loyal servant of the club who has now been a Burgos player for 10 years.

TANJU, Colak (Fenerbahce, Tur)

• 10.11.63 • Striker
• Turkey 30 full caps, 10 goals

The most talked-about player in Turkey. Caused a sensation in July 1991 when he transferred from Galatasaray to Fenerbahce - the equivalent of Ally McCoist joining Celtic - for a domestic record £1 million. He first came to the fore with Samsunspor, when he was the League's top scorer with 33 goals in 1985/86. He moved to Galatasaray in 1987, and by the season's end had scored 39 goals and won Europe's Golden Boot and the Turkish League title. After a season badly affected by injury and illness he regained form in 1990/91, finishing as the League's top scorer once again. His 31 goal tally was almost twice as much as his nearest rivals, Feyyaz and Sabatic.

TARASIEWICZ, Ryszard (Nancy, Fra)

• 27.04.62 • Midfield
• Poland 56 full caps, 9 goals

Captain of the Polish national side and one of the finest players in the French First Division. Blessed with two good feet, and tremendous vision. Began with Wroclav (Pol) and moved to Neuchatel (Swi) before joining Nancy in 1990. Debut v Brest, 28th July 1990. Scored ten goals in 35 games during his first season at Nancy.

TASSOTI, Mauro
(Milan, Ita)

• 19.01.60 • Defender

full back who began with Lazio, making League debut aged 18. Signed by Milan in 1980 and has now made more than 250 appearances for the club.

TAUMENT, Gaston
(Feyenoord, Hol)

• 01.10.70 • Striker
• Holland U21

Product of Feyenoord youth team, made first team debut aged 18 v Den Bosch, April 1989. Spent 1989/90 season on loan to Second Division neighbours Excelsior. Former U21 international, voted Dutch PFA Young Player of the Year in 1991. Made full debut as sub v Portugal, February 1992.

TENDILLO, Miguel
(Real Madrid, Spa)

• 01.02.61 • Defender
• Spain youth, U21, 27 full caps

Tall central defender who joined Real from Real Murcia in June 1987.

TEPPERS, Patrick
(Waregem, Bel)

• 30.07.64 • Midfield

Experienced winger with more than 140 senior games under his belt. Signed from KFC Winterslag.

TERRACENERE, Angelo
(Bari, Ita)

• 22.09.63 • Midfield

A locally born ball-winner, Angelo made his League debut with Bari in Serie B during the 1981/82 season. Left the club to spend two years with Serie C side Monopoli before returning to Bari in the summer of 1985.

TEUBER, Ronny
(Dynamo Dresden, Ger)

• 01.09.65 • Goalkeeper
• East Germany 1 full cap

One of the two keepers with full international experience for Germany on Dresden's books last season. Signed from Union Berlin in 1986.

THAIRET, Patrick
(RWD Molenbeek, Bel)

• 21.08.60 • Striker

Originally signed from Daring CB as a wide midfielder, he has proved equally adept as an out and out striker. Helped the club to the Division Two Championship in 1989/90 and is approaching 300 senior appearances.

THANS, Benoit (Antwerp, Bel)

• 20.08.64 • Midfield

Bustling ball-winner who joined the club in the summer of 1991 from Standard Liege. Also previously with Biegny, Cercle Liege and French club Lens.

THERN, Jonas (Napoli, Ita)

• 20.03.67 • Midfield
• Sweden 35 full caps, 6 goals

Influential and talented midfielder who began his career in Sweden with Varnamo. Move on to Malmo in 1985 and broke into the Swedish international side against Germany in October 1987. Was a member of his country's Olympic side a year later and by 1989 he had earned himself a lucrative move abroad, joining Benfica in Portugal for £800,000. His fine performances in Sweden's Championship side brought him to the attention of Italian giants Napoli, who signed him in July 1992.

THETIS, Jean-Manuel (Montpellier, Fra)

• 05.11.71 • Defender
• France Schools; Youth; U21

At 6ft 4in Thetis is, not surprisingly, one of the strongest headers of the ball in France. Formerly with Racing Paris, he signed for Montpellier in 1990. Helped club to the French Cup in 1990.

THIJS, Peter (RWD Molenbeek, Bel)

• 10.04.64 • Goalkeeper

Signed from Lierse. Widely experienced in the lower Divisions with Schelle and FC Boom he joined the club in 1989. Shared the number one spot with Joszef Gaspar during his first couple of seasons at the club, but has now established himself as first choice.

THOELEN, Dirk (Beveren, Bel)

• 15.05.68 • Defender

Like team-mate Julien Lodders he was discovered playing for local minor League club Looi Sport, and signed in the wake of promotion in 1990/91.

THOLOT, Didier (St Etienne, Fra)

• 02.04.64 • Striker

Former Niort and Reims forward who joined the club in July 1991. Diminutive player who is lightning quick at snapping up half chances around the six-yard box. Scored a total of five League goals in the 1991/92 campaign.

THOM, Andreas (Bayer Leverkusen, Ger)

• 07.09.65 • Striker
• East Germany 51 full caps, 16 goals/Germany 2 full caps, 1 goal

One of the few players who have won caps for both East Germany and the recently unified Germany at full international level. Signed from Dynamo Berlin for £1.5m in 1989, to become first player to move from East to West Germany. Was expected to leave Bayer in 1992, but signed a new two year contract in April. Scored on his debut for the unified Germany, just minutes after coming on as substitute against Switzerland in December 1990.

THOMAS, Dominique (Lille, Fra)

• 13.03.63 • Defender
• France U21

Experienced player who is currently in his second spell at the club. Began with INF Vichy before joining Lille for the first time in 1984. His First Division debut came during that stay at Grimonprez-Jooris, away to Brest in August 1984. Transferred to Bordeaux before returning to Lille in July 1989. Is now approaching his 300th senior appearance. Failed to find the net once during the 1991/92 League campaign.

THOMAS, Jean-Christophe (Sochaux, Fra)

• 16.10.64 • Midfield
• France B

Striker turned midfielder who has socred over 30 goals in more than 200 League games for Sochaux. Signed from Meursault as a 15-year- old, he's settled well on the left of midfield.

THON, Olaf (Bayern Munich, Ger)

• 01.05.66 • Midfield
• Germany 35 full caps

Played for junior sides Beckhausen 05 and STV Horst Emscher before joining Schalke 04 in 1980. Signed by Bayern for then German record fee of £1.4m in 1988. Made his full international debut v Malta in December 1984 and was a member of 1986 World Cup squad. Played in 1990 World Cup finals, scoring the penalty that won the semi-final shoot-out against England. Did not play in the final.

THOUVENEL, Jean-Christophe (Le Havre, Fra)

• 08.10.58 • Defender
• France 4 full caps

Well-travelled full back who's a firm favourite with the fans at Stade Jules-

Deschaseaux for his raiding runs down the right flank. Formerly with Paris FC, Servette Geneva and Bordeaux, he joined Le Havre in the summer of 1991. Approaching 500 Division One games in France.

THYS, Phillipe
(Toulon, Fra)

• 30.08.59 • Defender

Experienced and widely travelled full back who has been playing at the top level for more than twelve years. Formerly with Metz, Racing Paris, Nantes and Marseille. Joined the club in 1990 and has made more than 300 senior appearances since his debut, for Metz v Nice, on 24th July 1980.

TIEHI, Joel
(Le Havre, Fra)

• 12.06.64 • Striker

One of the plethora of African footballers hitting the big-time in France. Born in Abidjan, on the Ivory Coast, he was signed from his home-town club, Stade d'Abidjan, in 1987.

van TIGGELEN, Adri
(PSV Eindhoven, Hol)

• 16.06.57 • Defender
• Holland 54 full caps

Unlikely, gangly looking footballer who began his Dutch League career with Sparta

in 1978/79 season and made over 150 First Division appearances before moving to Groningen in 1983. Joined Anderlecht of Belgium in 1986 and then moved on to PSV in July 1991.

TIHY, Benoit
(Lille, Fra)

• 06.07.59 • Defender

Highly experienced full back or central defender who began with Valenciennes in 1979. Moved on to the Paris club Racing and then Toulouse before joining Sochaux where he played probably the best football of his career. Lille snapped him up in the summer of 1991, and he was a major reason behind the club having one of the best defensive records in France in 1991/92 - just 34 goals conceded.

TILSON, David
(Bohemians, Eir)

• 17.05.68 • Midfield

Tenacious, hard-running midfield man who likes to get forward and help out up front. Previously with UCD.

TIMMERMAN, Piet
(Kortrijk, Bel)

• 11.05.70 • Midfield

Signed from minor League club Winkel Sport in 1988 he celebrated his 100th senior game during the 1991/92 season. Ferocious tackler in the midfield.

TIMOFTE, Yon
(Porto, Por)

• 16.12.67 • Midfield
• Romania 3 full caps, 1 goal

International midfielder who left Timisoara in his native Romania in 1991 to sign a three year contract in Portugal with Porto.

TIMOTHEE, Didier
(Caen, Fra)

• 20.06.70 • Midfield

Has come up through the ranks at the club, and made his senior debut against St Etienne on 2nd February 1991.

TIPURIC, Jerko
(Cercle Brugge, Bel)

• 14.06.60 • Defender

Yugoslavian-born defender who signed from Hajduk Split in the summer of 1990, and has been the mainstay of the back four ever since.

TITTEL, Dusan
(Nimes, Fra)

• 17.12.66 • Defender
• Czechoslovakia 8 full caps

Experienced central defender who was one of several players to join the club at the beginning of 1991/92. Previously with Slovan Bratislava. At 6ft 3in tall, he is very strong in the air. His international debut came against Finland in August 1990 (drew 1-1).

TJIN-ASJOE, Rick
(Den Haag, Hol)

• 23.08.62 • Defender

Born in Surinam and signed by Den Haag in June 1988. Has made just over 30 appearances in his four years with the club.

TOAL, John
(Drogheda United, Eir)

• 05.11.67 • Midfield

Signed from Shamrock Rovers. A versatile performer who can play anywhere across the back four, or in midfield.

TODOROV, Nicolai
(Montpellier, Fra)

• 26.09.64 • Midfield
• Bulgaria 11 full caps, 3 goals

Former Lokomotiv Sofia player who jumped at the chance to move overseas once travel restrictions were eased in Bulgaria. Joined Montpellier in 1991, and was so impressed he immediately signed a deal keeping him at La Mosson for four years. Prefers to play wide on the left, but can also fill a role in central midfield or defence.

TOMAS Gonzalez Rivera
(Valencia, Spa)

• 03.03.63 • Midfield

Well-built player who scores his fair share of goals from midfield. Signed from Oviedo in 1989.

TOMAS Renones Crego
(Atletico Madrid, Spa)

• 09.08.60 • Defender
• Spain 13 full caps

Veteran right back who has been with Atletico for the past nine seasons.

TONI
(Valencia, Spa)

• 25.10.65 • Striker
• Brazil youth

South American whose real name is Antonio Jose Gomes. Joined Valencia from Brazilian side San Jose in 1989.

TONNIES, Michael
(MSV Duisburg, Ger)

• 19.12.59 • Striker

Prolific goal scorer who topped the Second Division charts during Duisburg's 1991 promotion season. Originally began his career with Schalke, before arriving at MSV in 1986 via Bayreuth, Bocholt and Rot-Weiss Essen.

TORKEN, Remco
(Den Haag, Hol)

• 03.01.72 • Striker

Previously with junior sides Leiden and UVS, Remco joined Den Haag as a 16-year-old and made his first team debut a year later.

TORRENTE, Vincenzo
(Genoa, Ita)

• 12.02.66 • Defender

Right-back who joined Genoa from Nocerina in 1985.

TORRES, Jose Miguel
(Valencia, Spa)

• 31.03.62 • Defender

Experienced defender who joined Valencia from Gardia.

TOURSOUNIDIS, Yorgos
(PAOK Salonika, Gre)

• 21.08.70 • Midfield
• Greece 5 full caps

Likes to play wide on the right of midfield, and is widely expected to become one of the country's leading lights over the next two or three seasons. Made his international debut v Italy in May 1990.

TOZE
(Porto, Por)
• 04.09.65 • Striker
• Portugal 1 full cap

Made his Portuguese League debut for Penafiel during the 1983/84 season. Later had spells with Vitoria Guimaraes, Maritimo and Biera-Mar before joining Porto in the summer of 1991.

TRAUTNER, Eberhard
(VfB Stuttgart, Ger)
• 07.02.67 • Goalkeeper

Reserve keeper to Eike Immel at Stuttgart. Although he has been with the club over ten years he has not played more than a handful of games for the first team.

TREACY, Derek
(Shamrock Rovers, Eir)
• 06.04.71 • Striker

Tricky winger who was discovered playing for minor League side Belvedere in 1989. His League of Ireland debut came at home to Dundalk on November 19, 1989 (drew 0-0).

TREACY, John
(St Patrick's Athletic, Eir)
• 16.04.59 • Midfield

Experienced central midfielder who chips in with the odd goal.

TRESSON, Colm
(Bray Wanderers, Eir)
• Midfield

Joined the club from junior side St Joseph's Boys, and played a big part in the 1990/91 promotion season which saw Wanderers return to the Premier Division.

TROOST, Sjaak
(Feyenoord, Hol)
• 28.08.59 • Defender
• Holland 4 full caps

Made more than 300 League appearances for Feyenoord since making debut during 1978/79 season. Member of Dutch European Championship winning squad in 1988. Has twice broken his leg.

TRUJILLO, Jose Carmelo
(Betis, Spa)
• 17.05.66 • Goalkeeper

Joined Betis in 1988 from Recreativo de Huelva and took over the first team spot from Argentinian international Nery Pumpido during the 1989/90 season.

TRULSEN, Andre (Cologne, Ger)
• 28.05.65 • Midfield

Was snapped up by St Pauli after spells in junior football with Osdorfer Born, HEBC Hamburg and SV Lurup. He joined Cologne in 1991 and has since gone on to make over 100 First Division appearances.

TSCHISKALE, Uwe (Wattenscheid, Ger)
• 09.07.62 • Striker

Signed from FC Schalke 04 in 1988. Previously with Bayern Munich.

TSIFOUTIS, Yorgos (Panathinaikos, Gre)
• Midfield
• Greece 2 full caps

Signed from Panseraikos in the summer of 1990. Made his national team debut while still a Panseraikos player, against Portugal in January 1989 (lost 2-1).

TSVEIBA, Akhrik (Dynamo Kiev, Ukr)
• Defender
• USSR full caps

Sweeper who captained Kiev to the USSR League title in 1991.

TUEBA Menayame (Farense, Por)
• 13.03.63 • Midfield

One of a number of Zairean players in Portugal, he started his career with Benfica but made jsut 28 appearances before moving to Vitoria Setubal in 1988 and then on to Tirsense. Was ever-present there for two seaons before moving to Farense.

TUGAY, Kerimoglu (Galatasaray, Tur)
• 24.08.70 • Defender
• Turkey 5 full caps; U21

The club's youth policy was completely re-organised on the advice of national coach Sepp Piontek three years ago, and they have been rewarded with a string of fine young players. Pick of the current bunch is Tugay, who's international debut came v Eire in 1990.

TUITE, Marcus (Bohemians, Eir)
• 11.05.68 • Midfield

Dublin-born player who began with Luton Town. Failed to make the grade at Kenilworth Road and returned to his home country with Limerick City in February 1987. His League of Ireland debut came later that month, at Dundalk. He spent nearly four seasons with Limerick before transferring to Bohemians in November 1990.

TULLY, Michael (Larne, N.Ir)

• Midfield

Solid performer, who is equally happy to play in central defence or midfield. Signed from Distillery at the start of the 1991/92 campaign, he played a huge part in the club's most successful season ever, as they finished fourth in the Irish League.

TURHAN, Sofuoglu (Fenerbahce, Tur)

• 19.08.65 • Midfield
• Turkey 3 full caps

Made his national debut as substitute in a 1-0 win over Greece in March 1989.

TURR, Frank (Bochum, Ger)

• 16.09.70 • Midfield

Made 54 League appearances from Nuremburg before moving to Bochum at the start of the 1991-92 season.

UGUR, Tutuneker (Galatasaray, Tur)

• 02.08.63 • Midfield
• Turkey 16 full caps, 1 goal; Olympic

Dortmund-born player who was spotted playing in the German minor leagues by Ordurspor in 1987. Signed for Galatasaray in 1990. After six months out injured he earned a recall to the national side in the spring of 1991.

UNAL, Karaman (Trabzonspor, Tur)

• 18.08.66 • Midfield
• Turkey 21 full caps, 1 goal

His international bow came against Romania in the 1990 World Cup qualifiers (lost 3-1). Signed from minor League club Malatyaspor.

UNZUE Labiano, Juan Carlos (Seville, Spa)

• 22.04.67 • Goalkeeper

Joined Seville from Barcelona where he had previously been understudy to Zubizarreta.

UPRICHARD, Stephen (Crusaders, N.Ir)

• Defender

Joined the club from Armagh in November 1989, but has suffered with several injuries since then. Previously with Glenavon. Known as 'Scobie' at Crusaders.

URBAN, Jan
(Osasuna, Spa)

• 15.02.62 • Striker
• Poland 53 full caps, 5 goals

Has been with Osasuna for three seasons.

URIA Lekuona, Joaquin
(Real Sociedad, Spa)

• 12.02.65 • Defender

Joined Sociedad along with Aguirre from Sestao in 1989.

URTUBI, Ismael
(Atletico Bilbao, Spa)

• 24.05.61 • Midfield
• Spain 2 full caps

Ball winning midfielder who joined Bilbao in 1977.

UVENARD, Thierry
(Le Havre, Fra)

• 24.03.64 • Defender

Local boy, who signed for his home-town side straight from school in 1980. Got his chance in Le Havre's first team during the 1991/92 season.

VADO Osdvaldo Couto Pinto
(Maritimo, Por)

• 05.03.69 • Midfield

Born in Angola, he moved to Portugal in the 1988/89 season when he joined Portimonense. Played two seasons there before switching to Maritimo.

VAHIRUA, Pascal
(Auxerre, Fra)

• 9.3.66 • Striker
• France 14 full caps, 1 goal

Became the first Tahitian to play for France when he made his International debut v Kuwait in January 1990. Joined from Tahiti club Mataia in 1983 and in 1986/87 formed a lethal partnership with Eric Cantona as Auxerre finished fourth in the League. Old-fashioned winger who likes to run at the defence, and possesses a fierce left foot shot.

VALCKX, Stan
(Sporting Lisbon, Por)

• 20.10.63 • Midfield
• Holland 3 full caps

Made his First Division debut in 1985/86 with Venlo. Signed by PSV in July 1988. Made his full international debut against Italy in September 1990 (lost 1-0). Followed ex-PSV Eindhoven boss Bobby Robson to Lisbon in June 1992.

VALERY, Patrick
(Monaco, Fra)

• 03.07.69 • Defender
• France U21

Born in Brignoles, he joined his home town club, AS Brignoles, straight from school. Has been with Monaco since 1984. His first Division One game came on 18th July 1987, against Marseille. Failed to find the net once during the 1991/92 League campaign.

VALIDO, Pedro
Manuel
(Benfica, Por)

• 13.03.70 • Defender
• Portugal youth, U21

Born in Lisbon, but overlooked by the city's big clubs and began his career instead with Ferense. Later moved onto Gil Vicente, before returning to the capital and signing for Benfica in a big money move in 1991.

VALK, Marcel
(Den Haag, Hol)

• 18.04.67 • Midfield

Previously with UVS, Marcel joined Den Haag in July 1990 and immediately established himself in the first team.

VALVERDE Tejedor,
Ernesto
(Atletico Bilbao, Spa)

• 09.02.64 • Striker
• Spain U21

Learnt his trade with Barcelona and Espanol before finally arriving at Atletico Bilbao in 1991.

VANDENBERGH,
Erwin
(Gent, Bel)

• 26.01.59 • Striker
• Belgium 48 full caps, 20 goals

Born-again goal-getter who returned to his homeland in 1990/91 after a four-year spell at French club Lille. Was the Belgian League's leading scorer (23 goals in 34 games) in his first season back in the country, after signing for little Gent in June 1990. His goals earned Gent a place in the UEFA Cup for 1991/92 and himself a recall to the international side. Formerly with Ramsel, Lierse and Anderlecht. He shot to fame during the 1982 World Cup, when he scored Belgium's winner v holders Argentina.

VANDERBEKEN, Dirk
(Eendracht Aalst, Bel)

• 30.12.65 • Defender

After injury ruled him out of much of the 1990/91 season, he signed for Aalst to help strengthen the side for their first season back in the top flight since 1962. Previously with Waregem, Gent and Deinze.

VANDERMISSEN, Guy (Germinal Ekeren, Bel)

• 25.12.57 • Midfield
• Belgium 17 full caps

Highly experienced central midfielder who has spent the bulk of his career with Standard Liege, where he won two League Championships and the Belgian Cup. Apart from a brief spell at Stade Warremmien, Ekeren is his only other club. He signed in July 1991. His international debut came in June 1982, against Argentina, in the opening game of the Spanish World Cup finals. Belgium beat the reigning World Champions 1-0.

VANENBURG, Gerald (PSV Eindhoven, Hol)

• 05.03.64 • Midfield
• Holland 41 full caps, 1 goal

Made League debut in 1980/81 season and spent six years with Ajax before joining PSV in July 1986. Now made more than 300 First Division appearances.

VAUDEQUIN, Pascal (Derry City, Eir)

• Defender

Something of a rarity in the League of Ireland, having come from outside Eire or the United Kingdom. Born in Paris, he signed from Dunkirk in June 1987. Made his debut two months later, September 13, v Bray Wanderers and has established himself as a firm favourite at The Brandywell. Helped the club to their glorious League and Cup double in season 1988/89.

VAVADIO, Christian (Charleroi, Bel)

• 14.02.65 • Midfield

One of a plethora of overseas players with Belgian nationality to be playing at the Gemeentelijk Stadium. Originally from Zaire this ball-winning central midfielder was signed from La Louviere in 1988. Also previously with Mont-Marchienne and Marcinelle.

VECRUYSSE, Phillipe (Nimes, Fra)

• 28.01.62 • Midfield
• France full caps

Goalscoring left-sided midfielder who was one of several players to join the club after promotion to Division One in 1990/91. Previously with Lens (twice), Bordeaux and Marseille. Has made more than 350 First Division appearances. His six League goals during the 1991/92 League campaign made him Nimes' highest scorer, one ahead of Bernadet.

van VEIRDEGHEM, Patrick (Antwerp, Bel)

• 19.01.63 • Defender

Discovered by minor League club Eendracht Doornzele, he signed for Antwerp in 1984/85 and has now made more than 250 First Division appearances.

VELOSO, Antonio Augusto da Silva (Benfica, Por)

• 31.01.57 • Defender
• Portugal 14 caps

Long serving defender who joined Benfica from Beira-Mar in 1980 and made his international debut against Scotland the following year. Originally a left-back, he now plays the sweeper role and is approaching his 300th League appearance for the club.

VENANCIO, Pedro Manuel Regateiro (Sporting Lisbon, Por)

• 21.11.63 • Defender

Born in Setubal and began his career with his local club Vitoria. Sporting stepped in to sign the teenage defender and gave him his First Division debut during the 1982/83 season. Has now made 200 appearances for the Lisbon club.

VERBRUGGEN, Marc (Eendracht Aalst, Bel)

• 22.06.59 • Defender

Vastly experienced with University Merelbeke, Lokeren, Molenbeek, RC Jet and Gent. Injury kept him out of the Gent line-up for much of 1990/91 and he decided to make a fresh start with newly-promoted Alast for the 1991/92 campaign.

VERCAUTEREN, Frank (RWD Molenbeek, Bel)

• 28.10.56 • Midfield
• Belgium 63 full caps, 9 goals

Hugely experienced striker or central midfielder who is the lynch-pin of the Molenbeek side. Veteran of two World Cups (1982 and 1986) and countless European adventures with Anderlecht, his first club. Signed from Nantes after Molenbeek were promoted from Division Two in 1990. Has played more than 400 senior games. The 8th most-capped player in Belgian history. His international debut came against Northern Ireland in 1977.

VERDEGEM, Tom (Gent, Bel)

• 13.09.67 • Midfield

Home grown winger who signed pro with the club in 1984. Has helped the club to promotion twice (1987 and 1989) and is approaching 100 senior games.

VERDELLI, Corrado (Cremonese, Ita)

• 30.09.63 • Defender

Had spells with Fanfulla, Lodi Vecchio, Oltrepo and Monza before breaking into the Internazionale first team in 1988. Moved to Cremonese in 1990.

VERHEYDEN, Lee (Germinal Ekeren, Bel)

• 29.03.73 • Goalkeeper

Young 'keeper signed as back-up for first choice Philippe van de Walle in the summer of the 1991. Formerly with Beerschot for whom he made four First Division appearances.

VERKUYL, Marc (Gent, Bel)

• 19.11.63 • Defender

Dutch-born full back who began who had experience at home with Sparta, Groningen and Ajax before joining Gent in the summer of 1990. His tough tackling performances played a big part in the club's sound defensive record for season 1991/92.

VERLINDEN, Dany (Club Brugge, Bel)

• 15.08.63 • Goalkeeper

Began his career with Ourodenberg Sport as a 17-year-old, before moving to the top flight with SK Lierse. It was his tremendous form in goal which helped the club to their 1991 Belgian Cup win.

VERSTRAETEN, Mike (Germinal Ekeren, Bel)

• 12.08.67 • Defender

Former Olympia Haacht and Mechelen player who signed from Beerschot. Another central defender who likes to get forward and chip in with his share of goals.

VERSAVEL, Bruno (Anderlecht, Bel)

• 17.08.67 • Midfield
• Belgium 25 full caps, 3 goals

The most widely talked about player in Belgium. He represented his country at World Cup Italia '90. Began with Diest before moving to Lokeren, and then on to Mechelen in 1988. It was at Mechelen, where he played alongside older brother Patrick, that he really established himself. Originally signed as a full back, he was switched to midfield, and the move proved to be a masterstroke. Scored 13 goals in 34 games in 1990/91, making him joint top scorer at Mechelen, and that prompted a big money bid from Anderlecht midway through the following season.

VERSAVEL, Patrick
(Mechelen, Bel)
• 07.01.61 • Striker

Elder brother of Belgium's bright, up-and-coming star Bruno Versavel. Formerly with KFC Diest and Lokeren he followed his brother to Mechelen in 1989, Bruno having made the switch the previous year. Equally happy in midfield, on the wing or as a traditional striker.

VEYT, Danny
(Lokeren, Bel)
• 09.12.56 • Midfield
• Belgium 12 full caps, 1 goal

Played a huge part in Belgium's glorious run to the Semi-final of the 1986 World Cup in Mexico, where they lost out to eventual winners Argentina. Made his international debut v Holland in November 1985. Formerly with Sint-Amands, FC Boom, Sint-Niklaas, Waregem, Cercle Liege and Gent. Joined the club prior to the 1991/92 season.

VIALLI, Gianluca
(Juventus, Ita)
• 09.07.64 • Striker
• Italy 53 full caps, 14 goals

Signed by Sampdoria from Cremonese in 1984. Runner-up in 1986 European U21 Champs. Played for Italian full side in 1988 European Champs and 1990 World Cup. Italian League's top scorer in 1991 as Sampdoria won title. Transferred to Juventus in the summer of 1992 for a then world record £11 million. His transfer record lasted a matter of days before Gianluigi Lentini moved from Torino to Milan for £12 million.

de VICENTE, Adrian
(Grasshoppers, Swi)
• 25.07.64 • Striker

An Argentinian-born forward who arrived in Switzerland via Talleres of Cordoba in the summer of 1989. Helped Grasshoppers to the Swiss Championship in 1991.

VICTORIA, Raymond
(Bayern Munich, Ger)
• 10.10.72 • Striker
• Holland U18

Former youth player with Feyenoord. Joined Bayern in 1991.

VIERCHOWOD, Pietro
(Sampdoria, Ita)
• 06.04.59 • Defender
• Italy 40 full caps, 1 goal

Played Serie A soccer with Como, Fiorentina, Roma and, since 1983, Sampdoria. Made International debut v Holland in January 1981. Central defender, but has been used as centre-forward on occasions.

VILCHEZ Ortiz, Eduard
(Espanol, Spa)

• 22.09.67 • Midfield
• Spain youth

Began his career with Real Madrid's reserve side, Castilla, and joined Espanol from Logrones in 1991.

VILFORT, Kim
(Brondby, Den)

• 15.11.62 • Midfield
• Denmark 46 full caps, 7 goals

Scored Denmark's decisive goal against Germany in the 1992 Euopean Championship final - and won the hearts of his nation. After the Danes' econd ame of the tournament - gainst Sweden - he was recalled home to be at the bedside of his 7-year-old daughter, Line, who suffers from leukaemia. Happily, her condition impoved and Kim returned to Sweden, and soccer immortality.

VILLARROYA, Francisco Javier Perez
(Real Madrid, Spa)

• 06.08.66 • Defender
• Spain youth, 14 full caps

Signed by Real Madrid from Real Zaragoza in May 1990.

VINCENTE Fanguera Pereira
(Uniao, Por)

• 01.01.65 • Midfield

A bit part player even in an inexperienced side like Uniao. He signed for the club at the start of the 1990/91 season but has struggled to be included in the first team.

VINK, Marciano
(Ajax, Hol)

• 17.10.70 • Defender
• Holland 2 full caps

Has spent all his career with Ajax and made his first team debut v Sparta Rotterdam in August 1988. His international debut came against Malta in a European Championship qualifier in December 1990 (won 8-0).

VISCAL, Eric
(Gent, Bel)

• 20.03.68 • Striker

Dutch-born front man who signed from Lierse at the beginning of the 1990/91 season. Scored 12 goals in 31 games in his first year. Ex-Tongeire, PSV and Beveren.

VITI
(Oviedo, Spa)

• 09.07.59 • Goalkeeper

Real name is Victor Martin Garcia Rodriguez and has spent the past 14 seasons with Oviedo.

VITOR BAIA
(Porto, Por)

• 15.10.69 • Goalkeeper
• Portugal 5 full caps

Has spent his entire League career with Porto after making his debut during the 1988/89 season. Has now made over 100 appearances for the club and has won the Portuguese League and cup during that time.

VITOR DUARTE
(Beira-Mar, Por)

• 31.08.59 • Defender

Made his First Division debut with Benfica during the 1985/86 season, but moved on to Farense after just one appearance. Signed by Sporting Braga in 1987 and joined Beira-Mar four years later.

VITOR PANEIRA
(Benfica, Por)

• 16.02.66 • Midfield
• Portugal U21, 23 full caps, 3 goals

Right sided player whose real name is Vitor Manuel da Costa Araujo. Made his League debut at the start of the 1988/89 season and broke into the international side a short while later, making his debut against Sweden in October 1988.

VIZCAINO Morcillo, Juan
(Atletico Madrid, Spa)

• 06.08.66 • Midfield
• Spain 4 full caps

Moved to the Spanish capital in 1990 from Zaragoza. Made his international debut against Portugal in January 1991 (won 1-0).

de VLIEGER, Geert
(Beveren, Bel)

• 16.10.71 • Goalkeeper

Highly regarded young 'keeper who had just enough time to make his First Division debut before Beveren were relegated in 1990. Stayed to fight on, though, and guided the club back into the top flight at the first attempt. Was a major reason behind Beveren's excellent defensive record in that promotion campaign, when they conceded just 21 goals all season.

VOLKERICK, Dirk
(Beveren, Bel)

• 26.06.68 • Defender

Former KSV Temse player who remained at Beveren despite relegation in 1989/90 and helped the club back into Division One at the first attempt.

VOLLBORN, Rudiger (Bayer Leverkusen, Ger)

• 12.02.63 • Goalkeeper
• West Germany youth

Won a junior World Cup winners medal with West Germany in 1981 and moved from Blau-Weiss to Leverkusen that same year. Has now made over 250 Bundesliga appearances for Bayer and was a UEFA Cup winner with the club in 1988.

VOLLER, Rudi (Marseille, Fra)

• 13.04.60 • Striker
• Germany 83 full caps, 42 goals

Began his career with Kickers Offenbach, later joining TSV 1860 Munich and then moving to Werder Bremen in 1982. Joined Roma in 1987 and helped them to win the Italian Cup in 1991. Won a World Cup runners-up medal in 1986 and a winners' medal in 1990. Was appointed German captain, in the absence of Lothar Matthaus, for the 1992 European Championships in Sweden, but broke his arm in the first game of the tournament, v CIS, and was forced to sit out the rest of the tournament. Snapped up by Marseille in July 1992.

VONCKX, Peter (Germinal Ekeren, Bel)

• 31.10.69 • Defender

Began with Lierse, where he made just one appearance - as substitute - before being signed by Ekeren in the summer of 1991.

VOS, Henk (Standard Liege, Bel)

• 05.06.68 • Striker

Dutch-born forward who joined the club from Germinal Ekeren in December 1989. Played just 24 games for Standard before being loaned to French club Metz for the duration of season 1990/91. Also previously with Breda, PSV Eindhoven and Willem II Tilburg.

van VOSSEN, Peter (Anderlecht, Bel)

• 21.04.68 • Striker

Formerly with Zierikzee and Vlissingen, his goals carried Beveren to the Second Division title in 1990/91. Signed by Anderlecht at the end of the 1991/92 season.

VOTAVA, Mirko (Werder Bremen, Ger)

• 25.04.56 • Midfield
• West Germany 5 full caps, 1 goal

Bremen captain and play-maker. Began his career with Dukla Prague in Czechoslovakia before defecting to Germany and joining VfL Witten. Later became a naturalized German, moving on to Borussia Dortmund and making international debut. Had a spell in Spain with Atletico Madrid before returning to Germany with Bremen in 1985.

VRIESEDE, Anton (Den Haag, Hol)
• 18.10.68 • Defender

One of two twins in the Den Haag side, Anton joined Den Haag from Ajax in July 1990. Previously with junior side Zoetermeer.

VRIESEDE, Edmund (Den Haag, Hol)
• 18.10.68 • Defender

Like his twin brother, Edmund also played for junior club Zoetermeer, but he arrived at Den Haag twelve months earlier than Anton, signing in July 1989.

VUJOVIC, Zoran (Cannes, Fra)
• 26.08.58 • Defender

Born in Sarajevo, has dual French/Yugoslav nationality. Experienced defender with Hajduk Split, Bordeaux and Vallauris, before joining Cannes in the summer of 1991. Good knowledge of French football - he first played for Bordeaux back in 1986.

VULIC, Zoran (Nantes, Fra)
• 04.10.61 • Defender
• Yugoslavia 25 full caps, 1 goal

Began with home town club Hadjuk Split before moving to Spanish First Division club Mallorca where he was a huge success. Nantes swooped for his signature in the summer of 1991, and the international central defender was a major factor behind the club's sound defensive record last season.

WADDLE, Chris (Marseille, Fra)

- 14.12.60 • Midfield
- England 61 full caps, 6 goals

Former sausage factory worker who joined Newcastle United from local club Tow Law Town. Often criticised for a lazy approach, mainly due to a peculiar running style, he joined Tottenham for a cut-price £590,000 in July 1985. Went on to become one of the finest players in England before joining Marseille for a then British- record £4.25m in July 1989. He suffered penalty shoot-out heartbreak twice in a year. First losing to W.Germany in World Cup Semi-final, July 1990, and then to Red Star Belgrade in Champions' Cup final, June 1991. Returned to England in July 1992, when he transferred to Sheffield Wednesday for £1 million.

WADE, Ricky (Linfield, N.Ir)

- Midfield
- Irish League Representative

Signed from Coleraine for £20,000 in 1991, he is widely regarded as one of the top players in the Irish League. A creative midfield player and regular goalscorer, he's become a fixture in the Irish League Representative XI.

WAGENHAUS, Andreas (Dynamo Berlin, Ger)

- 29.10.64 • Defender
- East Germany 3 full caps

Big central defender who joined Dresden from Chemie Halle in 1989. Played for RSK Freyburg as a junior.

WAGNER, Martin (Kaiserslautern, Ger)

- 24.02.68 • Midfield

Joined Nuremburg from Offenburger FV in 1988. Has a cultured left foot and is very dangerous from dead ball situations. With Nuremburg in danger of suspension from the Bundesliga due to financial problems, Wagner was sold to Kaiserslautern at the end of the 1991/92 season.

WALKER, Des (Sampdoria, Ita)

- 26.11.65 • Defender
- England U21; 46 full caps

Tottenham used to pay Des 20p a week - the price of his bus fare - to play for their youth team, but decided not to sign him as a pro. Brian Clough took him to Nottingham Forest and turned him into one of the world's top defenders. Very quick, and a superb reader of the game, he shot to prominence during Italia '90.

Juventus bid £5 million for him in July 1990. Eventualy signed for Sampdoria for cut-price £1.5 million in May 1992.

WALLEMME, Jean-Guy
(Lens, Fra)

• 10.08.67 • Defender

Has now played more than 100 senior games since signing for the club straight from school in 1984. Had to wait two years for his debut, which came at home to Paris St Germain in November 1986. Solid central defender, who uses his height to great advantage.

van de WALLE, Philippe
(Germinal Ekeren, Bel)

• 22.12.61 • Goalkeeper

Experienced 'keeper with more than 200 First Divsion games under his belt. Signed from Club Brugge he was also previously with Charleroi.

WALSH, Ollie
(Bohemians, Eir)

• Striker

Signed from Kilkenny City in 1990.

WALSH, Pierce
(Sligo Rovers, Eir)

• 16.08.64 • Midfield

Hard-working midfielder who joined the club from Athlone Town in August 1989.

WALTER, Fritz
(VfB Stuttgart, Ger)

• 21.07.60 • Striker

The man whose goals took Stuttgart to their first Bundesliga Championship title for eight years in 1991/92. Joined VfB from Waldhof Mannheim in 1987 and has now scored more than 100 First Division goals.

WANDZIK, Joszef
(Panathinaikos, Gre)

• Goalkeeper
• Poland 43 full caps, U21, Youth

One of only a handful of players to have appeared in two World Youth Cups - in Australia in 1981 and Mexico two years later. He began his senior career with LZS Bytom, in his native Poland, but really made his name with Ruch Chorzow. He collected a one year suspension when he transferred, amid much controversy, to Gornik Zabrze in 1984. Moved to Panathinaikos in the summer of 1990. His full international debut came against Tunisia in December 1985 (lost 1-0).

WAPENAR, Harold
(Feyenoord, Hol)

• 10.04.70 • Goalkeeper

Home grown player who has come up

through the ranks at the club. Understudy to first choice 'keeper Ed de Goey..

WARD, Damien
(Shamrock Rovers, Eir)

• 17.12.71 • Defender

Promising young defender who was spotted playing for local minor League side St Kevin's and snapped up in July 1990. He took his senior bow on April Fool's Day, 1991, at Galway United.

WARD, Sean
(Shamrock Rovers, Eir)

• Goalkeeper

Understudy to first choice 'keeper Paul Kavanagh, he has played only a handful of first team games.

WARZYCHA, Krysztof
(Panathinaikos, Gre)

• Striker
• Poland 34 full caps, 4 goals

Brother of Everton's Robert, he was Poland's "Footballer of the Year" in 1988. Began with Ruch Chorzow, but really set Greek football alight when he joined Panathinaikos at the beginning of the 1990/91 season. He was the club's leading scorer, with 14 goals, as they romped to the League and Cup double. Suffered three years in the international wilderness after making his debut, v Switzerland, back in March 1984.

WASEIGE, Frederic
(Gent, Bel)

• 11.05.65 • Midfield

Solid central midfielder who chips in with the odd goal. Signed from Cercle Liege at the beginning of season 1991/92.

WAWA, Lambic
(RWD Molenbeek, Bel)

• 12.04.61 • Striker

Burly, Zaire-born forward who is currently in his second spell at the club. Began with Zairese club Kalamu before moving to Belgium with Molenbeek. Moved to Farense, but returned to the Edmond Machtensstadion in 1990.

WEAH, George
(Monaco, Fra)

• 01.10.66 • Striker
• Liberia full caps

Born in Monrovia, Liberia, he was snapped up by the club from Tonnerre Yaounde in July 1988, and has been a huge hit in France. Was the club's leading scorer in 1990/91, with ten League goals. French Cup winner 1991.

WEBER, Josip
(Cercle Brugge, Bel)

• 16.11.64 • Striker

One of three Yuogslavs currently plying their trade at Cercle. Signed from Dinamo Vinkovi in 1989, he was previously with Slavonski Brod and Hajduk Split. Had a particularly successful year in 1990/91, when he scored 20 goals in 34 League games - and still Cercle finished only narrowly clear of relegation.

WEBER, Ralf
(Eintracht Frankfurt, Ger)

• 31.05.69 • Midfield

Signed from Kickers Offenbach 1989, but struggled to make an early impression at Frankfurt.

WEGMANN, Jurgen
(Borussia Dortmund, Ger)

• 31.03.64 • Striker

Originally joined Dortmund from Rot-Weiss Essen, but quit the club to try his luck at Schalke 04 and Bayern Munich. Returned to Dortmund in 1989 and has now made over 200 First Division appearances for his assorted clubs.

WEGMANN, Uwe
(Bochum, Ger)

• 14.01.64 • Midfield

Now in his second spell with Bochum, Uwe is nicknamed 'The Cobra' by supporters.

Originally left Bochum for Rot-Weiss Essen, but returned home in 1989.

WEGRIA, Bernard
(RC Liege, Bel)

• 07.03.63 • Defender
• Belgium U21; Olympic

Home-grown hero, and club captain. Lead the side to their best season of recent years, when they won the Belgian Cup in 1990, and also to their creditable third place in the League the previous year. Has now played more than 320 senior games for Liege, his only senior club. Father Victor (Belgian international 1959-61) also played for the club.

WEIDEMANN, Uwe
(Nuremburg, Ger)

• 14.06.63 • Midfield
• East Germany 10 full caps

Signed from RW Erfurt in 1990. Previously with Lokomotiv Leipzig.

WELLENS, Willy
(Cercle Brugge, Bel)

• 23.09.54 • Striker
• Belgium 7 full caps

Veteran goalscorer who's international debut came way back in May 1976, against Holland. Thirteen goals in 24 games for Molenbeek in 1990/91 wasn't good enough and he transferred to Cercle in June 1991. Widely travelled, he has played at Westerlo, Lierse, Molenbeek (twice), Standard Liege, Club Brugge, Beerschot and Kortrijk. Approaching his 600th senior game.

WENSCHLAG, Kay (Werder Bremen, Ger)

• 25.02.70 • Striker

Ex-Dynamo Berlin, Stahl Brandenburg and Rotation Berlin. Joined Bremen in 1991.

WESSELS, Andreas (Bochum, Ger)

• 06.07.64 • Goalkeeper

Signed from Viktoria Goch in 1986 as cover for the very experienced first choice keeper Ralf Zumdick.

WEST, David (Glentoran, N.Ir)

• Striker

Promising youngster who has come up through the ranks at The Oval. Made his senior debut at the back end of 1990/91, and has struggled to establish himself in the first team. Likes to play wide on the left and take players on, using his speed and crossing ability to cause great problems.

WESTERBEEK, Oliver (Karlsruher, Ger)

• 08.02.66 • Midfield

Signed from FC Homburg in 1990. Previously with VfL Bochum.

WHELAN, Anto (Shelbourne, Eir)

• 05.02.64 • Midfield

Signed from Bray Wanderers in the summer of 1988. Likes to get forward and help out his attackers.

WHELAN, Paul (Bohemians, Eir)

• Defender

Solid and reliable defender who has come up through the ranks at Dalymount Park to stake his claim in the first team.

WIEDERKEHR, Andrew (Grasshoppers, Swi)

• 20.04.70 • Striker

Made his Grasshoppers debut against Lausanne in 1988.

de WILDE, Ivan (Kortrijk, Bel)

• 09.05.66 • Goalkeeper

Has played all his football in the top flight since joining Beveren straight from school. Joined Kortrijk from Mechelen at the beginning of the 1991/92 season.

WILLEMS, Ron
(Ajax, Hol)

• 20.09.66 • Midfield

Began his career with PEC Zwolle and made his League debut during the 1983/84 season. Signed by Ajax in 1988.

WILLIAM de Andrade
(Benfica, Por)

• 21.12.67 • Defender

Brazilian-born central defender who began his career in Portugal with Nacional in 1988. Later signed by Vitoria Guimaraes and bought to Benfica in 1990 as a replacement for another Brazilian, Aldair, who had moved to Italy.

WILMOTS, Marc
(Standard Liege, Bel)

• 22.02.69 • Striker
• Belgium 13 full caps, 2 goal; U21

Described by coach Arie Haan as "the transfer of the year" when he signed at the beginning of 1991/92. Formerly with Jodoigne, St Truidense and Mechelen, he has made more than 130 First Division appearances.

WINKELS, Guy
(Genk, Bel)

• 01.02.64 • Defender

Attacking full back who signed from Gent in July 1991. Formerly with Patro Eisden.

WINTER, Aaron
(Lazio, Ita)

• 01.03.67 • Midfield
• Holland 25 full caps, 1 goal

Has spent all his career with Ajax and made his first team debut v FC Utrecht in April 1986. Has now made over 200 appearances for the club. Played a big part in Ajax's UEFA Cup final victory over Italian side Torino. Moved to Lazio in June 1992.

WITECZEK, Marcel
(Kaiserslautern, Ger)

• 18.10.68 • Striker

Made over 140 appearances for Bayer Uerdingen before moving to Kaiserslautern at the start of the 1991/92 season.

WITSCHGE, Richard
(Barcelona, Spa)

• 20.09.69 • Midfield
• Holland 17 full caps, 1 goal

Former Dutch Young Player Of The Year who joined Barcelona from Ajax for £3m in 1991. Injury forced him to withdraw from the Dutch squad for the 1992 European Championship in Sweden.

WITSCHGE, Rob
(Feyenoord, Hol)

• 22.08.66 • Midfield
• Holland 10 full caps, 1 goal

Son of well-known Dutch player Piet
Witschge, both Rob and younger brother
Richard have been capped at full
International level. Won 1987 European
Cup-Winners' Cup with Ajax but later lost
his place in the side. Moved to St Etienne
in France for £2m in 1989, but returned
to Holland with Feyenoord 18 months
later. An injury to brother Richard earned
him a late call-up to Holland's 1992
European Championship squad.

WOELK, Lothar
(MSV Duisburg, Ger)

• 03.08.54 • Defender

Signed from Bochum in 1989. Made
400th Bundesliga appearance v
Nuremburg November 1991.

WOHLFARTH, Roland
(Bayern Munich, Ger)

• 11.01.63 • Striker
• Germany 2 full caps

Signed by Bayern from MSV Duisburg in
1984 for £350,000. Scored hat-trick in
1986 Cup final victory. Bundesliga joint-
top scorer in 1989 with 17, and top scorer
again in 1991 with 21. Has now scored
more than 100 senior goals, and is

regarded as one of the Bundesliga's
foremost goal poachers.

WOJTOWICZ, Rudolf
(Fortuna Dusseldorf, Ger)

• 09.06.56 • Defender
• Poland 1 full cap

Signed from Bayer Leverkusen in 1986.
Previously with Szombierki Beuthen.

de WOLF, John
(Feyenoord, Hol)

• 10.12.62 • Defender
• Holland 1 full cap

Started with Sparta Rotterdam before
moving on to Groningen. Won his only
international cap v Greece in 1987. Joined
Feyenoord in 1989 but injury delayed his
debut for 18 months. Uncompromising
central defender who is a cult hero with
the Feyenoord fans.

de WOLF, Michel
(Anderlecht, Bel)

• 19.01.58 • Defender
• Belgium 34 full caps, 1 goal

Widely travelled among the minor League
and smaller First Division clubs, he got his
first real shot at the big-time when he
joined Anderlecht in August 1990.
Formerly with Clabecq, Molenbeek, Gent
and Kortrijk. Helped the club to League

glory in 1991 and retained his place in the heart of the Belgian defence. Experience in two World Cups (1986, 1990) and one Euro Championship (1984).

WOLTER, Thomas (Werder Bremen, Ger)

• 04.10.63 • Midfield

Joined Bremen from HEBC Hamburg in 1984. Won 1988 League title with Bremen.

WOODHEAD, Marty (Omagh Town, N.Ir)

• Forward

Spent a short period with Glenavon before signing for home town club Omagh in 1984. Owns a sports shop and is now enjoying his eighth season with the club.

WOODS, Colin (Bangor, N.Ir)

• 19.12.62 • Midfield

Joined the club from Distillery in November 1989, and is equally happy playing in midfield or up front. Had a spell playing for Wellington City, in New Zealand.

WOODS, Ian (Athlone Town, Eir)

• 24.09.67 • Defender

Like so many Athlone players, he began his career at St Pat's Athletic, for whom he made his League of Ireland debut, v Waterford United, in November 1986. Signed from Kilkenny City in August 1990.

WORNS, Christian (Bayer Leverkusen, Ger)

• 10.05.72 • Defender
• Germany U21, 2 full caps

Had an excellent 1991/92 season with Leverkusen and also broke into the German national side. Signed by Bayer from Waldhof Mannheim for £800,000 in 1991.

WOSZ, Darius (Bochum, Ger)

• 08.06.69 • Midfield
• East Germany 7 full caps

Skilful wide player who joined Hallescher from Motor Halle in 1985 and then signed for Bochum in December 1991 for club record fee of £400,000. Made Bundesliga debut v Eintracht Frankfurt, February 1992.

WOUTERS, Jan (Bayern Munich, Ger)

• 17.07.60 • Midfield
• Holland 50 full caps, 4 goals

Left-sided midfielder. The youngest of nine children. Established himself with FC Utrecht and made full debut v France in 1982. Joined Ajax in 1986. European Championship winner 1988. Voted Holland's Players' Player Of The Year in 1990. Signed by Bayern for £1m in November 1991.

WRIGHT, Michael (Athlone Town, Eir)
• 28.05.60 • Defender

Experienced performer who has spent his entire pro career with Athlone. Very dependable stopper who is a great favourite at St Mel's, where he won the Championship in 1981 and 1983.

WUCK, Christian (Nuremburg, Ger)
• 09.06.73 • Striker

Talented young striker who broke into the Nuremburg side last season, often coming off the substitute's bench to score vital goals.

WUYTS, Marc (Charleroi, Bel)
• 12.09.67 • Striker

Young striker who is at last finding his feet in the top flight, having struggled for goals during his first two seasons as a senior. Formerly with Olympia Stokkel and Anderlecht, he signed from Mechelen.

WYNHOFF, Peter (Borussia Moenchengladbach, Ger)
• 29.10.68 • Striker

Joined Gladbach from Reinickendorfer Fuchse in 1989.

WYSE, Larry (Galway United, Eir)
• 13.11.56 • Midfield

Highly experienced player who was signed from Dundalk in August 1990. Began with Shamrock Rovers. Won Championship medals with Athlone Town in early 1980s before moving, via Bohemains, to Dundalk.

XUEREB, Daniel (Marseille, Fra)
• 22.05.59 • Striker
• France 8 full caps; ?? goals

Highly experienced player who was signed as cover for the extraordinary Papin in the summer of 1991. Is approaching his 500th League appearance in a career which began for Lyon, v Nancy, in October 1977. Also played for Lens, Paris St Germain and Montpellier.

YEBOAH, Anthony (Eintracht Frankfurt, Ger)

• 06.06.64 • Striker
• Ghana 25 full caps

Brought to Germany by Saarbrucken after starring for his national side and Okawu United in domestic competition. Signed by Frankfurt in 1990.

YORDANOV, Ivailo (Sporting Lisbon)

• 22.04.68 • Striker
• Bulgarian 1 full cap

The third Bulgarian to star in the Sporting side last season although, unlike Balacov and Guentchev, he did not come from the Etar club. Yordanov joined Sporting in the summer of 1991 from Lokomotiv Gorna. He is the brother of Sporting Gijon and Bulgaria star Georgi.

YORGAMLIS, Lysandros (Panathinaikos, Gre)

• Defender
• Greece 3 full caps

Versatile performer who is happy playing in defence or as a midfielder. His long-overdue international debut came against Canada in May 1989 (won 1-0).

YOUM, Thierno (Nantes, Fra)

• 17.04.60 • Striker
• Senegal full caps

Born in the Ruffisque region of Senegal, he began his career with Diaraf Dakar, before moving to Laval in 1984. He introduced himself to French football by scoring on his debut, at Sochaux, and has proceeded to become one of the French League's top strikers.

ZAHOUI, Francois (Toulon, Fra)

• 21.07.61 • Midfield
• Ivory Coast full caps

Experienced central midfielder who began his pro career with Italian side Ascoli. Has played more than 220 senior games since moving to France with Nancy in July 1983. Signed for Toulon in summer 1987 and helped the club to its best season of recent years, when it finished 5th in the League in 1987/88.

ZAINI, Pietro (Ascoli, Ita)

• 19.09.69 • Midfield

Born in Ascoli and joined his local side in 1987. Made his Italian First Division debut during the 1989/90 season, but could not help the club avoid relegation that year.

ZAKKAS, Theodoros (Eendracht Aalst, Bel)

• 11.12.65 • Striker
• Greece 4 full caps

Former Panionios goal-getter who joined Aalst in the 1990/91 close- season, after the club had won promotion the previous campaign. In his second spell with the club, he is well known to Belgian fans, as he was also previously with Anderlecht.

ZAMORANO Zamora, Ivan (Seville, Spa)

• 18.01.67 • Striker
• Chile full caps

Powerful South American who has adopted well to life in the Spanish League during his two seasons with Seville.

ZANON, Jean-Louis (Nancy, Fra)

• 30.11.60 • Midfield
• France Olympic; B; 1 full cap

Experienced campaigner with St Etienne, Marseille, Metz and Nimes before signing for Nancy in 1991. Unfortunate to be at his peak when Platini, Giresse, Tigana and Fernanadez formed the French International midfield - otherwise would have won many caps. Cultured passer of the ball, good left foot. Has won French Championship and Cup.

ZANUTTA, Michele (Sampdoria, Ita)

• 20.10.67 • Midfield

Made his League debut for Sampdoria during the 1986/87 season, but has since been loaned out to Parma and Reggiana.

ZARATE, Sergio (Nuremburg, Ger)

• 14.01.69 • Striker

Very quick and skilful Argentinian who joined Nuremburg from Velez Sarsfield in 1990. His 17 year-old brother was also on trial with Nurnberg last season. A German pop record called 'Samba On The Football Pitch' was also recorded last season in his honour.

ZENGA, Walter (Internazionale, Ita)

• 28.04.60 • Goalkeeper
• Italy 56 full caps

Colourful character who used to host his own show on Italian TV. Joined Inter as a 17-year-old but had to move on to Salernitana before making his League debut. Also had spells with Savona and Sambenedettese before returning to Inter in 1982.

ZERE, Patrice (Lens, Fra)

• 29.12.70 • Defender

From Abidjan, on the Ivory Coast, Patrice joined the club in 1986, and was immediately loaned out to Abbeville. Former striker who has been converted into a lightning fast attacking full back by Lens. Made his League bow away to Metz in April 1989.

ZIDANE, Zinedine (Cannes, Fra)

• 23.06.72 • Midfield
• France U21

Skilful young left-side player who was snatched from under the noses of home-town club Marseille. Made his debut, v Auxerre, in August 1990 and is widely tipped as a future International star.

ZIEGE, Christian (Bayern Munich, Ger)

• 01.02.72 • Midfield

Left sided midfielder who joined Bayern from Hertha 03 Zehlendorf for £12,000 in 1990.

ZINETTI, Giuseppe (Roma, Ita)

• 22.06.58 • Goalkeeper

Joined Bologna in 1974, but made his League debut while on loan to Fourth Division Imola. finally made his Serie A debut in 1978. Joined Pescara in 1978 and then moved on to Roma in 1990.

ZIOBER, Jacek (Montpellier, Fra)

• 18.11.65 • Striker
• Poland 32 full caps, 7 goals

Signed from LKS Lodz in July 1990, his French League debut came at home to Toulouse that same month. Didn't enjoy a particularly productive first season, with four goals in 26 games.

ZITELLI, David (Nancy, Fra)

• 30.10.68 • Striker
• France B

Has only really been given his chance since Marcel Husson was appointed trainer at the beginning of 1991/92. Husson was immediately impressed with Zitelli's partnership with Carmelo Micciche. Debut v Lens, 25th October 1986.

ZOLA, Gianfranco (Napoli, Ita)

• 05.07.66 • Midfield
• Italy 3 full caps

Began his career with minor club Nuorese and played there for three years before joining Third Division Torres in 1986. Signed by Napoli in 1989.

ZONDERVAN, Romeo (NAC Breda, Hol)

• 04.03.59 • Midfield
• Holland 4 full caps

Born in Surinam, a former Dutch international who returned to Holland in May 1992 after eight years with Ipswich in England. Originally moved to England with West Brom in 1983 after playing for Den Haag and FC Twente in Holland.

ZORATTO, Daniele (Parma, Ita)

• 15.11.61 • Midfield

After learning his trade in the lower Leagues with Piobbico, Casale and Bellaria, Daniele got his chance in Serie A with Cesena in 1981. Made just seven League appearances before moving onto Brescia, via Rimini, in 1983. Picked up by Parma in 1989 and helped the club win promotion from Serie B in his first year.

ZORC, Michael (Borussia Dortmund, Ger)

• 25.08.62 • Midfield

First came to Dortmund as 16-year-old and has now set a club record with over 270 First Division appearances. Also ranks third in the club's top Bundesliga scoring list.

ZUBIZARRETA, Andoni (Barcelona, Spa)

• 23.10.61 • Goalkeeper
• Spain U21; 61 full caps

Began his career with Alaves and then got his chance in the First Division when signed by Atletico Bilbao in 1981. Won League titles with Bilbao in 1983 and 1984 before joining Barcelona in 1986 for goalkeeping world record fee of £1.2m. Member of the Spanish team beaten by England in the European U21 Championship final in 1984. Made full international the following year against Finland.

ZUMDICK, Ralf (Bochum, Ger)

• 10.05.58 • Goalkeeper

With over 250 games for the club, Ralf is fifth in Bochum's all-time League appearance list. Originally joined the club from Preussen Munster in 1981.

ZUTA, Audrius (Dynamo Minsk, Bye)

• Midfield
• Lithuania full caps

Began his career with Atlantis of Klaipeda in Lithuania and now plays his football with Minsk in Byelorussia. Voted runner-up in the 1991 Lithuania Player of Year poll. Skilfull with strong shot.